SMP AS/A2 Mathematics

Core 1
for AQA

CAMBRIDGE
UNIVERSITY PRESS

The School Mathematics Project

SMP AS/A2 Mathematics writing team David Cassell, Spencer Instone, John Ling, Paul Scruton, Susan Shilton, Heather West

SMP design and administration Melanie Bull, Carol Cole, Pam Keetch, Nicky Lake, Jane Seaton, Cathy Syred, Ann White

The authors thank Sue Glover for the technical advice she gave when this AS/A2 project began and for her detailed editorial contribution to this book. The authors are also very grateful to those teachers who advised on the book at the planning stage and commented in detail on draft chapters.

PUBLISHED BY THE PRESS SYNDICATE OF THE UNIVERSITY OF CAMBRIDGE
The Pitt Building, Trumpington Street, Cambridge, United Kingdom

CAMBRIDGE UNIVERSITY PRESS
The Edinburgh Building, Cambridge CB2 2RU, UK
40 West 20th Street, New York NY 10011–4211, USA
477 Williamstown Road, Port Melbourne, VIC 3207, Australia
Ruiz de Alarcón 13, 28014 Madrid, Spain
Dock House, The Waterfront, Cape Town 8001, South Africa

http://www.cambridge.org/

© The School Mathematics Project 2004
First published 2004

Printed in the United Kingdom at the University Press, Cambridge

Typeface Minion   *System* QuarkXPress®

A catalogue record for this book is available from the British Library

ISBN 0 521 60525 3 paperback

Typesetting and technical illustrations by The School Mathematics Project

The authors and publisher are grateful to the Assessment and Qualifications Alliance for permission to reproduce questions from past examination papers. Individual questions are marked AQA.

Using this book

Each chapter begins with a **summary** of what the student is expected to learn.

The chapter then has sections lettered A, B, C, ... (see the contents overleaf). In most cases a section consists of development material, worked examples and an exercise.

The **development material** interweaves explanation with questions that involve the student in making sense of ideas and techniques. Development questions are labelled according to their section letter (A1, A2, ..., B1, B2, ...) and answers to them are provided.

D Some development questions are particularly suitable for discussion – either by the whole class or by smaller groups – because they have the potential to bring out a key issue or clarify a technique. Such **discussion questions** are marked with a bar, as here.

K **Key points** established in the development material are marked with a bar as here, so the student may readily refer to them during later work or revision. Each chapter's key points are also gathered together in a panel after the last lettered section.

The **worked examples** have been chosen to clarify ideas and techniques, and as models for students to follow in setting out their own work. Guidance for the student is in italic.

The **exercise** at the end of each lettered section is designed to consolidate the skills and understanding acquired earlier in the section. Unlike those in the development material, questions in the exercise are denoted by a number only.

Starred questions are more demanding.

After the lettered sections and the key points panel there may be a set of **mixed questions**, combining ideas from several sections in the chapter; these may also involve topics from earlier chapters.

Every chapter ends with a selection of **questions for self-assessment** ('Test yourself').

Included in the mixed questions and 'Test yourself' are **past AQA exam questions**, to give the student an idea of the style and standard that may be expected, and to build confidence. Occasionally, exam questions are included in the exercises in the lettered sections.

A calculator is not required for 'Test yourself' questions in this book (in line with the current examination requirements for this module); but a scientific or graphic calculator may be appropriately used elsewhere; there are many opportunities to use a graph plotter or a spreadsheet facility.

Contents

1 Linear graphs and equations

In this chapter you will
- revise work on linear graphs and their equations
- change a given linear equation to a different form
- solve problems by using intersecting linear graphs
- revise and extend work on simultaneous equations

A Linear graphs (answers p 153)

K On any part of a straight line graph, the gradient is the ratio $\dfrac{\text{increase in } y}{\text{increase in } x}$.

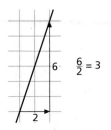

$6 \quad \dfrac{6}{2} = 3$

2

A gradient can be a fraction. It is negative if the line goes down as it goes to the right (since the increase in y is negative).

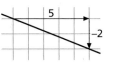

5

$-2 \quad \dfrac{-2}{5} = -\dfrac{2}{5} \text{ (or } -0.4)$

K Lines that have the same gradient are parallel.

A1 Give the gradients of each of these straight lines. Draw sketches if you need to. Are any of the lines parallel?

    A The line from $(2, 1)$ to $(4, 6)$ **B** The line from $(-4, -2)$ to $(-1, -5)$

    C The line from $(-1, 0)$ to $(2, -1)$ **D** The line from $(-3, -3)$ to $(1, 7)$

K An equation of the form $y = mx + c$ is a straight line.
m is the gradient and c is the y-intercept.
The y-intercept is the value of y where the line cuts the y-axis.

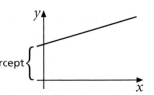

y-intercept

A2 Draw these straight lines on squared paper.

    (a) $y = 2x + 4$ **(b)** $s = -2t + 7$ **(c)** $y = 3x - 5$ **(d)** $y = 5$

A3 A graph has the equation $3x + 4y - 24 = 0$.

    (a) Substitute 0 for x in the equation.
        Solve the equation you get.
        What point does this tell you the graph goes through?

    (b) Substitute 0 for y in the equation.
        Solve the equation you get.
        What point does this tell you the graph goes through?

The results from question A3 tell you where the graph cuts the axes, enabling you to sketch the graph.

A sketch graph is not drawn on graph paper, but key points are labelled.

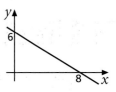

A4 Use the above method to sketch a graph of each of these equations.

(a) $2x + 5y - 20 = 0$ (b) $7x + 4y - 28 = 0$ (c) $2x - 4y + 8 = 0$

(d) $4x - 3y - 12 = 0$ (e) $6x + 5y + 30 = 0$ (f) $x + 5y + 5 = 0$

A5 Sketch graphs of these.

(a) $3x + 7y = 21$ (b) $5x + y = -5$ (c) $2x - 2y = -9$

D **A6** A straight line goes through $(0, 8)$ and $(6, 0)$. Write its equation in the form $ax + by = c$, where a, b and c are constants.

You will often find it useful to change the equation of a linear graph into an equivalent form, as in the following example.

Example 1

Find the gradient of the straight line graph $4x + 5y - 3 = 0$.

Solution

Make y the subject of the equation.

$$5y = -4x + 3$$
$$y = -\tfrac{4}{5}x + \tfrac{3}{5}$$

Look at the coefficient of x.   So the gradient is $-\tfrac{4}{5}$.

A7 Write each of these equations in the form $y = mx + c$.

(a) $3x + y - 2 = 0$ (b) $x - 2y + 6 = 0$ (c) $3x + 5y - 2 = 0$

A8 Sort these into three sets of parallel lines, giving the gradient for each set.

$3x - y - 4 = 0$ $y = -\tfrac{1}{2}x + 2$ $y = 3x + \tfrac{1}{2}$ $y = -3x + 4$

$y = 7 - \tfrac{1}{2}x$ $3x + y - 7 = 0$ $y = -\tfrac{1}{2} + 3x$ $y = -2 - 3x$

A9 There are some pairs of **perpendicular** lines here (one line at right angles to the other).

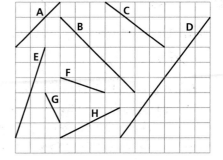

(a) Record the gradients of each pair of perpendicular lines.
   Describe how the gradients in any pair are related.

(b) What is the gradient of any line perpendicular to a line that has gradient $\tfrac{2}{3}$?

(c) What is the gradient of any line perpendicular to a line with gradient -4?

(d) If two lines with gradients p and q are perpendicular, what is the value of pq?

K If two lines with gradients m_1 and m_2 are perpendicular,

$$m_2 = -\frac{1}{m_1} \text{ or } m_1 m_2 = -1.$$

A10 Which of these lines are perpendicular to one another?

    A The line from $(1, 3)$ to $(7, 4)$ **B** The line from $(0, 0)$ to $(5, 4)$

    C The line from $(4, 2)$ to $(8, -3)$ **D** The line from $(0, 0)$ to $(12, 2)$

A11 Which of these lines are perpendicular to one another?

    A $y = 2x + 4$ **B** $5x + y = 2$ **C** $y = -\frac{1}{2}x - 3$ **D** $y = \frac{1}{5}x - 2$

    E $y = \frac{3}{4}x$ **F** $y = 3 - 2x$ **G** $y = \frac{1}{2}x + 5$ **H** $3x + 4y - 1 = 0$

A12 Can you think of any perpendicular lines for which the
rule $m_1 m_2 = -1$ will not work?

Example 2

Identify any parallel or perpendicular lines among these.

    A $y = 3x + 2$ **B** $3y = 2x$ **C** $3x - y - 5 = 0$ **D** $3x + 2y = 5$

Solution

Write the equations in the form $y = mx + c$.   A $y = 3x + 2$
                                               B $y = \frac{2}{3}x$
                                             C $y = 3x - 5$
                                             D $y = -\frac{3}{2}x + \frac{5}{2}$

Examine the x-coefficients (gradients).   A and C are parallel (with gradient 3).
B and D are perpendicular because $\frac{2}{3} \times -\frac{3}{2} = -1$.

Example 3

Sketch the graph of $\frac{x}{2} + \frac{y}{3} = 5$.

Solution

Multiply through by 6 to avoid the fractions. $3x + 2y = 30$

Find where the graph cuts the x-axis (where $y = 0$) by substituting 0 for y.

$$3x + 0 = 30$$
$$x = 10$$

So the graph cuts the x-axis at $(10, 0)$.

Similarly for the y-intercept substitute 0 for x. $0 + 2y = 30$
$$y = 15$$

So the graph cuts the y-axis at $(0, 15)$.

Sketch the graph and label key points.

Exercise A (answers p 153)

1 Which of the following graphs are parallel to the graph of $5x + 6y = 15$?

$y = \frac{5}{6}x - 15$ $\qquad$ $\frac{x}{6} + \frac{y}{5} = 1$ $\qquad$ $y = -\frac{5}{6}x + 4$ $\qquad$ $y = 30 + \frac{5}{6}x$

2 Draw a sketch of each of these graphs.

(a) $y = 2x - 7$ $\qquad$ (b) $7x + 6y - 42 = 0$ $\qquad$ (c) $2x - 3y = 12$

3 There are three sets of parallel lines here.
Match them up and say what the gradient is for each set.

A $x + 7y = 1$ $\qquad$ B $y = -\frac{2}{7}x + 3$ $\qquad$ C $\frac{x}{7} + y = 3$ $\qquad$ D $2y = 7x - 3$

E $2x + 7y = 1$ $\qquad$ F $2y - 7x - 1 = 0$ $\qquad$ G $x + 7y + 2 = 0$ $\qquad$ H $\frac{x}{2} - \frac{y}{7} + 3 = 0$

4 For each of these equations,

    (i) rearrange it into the form $y = mx + c$

    (ii) give the gradient

    (iii) give the intercept on the y-axis

(a) $3x + y + 7 = 0$ $\qquad$ (b) $x + 2y - 8 = 0$ $\qquad$ (c) $4x + 5y + 1 = 0$

(d) $3x - 2y - 6 = 0$ $\qquad$ (e) $-7x + 2y + 3 = 0$ $\qquad$ (f) $-4x - 6y + 9 = 0$

5 What is the gradient of a straight line of the form $ax + by + c = 0$,
where a, b and c are constants?

6 Which of these lines are parallel to the line $y = 4x - 2$?

$y = 2 - 4x$ $\qquad$ $y = 4x + 8$ $\qquad$ $4x + y + 6 = 0$ $\qquad$ $-8x + 2y - 7 = 0$

7 Which of these lines are parallel to the line $2x + 3y = 4$?

$3x - 2y + 1 = 0$ $\qquad$ $y = \frac{2}{3}x + 6$ $\qquad$ $4x + 6y + 3 = 0$ $\qquad$ $y = -\frac{2}{3}x$

8 Which of these lines are perpendicular to the line $y = 3x + 1$?

$y = \frac{1}{3}x - 1$ $\qquad$ $6x - 2y + 3 = 0$ $\qquad$ $y = -\frac{1}{3}x + 2$ $\qquad$ $x + 3y = 1$

9 Which of these lines are perpendicular to the line $5x - 3y + 2 = 0$?

$-3x - 5y + 1 = 0$ $\qquad$ $3x - 5y - 10 = 0$ $\qquad$ $y = 6 - \frac{3}{5}x$ $\qquad$ $y = \frac{3}{5}x + 4$

10 A triangle has vertices A $(-2, 1)$, B $(-1, -4)$ and C $(9, -2)$.
Find the gradients of its sides AB, BC and CA.
What does this tell you about the triangle?

11 A quadrilateral has vertices A $(1, 4)$, B $(4, 2)$, C $(9, 3)$ and D $(3, 7)$.
Find the gradients of its sides AB, DC, AD and BC.
What special kind of quadrilateral is it?

B Finding the equation of a linear graph (answers p 154)

Here a straight line with gradient 3 goes through the point $(1, 2)$.

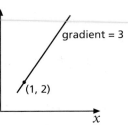

D

B1 Give the coordinates of three other points on the line.

B2 What do you think the line's equation is?

Although you can probably spot the equation mentally in a simple case like this, it is a good idea to have a written method that also works for less obvious equations.

One such method is as follows.

Consider the standard form of a straight line $y = mx + c$.

Substitute the values given above.

$$2 = 3 \times 1 + c$$
$$2 = 3 + c$$
$$c = -1$$

So the line's equation is $y = 3x - 1$.

This is a satisfactory method. However the following approach has the advantage of leading to a general formula that allows you to deal with some problems in a more direct way.

Here again is the line with gradient 3 going through $(1, 2)$.

The point labelled (x, y) is any point (a 'general point') on the line.

Whatever the value of y, the height of the triangle is $y - 2$.
Similarly the base of the triangle is $x - 1$.

Since the gradient is 3, $\qquad \dfrac{y - 2}{x - 1} = 3$

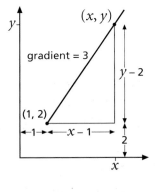

Multiply both sides by $(x - 1)$. $\quad y - 2 = 3(x - 1)$
$$y - 2 = 3x - 3$$
$$y = 3x - 1$$

K

In general, a straight line with gradient m passing through the point (x_1, y_1) has the equation $\dfrac{y - y_1}{x - x_1} = m$ or $y - y_1 = m(x - x_1)$.

B3 Use this formula to find the equation of each of these straight lines, in the form $y = mx + c$.

(a) Passing through $(3, 2)$ with gradient 4

(b) Passing through $(2, 4)$ with gradient -1

(c) Passing through $(-2, -5)$ with gradient 3

(d) Passing through $(-6, 1)$ with gradient $\frac{1}{4}$

(e) Passing through $(-3, 2)$ with gradient $-\frac{1}{2}$

Example 4

Find the equation of the line that passes through $(2, 3)$ and $(4, 8)$.

Solution

Find the height and width of the triangle made between the points.

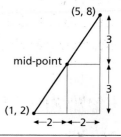

$$\text{gradient} = \tfrac{5}{2}$$

Substitute this gradient and one of the points in the formula $y - y_1 = m(x - x_1)$;
here the point $(2, 3)$ *has been chosen.*

$$y - 3 = \tfrac{5}{2}(x - 2)$$
$$y - 3 = \tfrac{5}{2}x - 5$$
$$y = \tfrac{5}{2}x - 2$$

Alternative solution (without use of the formula above)

Again, from the dimensions of the triangle, $\text{gradient} = \tfrac{5}{2}$

So the required line has the form $y = \tfrac{5}{2}x + c$.

Substitute the values of the point $(2, 3)$.

$$3 = \tfrac{5}{2} \times 2 + c$$
$$3 = 5 + c$$
$$c = -2$$

So the required line is $y = \tfrac{5}{2}x - 2$.

Mid-points

If a straight line is drawn between the points $(1, 2)$ and $(5, 8)$ it is easy
to see that their mid-point (the point halfway between them) is $(3, 5)$.

Adding the two given x-coordinates and dividing by 2 gives the
x-coordinate of the mid-point; similarly with the y-coordinates.

The mid-point of the points (x_1, y_1) and (x_2, y_2) is $\left(\dfrac{x_1 + x_2}{2}, \dfrac{y_1 + y_2}{2} \right)$.

Example 5

Find the equation of the perpendicular bisector of the line segment
between $P\,(12, 9)$ and $Q\,(16, 15)$.

Solution

The perpendicular bisector is the line perpendicular to PQ going through the mid-point of PQ.

The mid-point is $\left(\dfrac{12 + 16}{2}, \dfrac{9 + 15}{2} \right)$, which is $(14, 12)$.

The gradient of PQ is $\tfrac{6}{4}$, which is $\tfrac{3}{2}$.
So the perpendicular bisector has gradient $-\tfrac{2}{3}$.

Use the gradient and point P in the formula $y - y_1 = m(x - x_1)$.

$$y - 14 = -\tfrac{2}{3}(x - 12)$$
$$y - 14 = -\tfrac{2}{3}x + 8$$

This gives the equation of the required line. $\quad y = -\tfrac{2}{3}x + 22$

1 Find the equation of each of these straight lines in the form $y = mx + c$.

    (a) Passing through $(7, 2)$ with gradient 3

    (b) Passing through $(3, 0)$ with gradient $\frac{1}{2}$

    (c) Passing through $(-1, -1)$ and parallel to $y = 2x + 5$

    (d) Passing through $(-2, 4)$ and parallel to $3x + 2y + 7 = 0$

2 Find the equation of each of these straight lines in the form $y = mx + c$.

    (a) Passing through $(6, 4)$ and $(12, 6)$ **(b)** Passing through $(-2, 5)$ and $(4, -1)$

3 Find the mid-point of each of these line segments.

    (a) From $(1, 6)$ to $(7, 2)$ **(b)** From $(-3, 1)$ to $(5, 3)$ **(c)** From $(-3, -5)$ to $(4, -1)$

4 Find the equation of each of these straight lines in the form $y = mx + c$.

    (a) Perpendicular to the line $y = 4 - 2x$, passing through $(0, 0)$

    (b) Perpendicular to the line $3x + 4y = 5$, passing through $(3, -2)$

    (c) Perpendicular to the line $y = 2.5x + 0.5$, passing through $(-1, -2)$

5 For each pair of points,

    (i) find their mid-point

    (ii) find the equation of the line passing through them

    (iii) use Pythagoras's theorem to find the length of the line segment between them, leaving as exact values any square roots that don't 'work out'

    (a) $(4, 4)$ and $(6, 10)$ **(b)** $(4, -2)$ and $(8, 4)$ **(c)** $(-4, 5)$ and $(-1, 2)$

6 (a) Find the equation of the line passing through $(-4, -3)$ and $(2, 1)$.

    (b) Given that this line also passes through the point $(a, 5)$, find a.

7 $(-1, 2)$ is the mid-point of line segment AB. B is the point $(2, -0.5)$. What is point A?

8 A line segment is drawn from $(1, 2)$ to $(6, 4)$. Find the equation of a line that goes through its mid-point and is perpendicular to it.

C Problem solving with linear graphs (answers p 154)

Electricity companies send out bills every three months (every quarter).

  C1 Company P simply charges £0.09 per unit of electricity used.

    (a) Write a formula for C, the cost in £, in terms of E, the number of units used in the quarter.

    (b) Draw axes like these. Go up to 1000 units and £100. Draw a graph of company P's formula and label it.

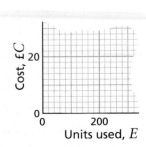

D **C2** Company Q has a different way of charging each quarter. The table shows examples of amounts charged.

Units used, E	100	500	700	1000
Cost, £C	22	50	64	85

(a) Draw a graph of this data on the same grid and label it Q.

(b) Write a formula for C in terms of E that fits this information.

(c) If you had to describe company Q's way of charging each quarter using words rather than a formula, what would you say?

Linear graphs like those you have drawn for C1 and C2 can help you see real-life problems clearly and make comparisons.

C3 For each of the following customers, use your graphs to decide which of the two electricity companies would give better value and what would it charge.

(a) A customer who uses 300 units a quarter

(b) One who uses 750 units a quarter

(c) One who uses 900 units a quarter

With some website research, comparing different suppliers' costs this way can save a consumer a lot of money.

Exercise C (answers p 154)

1 A couple opening a restaurant want some publicity leaflets printed.
Printer R quotes '£50 one-off charge plus £0.02 per leaflet'.
Printer S uses the formula $C = 0.05n + 40$, where C is the cost in £s and n is the number of leaflets.

(a) On a grid with n on the horizontal axis, draw graphs of what the printers charge.

(b) The couple plan to spend £65 on as many leaflets as possible.
Which printer should they choose and how many leaflets should they order?

2 Oil is being pumped out of a tank at a constant rate.
This graph shows the volume, V litres, of oil in the tank at a time t seconds from when the pumping starts.

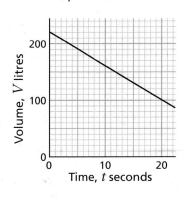

(a) At what rate, in litres per second, is oil leaving the tank?

(b) Write a formula for V in terms of t.
Substitute $V = 0$ into your formula and solve the equation to find when the tank will be empty.

(c) Use this information to complete the graph accurately on graph paper.

(d) A second tank is having oil pumped steadily out of it at the same time. The formula for the volume of oil it holds is $V = 250 - 8t$. Work out when it will be empty and draw its graph on the same grid.

(e) When will the two tanks hold the same amount?
What is this amount?

3 At a certain place in a cave, a stalactite and a stalagmite start to form.
The stalagmite grows up from the floor at 0.3 cm per year.

stalactite

   (a) Write a formula for the height H cm of its tip above the ground after t years.

The stalactite grows down from the ceiling at 0.2 cm per year.
The ceiling is 320 cm above the floor at this place.

stalagmite

   (b) Write a formula for the height H cm of the stalactite's tip above the ground after t years.

   (c) Draw graphs of these formulas on the same grid.
   (You will need several hundred years on the horizontal axis.)

   (d) From the graphs, when will the two tips be 100 cm apart?

   (e) When will the stalactite and stalagmite touch?
   How high above the floor will the point of contact be?

4 A school band makes a CD and investigates the cost of having copies made with a coloured design printed on them.

Company X quotes £110 for 20 copies or £190 for 100 copies.

Company Y quotes £50 for 10 copies plus £2 for each additional copy.

   (a) For each company, find a linear formula for the cost £C of n copies.
   Draw or sketch graphs if it helps.

   (b) Use the formulas to decide which company is cheaper for

       (i) 50 copies   **(ii)** 80 copies

D Solving simultaneous linear equations

Problems that involve finding where the graphs of two linear equations intersect can be dealt with by solving a pair of simultaneous equations.
This can be quicker and is more accurate than using the graphs.

There are several methods for solving a pair of simultaneous equations.
Which is best depends on the form of the equations.

The symbol $\Rightarrow$ appears in the examples on the opposite page.
It is used to connect two mathematical statements when the second one follows mathematically from the first (that is, the first statement **implies** the second).
In practice you can think of it as meaning 'So …'.

The symbol $\therefore$ ('therefore') is used in a similar way.

Example 6

Find where these two linear graphs intersect.

$3x + 4y = 26$
$7x - y = 9$

Solution (by equating coefficients)

Note the coefficient of y in the first equation. $3x + 4y = 26$
Multiply the second equation by 4 to get the
'same size' coefficient. $28x - 4y = 36$

Add the previous two equations together. $31x = 62$
$$\Rightarrow \quad x = 2$$

Substitute this in the simpler equation. $14 - y = 9$
$$\Rightarrow \quad y = 5$$

So the point of intersection is $(2, 5)$.

Check by substituting your values for x and y into the original equations.

$\text{LHS} = 3 \times 2 + 4 \times 5 = 26$, which equals RHS
$\text{LHS} = 7 \times 2 - 5 = 9$, which equals RHS

Example 7

Find where these two graphs intersect. $y = 7 - 3x$
$2x + 5y = 9$

Solution (by equating coefficients)

In the first equation get the x and y terms on the left-hand side. $3x + y = 7$
Multiply this equation by 5. $15x + 5y = 35$
Here is the second equation. $2x + 5y = 9$
Subtract it from the multiplied first equation. $13x = 26$
$$\Rightarrow \quad x = 2$$

Substitute into the first given equation. $y = 7 - 6 = 1$
So the graphs intersect at $(2, 1)$.

Check by substitution into the formulas for the graphs.

Solution (by substitution)

Here are the two given equations again. $y = 7 - 3x$
$2x + 5y = 9$

The first one states that the expression $7 - 3x$ is equal to y.
So replace y in the second equation by this expression. $2x + 5(7 - 3x) = 9$
Simplify. $2x + 35 - 15x = 9$
$$\Rightarrow \quad -13x = -26$$
$$\Rightarrow \quad x = 2$$

Then find y as in the previous method.

You have just seen two methods for solving simultaneous equations. There is a third method that is particularly suited to intersecting graphs that are in the form $y = \ldots$

Example 8

Find the point of intersection of these graphs.
$$y = 2x - 1$$
$$y = 4 - x$$

Solution (by equating the expressions for y)

At the point of intersection, both graphs have the same y value. Therefore the expression for y in the first graph must equal the expression for y in the second graph.

$$2x - 1 = 4 - x$$
$$\Rightarrow \quad 3x = 5$$
$$\Rightarrow \quad x = \frac{5}{3}$$

Substitute into the simpler equation.

$$y = 4 - \frac{5}{3} = \frac{7}{3}$$

So the point of intersection is $(\frac{5}{3}, \frac{7}{3})$.

The following example is not about graphs (though it could be solved by drawing a pair of intersecting graphs). It is still suited to the 'equating the expressions for y' approach (though here expressions for h are equated).

Example 9

A snail climbs up from the bottom of a garden wall at 0.5 cm per minute. Starting at the same time from a point 3.24 metres up the wall, a millipede walks down the wall at a steady rate of 4 cm per minute. When are the two at the same level, and what is that level?

Solution

Define the 'unknowns'.

Let h be the height up the wall in centimetres.
Let t be the time in minutes from the start.

Express each creature's height in terms of time.

$h = 0.5t$ (snail)
$h = 324 - 4t$ (millipede)

When they are at the same height,
$$0.5t = 324 - 4t \quad \text{(snail's } h = \text{millipede's } h\text{)}$$
$$\Rightarrow \quad 4.5t = 324$$
$$\Rightarrow \quad t = 72$$

Substitute in the snail's formula.

$$h = 0.5 \times 72 = 36$$

After 72 minutes they are both 36 cm from the bottom of the wall.

Exercise D (answers p 155)

1 Solve the following pairs of equations using the 'equating coefficients' method.

(a) $3p + q = 19$
    $5p + 2q = 32$

(b) $5a + 3b = 8$
    $3a - b = 9$

(c) $2h + 3j = 1$
    $7h + 4j = -16$

2 Solve the following pairs of equations using the 'substitution' method.

(a) $y = 2x$
$3x + y = 15$

(b) $3x + 2y + 12 = 0$
$y = x - 1$

(c) $q = 2p - 6$
$3p - 2q = 11$

3 Solve the following pairs of equations using the 'substitution' method. Where necessary, first make y the subject of one of the equations.

(a) $y = 5x$
$7x - 3y + 4 = 0$

(b) $x + y + 1 = 0$
$2x + 3y - 1 = 0$

(c) $y - x + 8 = 0$
$5x + 4y + 5 = 0$

4 Solve these pairs of equations by 'equating the expressions for y'.

(a) $y = 2 - \frac{1}{3}x$
$y = 3(x - 1)$

(b) $y = \frac{2}{3}x$
$y = 2(2 - x)$

(c) $s = 2t - 3$
$s = 1 + \frac{1}{2}t$

5 Solve these pairs of equations by 'equating the expressions for y'. Where necessary, first make y the subject of one of the equations.

(a) $x + y = 1$
$y = 2x - 14$

(b) $y = 1 - 3x$
$y = 5(1 + x)$

(c) $y - x = 1$
$y = 4x + 10$

6 Find the point of intersection of each pair of straight lines. Choose an appropriate method in each case.

(a) $y = 2x - 7$
$\frac{x}{3} + \frac{y}{5} - 3 = 0$

(b) $3x + 5y = 25$
$2x + 6y = 26$

(c) $y = 2x + 1$
$7x + 10y = 64$

7 What happens when you try to solve the following simultaneous equations? Give a graphical explanation in each case.

(a) $y = 2 - \frac{2}{3}x$
$2x + 3y = 18$

(b) $y = -5 - \frac{5}{3}x$
$5x + 3y + 15 = 0$

(c) $x - 2 - \frac{1}{2}y = 0$
$y = 2x + 5$

8 The straight lines represented by these equations form a triangle.

$y = 4x - 17$ $\qquad\qquad$ $y = 2x + 4$ $\qquad\qquad$ $2x + 3y = 5$

Find the coordinates of the vertices of the triangle.

9 Plumber A makes a £40 call-out charge and then charges £40 per hour. Plumber B makes a £29 call-out charge and then charges £44 per hour.

(a) For each plumber, write a formula for C, the total cost in £s, in terms of t, the time worked in hours.

(b) Find the length of job for which both plumbers charge the same amount.

(c) Which plumber is cheaper for jobs that take longer than the length of time you found for (b)?

10 Obtain an exact answer to exercise C question 2 (e) using simultaneous equations.

11 Obtain an exact answer to exercise C question 3 (e) using simultaneous equations.

Using a computer

In AS mathematics you need to solve simultaneous equations on paper. But for real-life problems people often use computers.

You can do this with Microsoft® Excel's Solver tool, which is available as an add-in. Here it has been set up for question 1 (a) of exercise D.

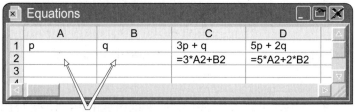

Solver will put the solutions in these blank cells.

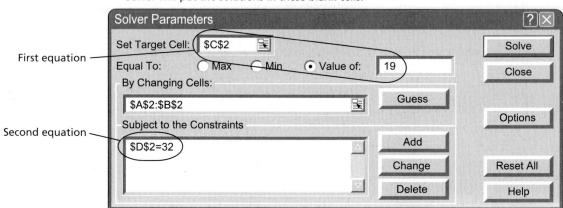

First equation

Second equation

Computers can solve larger groups of simultaneous equations, not just pairs. Their immense equation-solving power is put to good use in, for example, weather forecasting.

Key points

- For any part of a straight line graph, the gradient is the ratio $\dfrac{\text{increase in } y}{\text{increase in } x}$. (p 6)

- An equation of the form $y = mx + c$ is a straight line, where m is the gradient and c is the y-intercept. (p 6)

- Lines that have the same gradient are parallel. (p 6)

- If two lines with gradients m_1 and m_2 are perpendicular,
  $m_2 = -\dfrac{1}{m_1}$ or $m_1 m_2 = -1$. (p 8)

- A straight line with gradient m passing through the point (x_1, y_1) has
  the equation $\dfrac{y - y_1}{x - x_1} = m$ or $y - y_1 = m(x - x_1)$. (p 10)

- The mid-point of the points (x_1, y_1) and (x_2, y_2) is $\left(\dfrac{x_1 + x_2}{2}, \dfrac{y_1 + y_2}{2} \right)$. (p 11)

- The point of intersection of two graphs is found by treating their equations as simultaneous equations and solving them. (pp 14–16)

Mixed questions (answers p 155)

1 A quadrilateral is formed by the lines $y = 3x - 4$, $y = -\frac{1}{3}x$, $y = 3x + 5$ and $y = 7 - \frac{1}{3}x$.
What special type of quadrilateral is it?

2 A quadrilateral is formed by the lines $y = 0$, $3x + 5y = 15$, $x = 0$ and $3x + 5y = 30$.

(a) What special type of quadrilateral is it?

(b) Find its vertices.

3 The points A, B and C have coordinates $(1, 7)$, $(5, 5)$ and $(7, 9)$ respectively.

(a) Show that AB and BC are perpendicular.

(b) Find an equation of the line BC.

(c) The equation of the line AC is $3y = x + 20$ and M is the mid-point of AB.

   (i) Find an equation of the line through M parallel to AC.

   (ii) This line intersects BC at the point T. Find the coordinates of T.   AQA 2001

4 The line p has the equation $4x + 3y - 18 = 0$.
The line q has the equation $2y = 7 - x$.

(a) Sketch and label these lines on the same axes, showing clearly where
each of them meets the x- and y-axes.

(b) Find the coordinates of the point where p and q intersect.

(c) Find the equation of a third line, r, which is parallel to p and goes through
the point where q meets the x-axis.
Give the equation in the form $ax + by = c$, where a, b and c are integers.

5 Line p has the equation $3x + 4y + 8 = 0$.

(a) Sketch it, marking values where it crosses the axes.

Line q goes through the point $(6, 1)$ and is perpendicular to line p.

(b) Find the equation of line q, giving it in the form $y = mx + c$.

(c) Add line q to your sketch, marking values where it crosses the axes.

(d) Find the point of intersection of lines p and q, using
exact fractions in your answer.

6 A quadrilateral is drawn with its vertices at the points shown.

(a) Find the equations of its diagonals
AC and BD, and hence find their
point of intersection.

(b) Give the mid-points of the four sides.

(c) A new quadrilateral is formed by joining
the four mid-points. Work out the gradient
of each side of this new quadrilateral.

(d) What do your answers to (c) tell you about
this new quadrilateral?

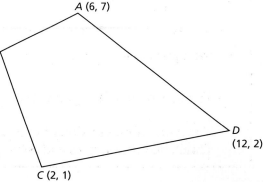

A (6, 7)

B
(0, 5)

D
(12, 2)

C (2, 1)

7 Find the equation of the line that goes through the origin $(0, 0)$ and is perpendicular to the line $8x + 6y - 50 = 0$.

Find where these two lines intersect and hence find the perpendicular distance of the line $8x + 6y - 50 = 0$ from the origin.

8 Determine, with reasons, whether the following points all lie on the same straight line.

$$(-3, -3) \quad (2, -1) \quad (9, 2)$$

9 The line AB has equation $5x - 2y = 7$, and the point A has coordinates $(1, -1)$ and the point B has coordinates $(3, k)$.

(a) (i) Find the value of k.

   (ii) Find the gradient of AB.

(b) Find an equation for the line through A which is perpendicular to AB.

(c) The point C has coordinates $(-6, -2)$, Show that AC has length $p\sqrt{2}$, stating the value of p.

AQA 2003

10 In a triangle, a median is a line from a vertex to the mid-point of the opposite side.

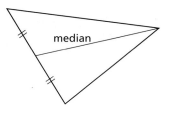

(a) Find the equations of the three medians of the triangle with vertices A (11, 1), B (9, 9) and C (1, 5).

(b) Show that these medians intersect at a single point, giving its coordinates.

*11 The diagram shows a kite. A is the point $(2, 9)$. C is the point $(8, 1)$.

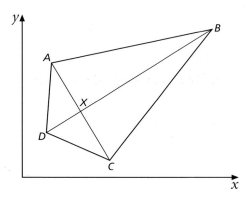

(a) Find the coordinates of X, where the diagonals intersect.

(b) Find the equation of the diagonal DB.

D is the point $(1, p)$ and B is the point $(q, 11)$

(c) Find p and q.

(d) Show that $\angle ADC$ is a right angle.

(e) Find the area of the kite.

Test yourself (answers p 156)

None of these questions requires a calculator.

1 Write the equations of the following lines in the form $y = mx + c$.

   (a) $5x + y = 4$ **(b)** $x - 2y + 6 = 0$ **(c)** $x + 2y = 3$ **(d)** $y - 6 = 2(x + 4)$

2 The line $y = 3x + 4$ is drawn. State whether each of the following lines is parallel to it, perpendicular to it, or neither.

   (a) $3x + y = 2$ **(b)** $y = 2 - \frac{1}{3}x$ **(c)** $3x - y - 7 = 0$ **(d)** $x + 3y - 2 = 0$

3 A straight line goes through the points $(2, 3)$ and $(6, 2)$.

   (a) What is its gradient?

   (b) Give its equation in the form $y = mx + c$.

4 Give the equation of the line joining the origin to the mid-point of $(5, 3)$ and $(-1, 7)$.

5 Find the length of the line joining $(1, -2)$ and $(-1, 1)$, leaving your answer as an exact value.

6 Line l has the equation $y = 6x + 1$.

   (a) Give the equation of the line through $(1, 0)$ parallel to l.

   (b) Give the equation of the line through $(3, -1)$ perpendicular to l.

7 Solve the following pairs of simultaneous equations by an appropriate method.

   (a) $4x + 5y - 6 = 0$ **(b)** $y = x + 1$ **(c)** $y = 3 - x$
       $y = x + 3$ $7x + 3y = 0$ $3x + 5y - 12 = 0$

   (d) $y = 2x + 5$ **(e)** $3x + 5y = 30$ **(f)** $y = \frac{2}{3}x - 1$
       $y = -3x$ $5x + 3y = 42$ $y = \frac{3}{2}x + 4$

8 The point A has coordinates $(2, 3)$ and O is the origin.

   (a) Write down the gradient of OA and hence find the equation of the line OA.

   (b) Show that the line which has equation

        $4x + 6y = 13$:

     (i) is perpendicular to OA;

     (ii) passes through the mid-point of OA.   AQA 2003

9 The equation of the line AB is $5x - 3y = 26$.

   (a) Find the gradient of AB.

   (b) The point A has coordinates $(4, -2)$ and a point C has coordinates $(-6, 4)$.

     (i) Prove that AC is perpendicular to AB.

     (ii) Find an equation of the line AC, expressing your answer in the form $px + qy = r$, where p, q and r are integers.

   (c) The line with equation $x + 2y = 13$ also passes through the point B.
      Find the coordinates of B.   AQA 2002

2 Surds

In this chapter you will
- learn how to manipulate surds and express them in different ways
- solve problems, leaving your solutions in surd form

A Understanding surds

$\sqrt{a}$ means the positive square root of a and it can be written as $\sqrt{a}$ or $\sqrt{a}$.
$\sqrt{a+b}$ is not the same as $\sqrt{a}+b$.
For example, $2\sqrt{16}+9 = (2\times\sqrt{16})+9 = 2\times 4+9 = 17$
However, $2\sqrt{16+9} = 2\sqrt{25} = 2\times 5 = 10$

A **rational** number is one that can be expressed in the fractional form $\frac{a}{b}$,
where a and b are integers. Examples are $\frac{3}{4}$ and $-\frac{4}{3}$.

An **irrational** number cannot be expressed in fractional form.
The square roots of all positive integers (except the perfect squares 1, 4, 9, 16, …)
are irrational. Examples are $\sqrt{3}$ and $\sqrt{7}$.

A number that involves an irrational root is said to be in **surd form**.
Examples are $2\sqrt{3}$ and $\sqrt{7}+1$.

We use surd form when we want to be **exact**.
For example, the length of a diagonal of a unit square is exactly $\sqrt{2}$,
but any decimal approximation of this value (such as 1.414) is not exact.

Example 1

Find in surd form the perimeter of isosceles triangle ABC.

Solution

By Pythagoras, the length of AB is $\sqrt{2^2+3^2} = \sqrt{4+9} = \sqrt{13}$.
So the perimeter is $6+\sqrt{13}+\sqrt{13} = 6+2\sqrt{13}$.   *This is an exact value.*

Exercise A (answers p 157)

1 Each of these is a rational number. Express each one as an integer, fraction or decimal.

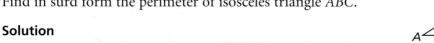

(a) $\sqrt{49}$ (b) $-\sqrt{81}$ (c) $\sqrt{\dfrac{1}{9}}$ (d) $6\sqrt{9}$

(e) $\sqrt{100}\times 4$ (f) $\sqrt{100\times 4}$ (g) $\sqrt{\dfrac{25}{4}}$ (h) $\dfrac{\sqrt{25}}{4}$

(i) $\sqrt{9}+7$ (j) $\sqrt{9+7}$ (k) $\sqrt{0.16}$ (l) $\left(\sqrt{7}\right)^2$

(m) $\left(\sqrt{3}\right)^4$ (n) $\left(2\sqrt{3}\right)^2$ (o) $2\sqrt{0.09}$ (p) $\sqrt{0.000001}$

2 A rectangle has a length of 10 cm and a width of 3 cm.
In surd form, find the length of one of its diagonals.

3 Write each of these in the form $p\sqrt{3}$ where p is an integer.

(a) $\sqrt{3} + \sqrt{3}$ (b) $6\sqrt{3} - 2\sqrt{3}$ (c) $\left(\sqrt{3}\right)^3$ (d) $\left(\sqrt{3}\right)^5$ (e) $\left(2\sqrt{3}\right)^5$

4 An isosceles triangle has a base length of 4 cm and a height of 5 cm.
Show that the perimeter of the triangle is $4 + 2\sqrt{29}$ cm.

5 A square has vertices with coordinates $(2, 1)$, $(4, 2)$, $(5, 0)$ and $(3, -1)$.
Show that the perimeter of this square is $4\sqrt{5}$.

6 In triangle PQR, $PQ = 4$ cm, $QR = 1$ cm,
$\angle PQR = 90°$ and $\angle QPR = \alpha°$.
Find the exact value of $\cos \alpha°$.

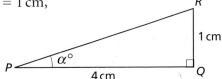

7 The shaded square has been constructed by
joining the mid-points of a larger square.
Find the perimeter of the larger square in surd form.

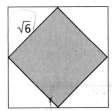

B Simplifying surds (answers p 157)

B1 Without using a calculator, decide which of these statements are true.

A $\sqrt{4} \times \sqrt{25} = \sqrt{100}$ B $\dfrac{\sqrt{36}}{\sqrt{9}} = \sqrt{4}$ C $\sqrt{50} + \sqrt{50} = \sqrt{100}$

D $\sqrt{2} \times \sqrt{18} = \sqrt{36}$ E $\sqrt{150} - \sqrt{50} = \sqrt{100}$ F $\dfrac{\sqrt{200}}{\sqrt{2}} = \sqrt{100}$

B2 Prove that each of these statements is true for all p and q.

(a) $\sqrt{p^2} \times \sqrt{q^2} = \sqrt{p^2 \times q^2}$ (b) $\dfrac{\sqrt{p^2}}{\sqrt{q^2}} = \sqrt{\dfrac{p^2}{q^2}}$

B3 How could you use the statements in B2 to prove that, for all a and b,

(a) $\sqrt{a} \times \sqrt{b} = \sqrt{ab}$ (b) $\dfrac{\sqrt{a}}{\sqrt{b}} = \sqrt{\dfrac{a}{b}}$

B4 How would you show someone that, in general, $\sqrt{a} + \sqrt{b}$ is not equivalent to $\sqrt{a+b}$?

K In general $\quad \sqrt{a \times b} = \sqrt{a} \times \sqrt{b}$

and $\quad \sqrt{\dfrac{a}{b}} = \dfrac{\sqrt{a}}{\sqrt{b}}$

When working in surd form, it is important to be able to manipulate expressions so they are as simple as possible. You can use the above rules to simplify many expressions.

Example 2

Simplify the product $\sqrt{3} \times \sqrt{2}$.

Solution

$\sqrt{3} \times \sqrt{2} = \sqrt{3 \times 2} = \sqrt{6}$

Example 3

Express $\sqrt{18}$ in terms of the simplest possible surd.

Solution

Begin by writing 18 as a product where one of the numbers is a square number.

$\sqrt{18} = \sqrt{9 \times 2} = \sqrt{9} \times \sqrt{2} = 3\sqrt{2}$

Example 4

Simplify the quotient $\dfrac{\sqrt{6}}{\sqrt{2}}$.

Solution

$\dfrac{\sqrt{6}}{\sqrt{2}} = \sqrt{\dfrac{6}{2}} = \sqrt{3}$

Example 5

Express $\sqrt{\dfrac{2}{9}}$ in terms of the simplest possible surd.

Solution

$\sqrt{\dfrac{2}{9}} = \dfrac{\sqrt{2}}{\sqrt{9}} = \dfrac{\sqrt{2}}{3}$ or $\dfrac{1}{3}\sqrt{2}$

Example 6

Expand and simplify $\sqrt{2}(\sqrt{2} - \sqrt{7})$.

Solution

$\sqrt{2}(\sqrt{2} - \sqrt{7}) = \sqrt{2} \times \sqrt{2} - \sqrt{2} \times \sqrt{7}$
$= 2 - \sqrt{14}$

Example 7

Expand and simplify $(\sqrt{3} + 1)(3\sqrt{3} - 5)$.

Solution

$(\sqrt{3} + 1)(3\sqrt{3} - 5) = \sqrt{3} \times 3\sqrt{3} - \sqrt{3} \times 5 + 3\sqrt{3} - 5$
$= 9 - 5\sqrt{3} + 3\sqrt{3} - 5$
$= 4 - 2\sqrt{3}$

You can set your working out in a table.

$\times$	$\sqrt{3}$	1
$3\sqrt{3}$	9	$3\sqrt{3}$
-5	$-5\sqrt{3}$	-5

Exercise B (answers p 158)

1 Simplify these products, writing your answers as simply as possible.

   (a) $\sqrt{5} \times \sqrt{2}$ **(b)** $\sqrt{2} \times \sqrt{8}$ **(c)** $2\sqrt{7} \times \sqrt{3}$ **(d)** $5\sqrt{3} \times 2\sqrt{2}$

2 Express each of the following in the form $a\sqrt{b}$ in terms of the simplest possible surds.

   (a) $\sqrt{8}$ **(b)** $\sqrt{54}$ **(c)** $\sqrt{32}$ **(d)** $\sqrt{50}$

   (e) $2\sqrt{150}$ **(f)** $5\sqrt{99}$ **(g)** $3\sqrt{200}$ **(h)** $2\sqrt{128}$

3 Simplify these, writing your answers as simply as possible.

   (a) $\dfrac{\sqrt{6}}{\sqrt{3}}$ **(b)** $\dfrac{\sqrt{27}}{\sqrt{3}}$ **(c)** $\dfrac{3\sqrt{14}}{\sqrt{2}}$ **(d)** $\dfrac{3\sqrt{24}}{\sqrt{6}}$

4 Express each of the following in terms of the simplest possible surds.

   (a) $\sqrt{\dfrac{4}{7}}$ **(b)** $\sqrt{\dfrac{3}{25}}$ **(c)** $3\sqrt{\dfrac{16}{5}}$ **(d)** $4\sqrt{\dfrac{7}{4}}$ **(e)** $3\sqrt{\dfrac{11}{81}}$

5 **(a)** Express each of these in the form $k\sqrt{3}$.   **(i)** $\sqrt{12}$ **(ii)** $\sqrt{75}$

   (b) Hence write $\sqrt{75} - \sqrt{12}$ in the form $n\sqrt{3}$ where n is an integer.

6 Express each of the following in the form $a\sqrt{b}$ in terms of the simplest possible surds.

   (a) $4\sqrt{3} + \sqrt{12}$ **(b)** $\sqrt{45} - \sqrt{20}$ **(c)** $\sqrt{200} + 9\sqrt{2} - \sqrt{72}$

   (d) $\dfrac{\sqrt{10} \times \sqrt{60}}{\sqrt{75}}$ **(e)** $\dfrac{\sqrt{108} - \sqrt{48}}{\sqrt{3}}$ **(f)** $\dfrac{2\sqrt{14} \times 4\sqrt{6}}{\sqrt{7}}$ **(g)** $\dfrac{\sqrt{98} + \sqrt{50}}{3\sqrt{2}}$

7 A rhombus has diagonals that measure $14\,\text{cm}$ and $2\,\text{cm}$.
   Show that the length of one of its edges is $5\sqrt{2}$ cm.

8 Expand the brackets and write each result in terms of the simplest possible surds.

   (a) $\sqrt{3}\left(\sqrt{3} + 3\sqrt{5}\right)$ **(b)** $\sqrt{10}\left(\sqrt{30} - \sqrt{2}\right)$

9 Expand the brackets and write each result as simply as possible.

   (a) $\left(\sqrt{2} + 9\right)\left(3\sqrt{2} - 1\right)$ **(b)** $\left(\sqrt{2} + \sqrt{3}\right)\left(\sqrt{5} - \sqrt{2}\right)$

   (c) $\left(\sqrt{5} + 6\right)\left(4 - 3\sqrt{5}\right)$ **(d)** $\left(\sqrt{3} + 7\right)^2$

10 Expand the brackets and write each result as simply as possible.

   (a) $\left(5 + \sqrt{11}\right)\left(5 - \sqrt{11}\right)$ **(b)** $\left(5 + 2\sqrt{3}\right)\left(5 - 2\sqrt{3}\right)$

   (c) $\left(\sqrt{5} - \sqrt{7}\right)\left(\sqrt{5} + \sqrt{7}\right)$ **(d)** $\left(2\sqrt{5} + 1\right)\left(2\sqrt{5} - 1\right)$

11 Expand the brackets and write each result as simply as possible.

   (a) $\left(\sqrt{a} + b\right)\left(\sqrt{a} - b\right)$ **(b)** $\left(x + \sqrt{y}\right)\left(x - \sqrt{y}\right)$ **(c)** $\left(\sqrt{p} - \sqrt{q}\right)\left(\sqrt{p} + \sqrt{q}\right)$

12 Prove that $\left(a\sqrt{b} + c\sqrt{d}\right)\left(a\sqrt{b} - c\sqrt{d}\right)$ is a rational number for all rational a, b, c and d.

C Rationalising the denominator

A pair of numbers such as $5 + \sqrt{2}$ and $5 - \sqrt{2}$ is called a pair of **conjugates**.

Another example of a pair of conjugates is $-\sqrt{2} - 3\sqrt{5}$ and $-\sqrt{2} + 3\sqrt{5}$.

The product of any pair of conjugates like these (which involve square roots of rational numbers) is always a rational number.

For example, $(5 + \sqrt{2})(5 - \sqrt{2}) = 25 - 5\sqrt{2} + 5\sqrt{2} - 2$

$$= 23$$

In general $(a + b)(a - b) = a^2 - ab + ba - b^2$
$$= a^2 - b^2$$

You can use this rule to multiply out conjugates.

For example, $(4\sqrt{3} - 1)(4\sqrt{3} + 1) = (4\sqrt{3})^2 - 1^2$

$$= 48 - 1$$

$$= 47$$

It can be useful to eliminate any surds from the denominator of a fractional expression. It often makes the expression simpler and hence easier to use in any subsequent calculation.

Example 8

Express $\dfrac{12}{5\sqrt{2}}$ in the form $a\sqrt{b}$, where a and b are rational numbers.

Solution

Multiply top and bottom by $\sqrt{2}$ to give a rational denominator.

$$\frac{12}{5\sqrt{2}} = \frac{12 \times \sqrt{2}}{5\sqrt{2} \times \sqrt{2}} = \frac{12\sqrt{2}}{10} = \frac{6\sqrt{2}}{5} = \frac{6}{5}\sqrt{2}$$

Example 9

By rationalising the denominator, simplify $\dfrac{\sqrt{3} - 5}{2\sqrt{3} + 1}$.

Solution

Multiply top and bottom by $2\sqrt{3} - 1$ to give a rational denominator.

$$\frac{\sqrt{3} - 5}{2\sqrt{3} + 1} = \frac{(\sqrt{3} - 5)(2\sqrt{3} - 1)}{(2\sqrt{3} + 1)(2\sqrt{3} - 1)}$$

$$= \frac{6 - \sqrt{3} - 10\sqrt{3} + 5}{12 - 2\sqrt{3} + 2\sqrt{3} - 1}$$

The product in the denominator is worked out in full here. Instead, you could evaluate $(2\sqrt{3})^2 - 1^2$ to obtain $12 - 1 = 11$.

$$= \frac{11 - 11\sqrt{3}}{11}$$

$$= 1 - \sqrt{3}$$

$1 - \sqrt{3}$ *is much simpler to use than* $\dfrac{\sqrt{3} - 5}{2\sqrt{3} + 1}$.

Example 10

Rationalise the denominator of $\dfrac{2}{1-\sqrt{5}}$.

Solution

*Multiply top and bottom by $1+\sqrt{5}$
to give a rational denominator.*
$$\frac{2}{1-\sqrt{5}} = \frac{2(1+\sqrt{5})}{(1-\sqrt{5})(1+\sqrt{5})}$$

$$= \frac{2+2\sqrt{5}}{-4}$$

*Multiply top and bottom by -1
to make the denominator positive.*
$$= \frac{-2-2\sqrt{5}}{4}$$

Divide top and bottom by 2 to simplify.
$$= \frac{-1-\sqrt{5}}{2} \qquad \text{This could be written as } -\tfrac{1}{2} - \tfrac{1}{2}\sqrt{5}.$$

Exercise C (answers p 158)

1 Rationalise the denominators of these. Simplify your answers where appropriate.

(a) $\dfrac{7}{\sqrt{6}}$ (b) $\dfrac{12}{\sqrt{3}}$ (c) $\dfrac{1}{\sqrt{5}}$ (d) $\dfrac{1-\sqrt{5}}{\sqrt{2}}$ (e) $\dfrac{8\sqrt{3}-2}{3\sqrt{2}}$

2 (a) Express each of these in the form $k\sqrt{7}$.   (i) $\sqrt{28}$ (ii) $\dfrac{21}{\sqrt{7}}$

(b) Hence write $\sqrt{28} + \dfrac{21}{\sqrt{7}}$ in the form $n\sqrt{7}$, where n is an integer.

3 Rationalise the denominators of the following.

(a) $\dfrac{1}{\sqrt{3}+1}$ (b) $\dfrac{5}{\sqrt{6}-1}$ (c) $\dfrac{7}{5\sqrt{2}-1}$ (d) $\dfrac{\sqrt{5}+4}{\sqrt{2}+1}$ (e) $\dfrac{6}{\sqrt{5}+\sqrt{2}}$

(f) $\dfrac{1}{\sqrt{3}+\sqrt{5}}$ (g) $\dfrac{\sqrt{3}}{3+\sqrt{13}}$ (h) $\dfrac{7\sqrt{2}}{3+2\sqrt{2}}$ (i) $\dfrac{\sqrt{10}+1}{\sqrt{5}-\sqrt{2}}$ (j) $\dfrac{\sqrt{11}-\sqrt{10}}{\sqrt{11}+\sqrt{10}}$

4 Show that $\dfrac{\sqrt{3}+5}{3-\sqrt{3}} = 3 + \tfrac{4}{3}\sqrt{3}$.

5 Given that $\dfrac{6-\sqrt{7}}{\sqrt{7}-2} = p + q\sqrt{7}$, where p and q are rational, find the value of p and q.

6 Given that $\dfrac{5-\sqrt{3}}{1+\sqrt{3}} = a + b\sqrt{3}$, where a and b are integers, find the value of a and b.

7 Rationalise the denominator of $\dfrac{1}{3\sqrt{2}-4}$ and hence prove that $\dfrac{1}{3\sqrt{2}-4} > 2$.

8 (a) Rationalise the denominator of these.   **(i)** $\dfrac{5\sqrt{3}}{4+\sqrt{11}}$ **(ii)** $\dfrac{4\sqrt{11}}{\sqrt{3}+1}$

(b) Hence simplify $\dfrac{5\sqrt{3}}{4+\sqrt{11}} + \dfrac{4\sqrt{11}}{\sqrt{3}+1}$ as far as you can.

9 Simplify each of these as far as you can.

(a) $\dfrac{6\sqrt{2}}{3+\sqrt{7}} + \dfrac{4\sqrt{7}}{\sqrt{2}-1}$ **(b)** $\dfrac{4\sqrt{5}}{\sqrt{3}-1} - \dfrac{4\sqrt{3}}{\sqrt{5}+1}$ **(c)** $\dfrac{\sqrt{2}}{2+\sqrt{3}} + \dfrac{\sqrt{3}}{1+\sqrt{2}}$

10 The area of a rectangle is 15 and its length is $2+\sqrt{7}$.

Find its width and write it in the form $a\sqrt{7}+b$.

11 Triangle ABC has an area of 5.

The length of base BC is $6\sqrt{2}-2\sqrt{3}$.
Find the height of this triangle, measured from base BC.
Write your answer exactly, in its simplest form.

*12 Rationalise the denominator of $\dfrac{1}{\sqrt{2}+\sqrt{3}+\sqrt{5}}$.

D Further problems

Example 11

Triangle PQR is isosceles.
$PR = 7\,$cm and $QR = 10\,$cm.

Find the exact area of the triangle.

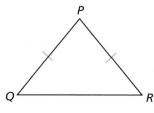

Solution

Since the triangle is isosceles, $QX = \frac{1}{2}QR = 5\,$cm.

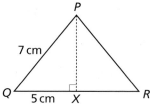

By Pythagoras, the length of PX is $\sqrt{7^2 - 5^2} = \sqrt{49-25}$
$$= \sqrt{24}$$
$$= \sqrt{4} \times \sqrt{6}$$
$$= 2\sqrt{6}\ \text{cm}$$ *Try to write your answer in terms of the simplest possible surds.*

So the area of PQR is $\frac{1}{2} \times 10 \times 2\sqrt{6} = 10\sqrt{6}$ cm².

The value π is an irrational number. All powers of π are irrational too.
For example, π^4 and $\sqrt{\pi}$ are also irrational.

Example 12

The area of a semicircle is 4π.
Show that the perimeter of this semicircle is $2\sqrt{2}(2+\pi)$.

Solution

The area of the semicircle is 4π.

The area of a semicircle is $\dfrac{\pi r^2}{2}$, where r is the radius, so $\dfrac{\pi r^2}{2} = 4\pi$.

So $\dfrac{r^2}{2} = 4$ and hence $r = \sqrt{8} = 2\sqrt{2}$.

So the diameter is $2 \times 2\sqrt{2} = 4\sqrt{2}$.

The length of the curved part of the semicircle is

$$\frac{\pi \times \text{diameter}}{2} = \frac{\pi \times 4\sqrt{2}}{2} = 2\sqrt{2}\,\pi.$$

Thus the perimeter of the semicircle is

    length of diameter + length of curved part

    $= 4\sqrt{2} + 2\sqrt{2}\,\pi = 2\sqrt{2}(2+\pi)$ as required.

Exercise D (answers p 159)

Give an exact answer to each problem.
Use π and the simplest possible surds where appropriate.

1 Find the length of the line joining the points with coordinates $(-3, -5)$ and $(5, -1)$.

2 A rectangle has vertices with coordinates $(0, 0)$, $(6, 4)$, $(4, 7)$ and $(-2, 3)$.
Find the area of the rectangle.

3 A circle has a radius of $3\sqrt{7}$. What is the area of this circle?

4 Show that triangle XYZ is a right-angled triangle.

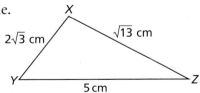

5 A circle has an area of 7π.
What is the circumference of the circle?

6 The two lines sketched here have equations
$y = \sqrt{2}x + 9$ and $y = 10 - x$.

Find the coordinates of the point of intersection.

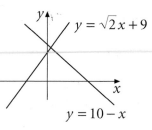

7 A quarter-circle has an area of 6π.
Show that the perimeter of the
quarter-circle is $\sqrt{6}(4 + \pi)$.

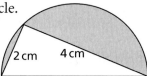

8 A circle has an area of $50\,\text{cm}^2$.

Show that the radius is $5\sqrt{\dfrac{2}{\pi}}$ cm and the circumference is $10\sqrt{2\pi}$ cm.

9 The diagram shows a triangle in a semicircle.

2 cm   4 cm

Work out

(a) the perimeter of the semicircle   **(b)** the total shaded area

10 The diagram shows a quarter-circle.
Length AB is $10\,\text{cm}$.

B

A

Show that the perimeter of the quarter-circle is $5\sqrt{2}\left(2 + \tfrac{1}{2}\pi\right)$ cm.

Key points

- A root such as $\sqrt{5}$ that cannot be written exactly as a fraction is **irrational**. (p 22)

- An expression that involves irrational roots is in **surd form**.
  Examples are $3\sqrt{5}$ and $\sqrt{10} - 7$. (p 22)

- $\sqrt{ab} = \sqrt{a} \times \sqrt{b}$ (pp 22–23)

- $\sqrt{\dfrac{a}{b}} = \dfrac{\sqrt{a}}{\sqrt{b}}$ (pp 22–23)

- The product of the two **conjugates** $\left(a\sqrt{b} + c\sqrt{d}\right)$ and $\left(a\sqrt{b} - c\sqrt{d}\right)$ is always
  a rational number (when a, b, c and d are rational).
  So, for example, to **rationalise the denominator** of the expression
  $\dfrac{6 + \sqrt{7}}{3 - 7\sqrt{2}}$ you need to multiply the numerator and denominator by $3 + 7\sqrt{2}$. (p 26)

Test yourself (answers p 159)

None of these questions requires a calculator.

1 Points A and B have coordinates $(-2, -1)$ and $(4, 1)$ respectively.
Show that AB has length $p\sqrt{10}$, stating the value of p.

2 (a) Express each of the following in the form $k\sqrt{5}$.

    (i) $\sqrt{45}$ **(ii)** $\dfrac{20}{\sqrt{5}}$ AQA 2003

  (b) Hence write $\sqrt{45} + \dfrac{20}{\sqrt{5}}$ in the form $n\sqrt{5}$, where n is an integer.

3 Points A, B and C have coordinates $(1, 2)$, $(3, 4)$ and $(9, -2)$ respectively.

  (a) (i) In surd form, find the lengths AB, BC and AC.

      (ii) Hence show that ABC is a right-angled triangle.

  (b) Find the area of triangle ABC.

4 Express each of the following in the form $p + q\sqrt{3}$.

  (a) $(2 + \sqrt{3})(5 - 2\sqrt{3})$

  (b) $\dfrac{26}{4 - \sqrt{3}}$ AQA 2002

5 (a) Express $(\sqrt{7} + 1)^2$ in the form $a + b\sqrt{7}$, where a and b are integers.   AQA 2001

  (b) Hence express $\dfrac{(\sqrt{7} + 1)^2}{(\sqrt{7} + 2)}$ in the form $p + q\sqrt{7}$, where p and q are rational numbers.

6 The shape shown is a sector ABC of a circle with centre A and radius AB.
The radius of the circle is 8 cm and the triangle ABC is equilateral.

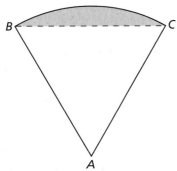

Show that the area of the shaded segment is $16\left(\frac{2}{3}\pi - \sqrt{3}\right)$ cm^2.

3 Quadratic graphs and equations

In this chapter you will

- multiply out brackets and factorise quadratic expressions
- write a quadratic expression in completed-square form and relate it to the sketch of the corresponding graph, noting the vertex and line of symmetry
- solve a quadratic equation by factorising, completing the square or using the formula
- relate the roots of a quadratic equation to where its graph crosses the x-axis
- evaluate and interpret the discriminant of a quadratic expression

A Expanding brackets: revision

Example 1

Multiply out $5x(x - 6)$.

Solution

$$5x(x - 6) = 5x \times x - 5x \times 6$$
$$= 5x^2 - 30x$$

Example 2

Multiply out $(3x + 2)(x - 6)$.

Solution

$$(3x + 2)(x - 6) = 3x(x - 6) + 2(x - 6)$$
$$= 3x^2 - 18x + 2x - 12$$
$$= 3x^2 - 16x - 12$$

You can set out your working in a table.

$\times$	x	-6
$3x$	$3x^2$	$-18x$
2	$2x$	-12

Exercise A (answers p 160)

1 Multiply out each expression.

  (a) $3(4x - 7)$ (b) $2x(x + 5)$ (c) $-x(3x - 1)$

2 Multiply out each expression and write the result in its simplest form.
Use a table for each one if you find it useful.

  (a) $(x + 5)(x + 6)$ (b) $(5 + x)(x - 3)$ (c) $(2x - 5)(x - 1)$

  (d) $(7 - x)(3x + 1)$ (e) $(2 - x)(6 - x)$ (f) $3(x - 5)(x + 8)$

  (g) $4(3 - x)(3x - 7)$ (h) $(x + 2)(x - 2)$ (i) $(4x + 3)(4x - 3)$

  (j) $(x + 3)^2$ (k) $2(x + 11)^2$ (l) $(x - 6)^2$

3 Multiply out each expression and write the result in its simplest form.

  (a) $(x + a)(x + b)$ (b) $(x + a)^2$ (c) $k(x + a)^2$

  (d) $(x + a)(x - a)$ (e) $(ax + b)^2$ (f) $(ax + b)(ax - b)$

B Factorising quadratic expressions: revision

Any expression of the form $ax^2 + bx + c$ (where $a \neq 0$) is called a **quadratic** expression.
Sometimes a quadratic expression can be factorised into the product of linear factors.

Example 3

Factorise $2x^2 - 8x$.

Solution

$2x^2 - 8x = 2x(x - 4)$

Example 4

Factorise $3x^2 + 8x + 5$.

Solution

$3x^2 = 3x \times x$

These two terms must
multiply to give 5.

5×1 and -5×-1 are
the possible products
for 5.

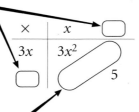

These two terms
must add to give $8x$.

$\times$	x	1
$3x$	$3x^2$	$3x$
5	$5x$	5

This table gives the correct
result so the factorisation is
$3x^2 + 8x + 5 = (3x + 5)(x + 1)$.

(handwritten:)
$15 \quad 3x^2 + 3x + 5x + 5 = 0$
$x(3x + 3 + 5) + 5 = 0$
$x(3x + 8) = -5$
$3x^2$
$(3x + 5)(x + 3)$
$(3x + 5)(x + 1)$

Example 5

Factorise $18x^2 - 32$.

Solution

Look for any common factors first.
$9x^2 - 16 = (3x)^2 - 4^2$ *is a difference of two*
squares so the factorisation is $(3x + 4)(3x - 4)$.

$18x^2 - 32 = 2(9x^2 - 16)$
$\qquad\qquad = 2(3x + 4)(3x - 4)$

A table confirms this.

$\times$	$3x$	-4
$3x$	$9x^2$	$-12x$
4	$12x$	-16

Exercise B (answers p 160)

1 Factorise each expression.

(a) $x^2 + 5x$ (b) $x^2 - 10x$ (c) $3x^2 - 6x$ (d) $4x^2 + 10x$

(e) $12x + 18x^2$ (f) $9x - x^2$ (g) $15x - 9x^2$ (h) $-x^2 + 7x$

2 Factorise each expression.

(a) $x^2 + 6x + 5$ (b) $x^2 - 6x + 5$ (c) $x^2 + 6x + 9$

(d) $x^2 + 10x + 9$ (e) $x^2 - 9x + 18$ (f) $x^2 + 4x - 21$

(g) $x^2 - x - 12$ (h) $x^2 - 14x - 15$ (i) $x^2 - 10x + 25$

3 Factorise each expression.

(a) $2x^2 + 5x + 3$ (b) $3x^2 + 16x + 5$ (c) $5x^2 - 8x + 3$

(d) $3x^2 - 20x - 7$ (e) $6x^2 + 27x - 15$ (f) $3x^2 + 11x + 6$

(g) $3x^2 + 19x + 6$ (h) $4x^2 - 22x + 24$ (i) $3x^2 - 22x - 16$

(j) $4x^2 - 4x + 1$ (k) $6x^2 - 29x - 5$ (l) $10x^2 - 29x + 12$

4 Factorise each expression.

(a) $x^2 - 9$ (b) $x^2 - 100$ (c) $x^2 - 1$

(d) $4x^2 - 25$ (e) $9x^2 - 1$ (f) $32 - 50x^2$

5 Where possible, factorise each expression fully.

(a) $2x^2 - 3x - 9$ (b) $x^2 - 2x + 7$ (c) $2x^2 - 2x - 60$

(d) $2x^2 + 5x + 1$ (e) $6x^2 + 9x - 15$ (f) $16x^2 - 8x - 3$

(g) $-x^2 - 2x + 15$ (h) $36x^2 - 25$ (i) $45 + x - 2x^2$

6 (a) Confirm that, when $x = 7$, the value of $x^2 + 10x + 25$ is a square number.

   (b) By factorising, show that the value of $x^2 + 10x + 25$ is a square number for any integer value of x.

7 (a) (i) Find the value of the expression $x^2 + 3x + 2$ when $x = 6$.

      (ii) Write this value as the product of two consecutive numbers.

   (b) Show that the value of $x^2 + 3x + 2$ can be written as a product of two consecutive numbers for any integer value of x.

*8 (a) Confirm that, when $x = 3$, the value of $16x^2 - 8x + 1$ is an odd square number.

    (b) Show that the value of $16x^2 - 8x + 1$ is an odd square number for any integer x.

*9 (a) (i) Find the value of the expression $4x^2 - 1$ when $x = 5$.

      (ii) Write this value as the product of two consecutive odd numbers.

    (b) Show that the value of $4x^2 - 1$ can be written as a product of two consecutive odd numbers for any integer value of x.

C Parabolas (answers p 160)

C1 Use a graph plotter on a computer or graphic calculator to plot the graph of
$y = ax^2 + bx + c$ for various values of a, b and c.
Note the effect of making a negative.

Curves with equations that can be written in the form $y = ax^2 + bx + c$ $(a \neq 0)$ are **parabolas**.

The curve seen when a plane cuts
a cone like this is a parabola.
The Ancient Greek mathematician
and astronomer Appollonius
(3rd century BCE) was the person
who named these curves 'parabolas'.

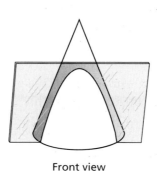

Front view

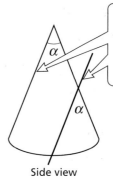

For a **para**bola,
these two lines
on a side view
are **para**llel.

Side view

You can see parabolas in various practical situations.

Parallel beams of light that shine on a parabolic reflector
are all reflected through the same point.

Car headlights and astronomical mirrors are modern
uses of parabolic reflectors.

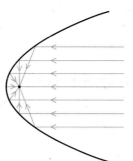

When the Romans invaded Syracuse on the coast of Sicily in 214 BCE, Archimedes
invented various devices to defend the city. These include the famous 'burning mirrors'
which are supposed to have set ships on fire. They were made as close as possible to
the shape of a parabolic mirror and focused the Sun's rays on to the invading ships.

Hundreds of years later, cannons were becoming widely used
in warfare and it was important to be able to judge accurately
where a cannon ball would land. Galileo (1564–1642)
determined that the path of a cannon ball (and indeed any
object moving under gravity such as a golf ball) follows a
parabolic curve.

The relationship between parabolic graphs and their equations is an important one.

The parabola with equation $y = x^2$ has a vertical line of symmetry along the y-axis and a **vertex** at the origin. The vertex of the graph of $y = x^2$ is a minimum point.

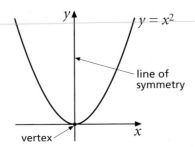

Use a graph plotter to draw the graphs in the problems below.

C2 (a) Plot the graph of $y = x^2$ and superimpose the graphs of $y = 2x^2$ and $y = \frac{1}{3}x^2$. Describe the relationship between the graphs.

  (b) Investigate graphs of the form $y = kx^2$ for both positive and negative values of k. How are they related to $y = x^2$?

C3 Investigate graphs of the form $y = x^2 + q$ for both positive and negative values of q. How are they related to $y = x^2$?

C4 Investigate graphs of the form $y = (x + p)^2$ for both positive and negative values of p. How are they related to $y = x^2$?

C5 Plot the graph of $y = x^2$ and superimpose the graph of $y = (x + 5)^2 + 2$.

  (a) What are the coordinates of the vertex of $y = (x + 5)^2 + 2$?

  (b) What is the equation of its line of symmetry?

  (c) (i) Show that the equation of the graph can be written as $y = x^2 + 10x + 27$.

   (ii) Hence write down where the graph crosses the y-axis.

C6 Investigate graphs with equations in the form $y = (x + p)^2 + q$. How are they related to $y = x^2$?

C7 What do you think is the vertex of the graph of $y = (x - 6)^2 + 9$?

C8 What do you think is the equation of the line of symmetry of $y = (x + 4)^2 - 3$?

C9 Investigate graphs of the form $y = 2(x + p)^2 + q$ for both positive and negative values of p and q. How are they related to $y = 2x^2$?

C10 How do you think graphs of the form $y = k(x + p)^2 + q$ are related to $y = kx^2$?

C11 (a) (i) What do you think are the coordinates of the vertex of $y = 3(x - 2)^2 - 5$?

(ii) What is the equation of its line of symmetry?

(b) (i) Show that the equation of the graph can be written as $y = 3x^2 - 12x + 7$.

(ii) Hence determine where the graph crosses the y-axis.

We can work algebraically when translating curves.

For example, the graph of $y = 2x^2$ is translated 3 units to the right and 4 units up.

Using vector notation this translation can be represented by $\begin{bmatrix} 3 \\ 4 \end{bmatrix}$.

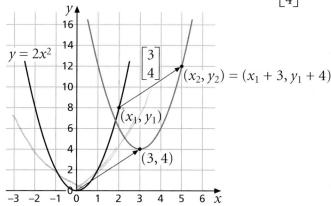

Let (x_1, y_1) be a point on $y = 2x^2$ and let (x_2, y_2) be its image on the translated curve.

Then $(x_2, y_2) = (x_1 + 3, y_1 + 4)$, giving

$x_1 = x_2 - 3$ *from rearranging* $x_2 = x_1 + 3$

and $y_1 = y_2 - 4$ *from rearranging* $y_2 = y_1 + 4$

We know that $y_1 = 2x_1{}^2$, so it must be true that

$$y_2 - 4 = 2(x_2 - 3)^2$$

and so $y - 4 = 2(x - 3)^2$ is the equation of the transformed curve.

This can be written as $y = 2(x - 3)^2 + 4$.

> So to find the equation of the curve that is the result of translating $y = 2x^2$ by $\begin{bmatrix} 3 \\ 4 \end{bmatrix}$ you can replace x by $(x - 3)$ and y by $(y - 4)$.

C12 What is the equation of the image of the curve $y = x^2$ after a translation of $\begin{bmatrix} 6 \\ 5 \end{bmatrix}$?

C13 What is the equation of the image of the curve $y = 2x^2$ after a translation of $\begin{bmatrix} -3 \\ 2 \end{bmatrix}$?

C14 Which translation will transform the curve $y = x^2$ to $y = (x - 9)^2 + 7$?

C15 Which translation will transform the curve $y = 3x^2$ to $y = 3(x + 1)^2 - 6$?

Example 6

The graph below is a translation of $y = x^2$.

What is its equation in the form
$y = ax^2 + bx + c$?

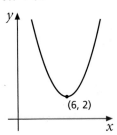

(6, 2)

Solution

The vertex is (6, 2) so the translation is $\begin{bmatrix} 6 \\ 2 \end{bmatrix}$.

So the equation can be written as
$$y - 2 = (x - 6)^2$$
$$\Rightarrow \quad y = (x - 6)^2 + 2$$
$$= x^2 - 12x + 36 + 2$$
$$= x^2 - 12x + 38$$

So the equation is $y = x^2 - 12x + 38$.

Example 7

Sketch the graph of $y = 3(x + 2)^2 - 1$, showing the vertex, the y-intercept and the line of symmetry.

Solution

The equation can be written $y + 1 = 3(x + 2)^2$.

The graph can be obtained by translating $y = 3x^2$ by $\begin{bmatrix} -2 \\ -1 \end{bmatrix}$. So the vertex is $(-2, -1)$ and the line of symmetry is $x = -2$.

When $x = 0$,
$y = 3 \times (0 + 2)^2 - 1 = 11$.
So the y-intercept is 11.

$x = -2$

11

$y = 3(x + 2)^2 - 1$

$(-2, -1)$

Exercise C (answers p 161)

1 Which translation will transform the curve $y = x^2$ to $y = (x - 4)^2 - 5$?

2 Which translation will transform the curve $y = x^2$ to $y = (x + 8)^2 + 1$?

3 What is the vertex of the graph with equation $y = (x - 5)^2 + 7$?

4 What is the equation of the line of symmetry for the graph of $y = (x + 2)^2 - 3$?

5 (a) (i) Write the equation $y = (x + 7)^2 - 5$ in the form $y = ax^2 + bx + c$.

   (ii) Hence write down the y-intercept.

   (b) Sketch the graph of $y = (x + 7)^2 - 5$.
   Show clearly the coordinates of the vertex and the y-intercept.

6 Sketch the graph for each of these equations, showing clearly the vertex and y-intercept.

   (a) $y = (x - 2)^2 + 5$ (b) $y = (x - 4)^2$ (c) $y = (x + 6)^2 - 20$

7 Show that the graph of $y = (x + 3)^2 + 1$ does not cross the x-axis.

8 Each of these graphs is a translation of $y = x^2$.
Find the equation of each one.

(a)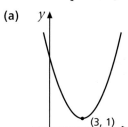
(3, 1)

(b)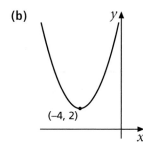
(–4, 2)

(c)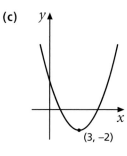
(3, –2)

9 (a) (i) Which translation will transform the curve $y = 2x^2$ to $y = 2(x + 1)^2 - 3$?

(ii) What are the coordinates of the vertex of $y = 2(x + 1)^2 - 3$?

(b) Write $y = 2(x + 1)^2 - 3$ in the form $y = ax^2 + bx + c$.

(c) Sketch the graph of $y = 2(x + 1)^2 - 3$, showing clearly the vertex, axis (line) of symmetry and the y-intercept.

10 Sketch the graph for each of these equations, showing clearly the vertex and y-intercept.

(a) $y = 2(x + 4)^2 + 1$ (b) $y = 3(x - 2)^2 - 7$ (c) $y = 4(x + 1)^2 - 3$

11 (a) (i) Which translation will transform the curve $y = -x^2$ to $y = -(x + 2)^2 + 5$?

(ii) What is the vertex of $y = -(x + 2)^2 + 5$?

(b) On the same set of axes, sketch the graphs of $y = -x^2$ and $y = -(x + 2)^2 + 5$, showing clearly the vertex of $y = -(x + 2)^2 + 5$.

(c) What is the y-intercept of $y = -(x + 2)^2 + 5$?

12 (a) Show that the expression $-2(x - 3)^2 + 11$ is equivalent to $-2x^2 + 12x - 7$.

(b) Sketch the graph of $y = -2(x - 3)^2 + 11$, showing clearly the vertex, axis of symmetry and the y-intercept.

*13 The parabola with equation $y = x^2$ is stretched by a factor of 3 in the y-direction.
Then it is translated by $\begin{bmatrix} 8 \\ 1 \end{bmatrix}$.
Write down the equation of the transformed graph.

*14 The parabola with equation $y = x^2$ is reflected in the x-axis.
Then it is stretched by a factor of 4 in the y-direction.
Finally, it is translated by $\begin{bmatrix} -5 \\ -3 \end{bmatrix}$.
Write down the equation of the transformed graph.

*15 Each of these graphs is a sketch of a parabola.
Determine the equation of each one.

(a)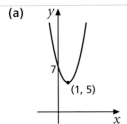

(b)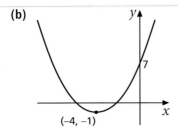

(c)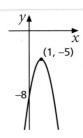

D Completing the square (answers p 162)

K The identity $(x + a)^2 = x^2 + 2ax + a^2$ is useful when dealing with squares.

For example, $(x - 3)^2 = x^2 + 2 \times (-3) \times x + 3^2$
$$= x^2 - 6x + 9$$

The expression $x^2 - 6x + 9$ is called a **perfect square** as it can be written as $(x - 3)^2$.

D1 Expand each expression.

(a) $(x + 4)^2$ (b) $(x - 9)^2$ (c) $(x + 20)^2$

(d) $(x - 1)^2$ (e) $(x + \frac{1}{4})^2$ (f) $(x - \frac{1}{3})^2$

D2 Decide which of the expressions below are perfect squares.

A $x^2 + 10x + 25$ B $x^2 + 6x + 12$ C $x^2 - 16x + 64$

D $x^2 - 2x + 2$ E $x^2 - 10x - 25$ F $x^2 - 12x + 36$

G $x^2 + x + \frac{1}{4}$ H $x^2 - 7x + 9\frac{1}{4}$

D3 What values of k make these expressions perfect squares?

(a) $x^2 + 14x + k$ (b) $x^2 + kx + 121$ (c) $x^2 - kx + 64$

D4 Multiply out the brackets and write each expression in its simplest form.

(a) $(x + 5)^2 - 25$ (b) $(x + 3)^2 - 9$ (c) $(x - 3)^2 - 9$ (d) $(x - 7)^2 - 49$

D5 (a) Express $x^2 + 6x + 9$ in the form $(x + p)^2$.

(b) Hence express $x^2 + 6x$ in the form $(x + p)^2 + q$.

(c) Hence express $x^2 + 6x + 5$ in the form $(x + p)^2 + q$.

(d) Sketch the graph of $y = x^2 + 6x + 5$.

D6 (a) Express $x^2 - 14x$ in the form $(x + p)^2 + q$.

(b) Hence express $x^2 - 14x + 50$ in the form $(x + p)^2 + q$.

(c) Sketch the graph of $y = x^2 - 14x + 50$.

Expressions in the form $(x + p)^2 + q$ are said to be in **completed-square form**.

___

Example 8

Write $x^2 - 8x + 3$ in completed-square form.
Hence find the minimum value of the expression $x^2 - 8x + 3$.
State the value of x that gives this minimum value.

Solution

Start with the first two terms.
The constant inside the brackets is found
by halving the coefficient of x.

$$x^2 - 8x = (x - 4)^2 - 16$$

Adjust your answer to take into account the
constant term.

$$x^2 - 8x + 3 = (x - 4)^2 - 16 + 3$$

$$\Rightarrow \quad x^2 - 8x + 3 = (x - 4)^2 - 13$$

You can check this by multiplying out the brackets and simplifying.

$(x - 4)^2 \geq 0$ for all values of x so the
minimum value of $x^2 - 8x + 3$ is -13.

The minimum value occurs when $(x - 4) = 0$. The minimum value occurs when $x = 4$.

___

D7 Write the following in completed-square form.

(a) $x^2 + 14x + 2$ (b) $x^2 - 6x + 12$ (c) $x^2 + 8x - 3$

D8 (a) Write $x^2 + 2x - 4$ in completed-square form.

(b) Hence sketch the graph of $y = x^2 + 2x - 4$.

D9 (a) Write $x^2 + 18x + 82$ in completed-square form.

(b) Hence show that $x^2 + 18x + 82 > 0$ for all values of x.

D10 (a) Write $x^2 + 4x + 11$ in completed-square form.

(b) (i) Hence show that the minimum value of $x^2 + 4x + 11$ is 7.

(ii) State the value of x that gives this minimum value.

D11 (a) Multiply out $(x - \frac{1}{2})^2$.

(b) Hence express $x^2 - x$ in the form $(x + p)^2 + q$.

(c) Write $x^2 - x - 5$ in completed-square form.

D12 Write the following in completed-square form.

(a) $x^2 + 3x + 1$ (b) $x^2 + 5x + 10$ (c) $x^2 - 9x - 3$

D13 (a) Write $x^2 - x + \frac{7}{4}$ in completed-square form.

(b) Hence show that the minimum value of $x^2 - x + \frac{7}{4}$ is $1\frac{1}{2}$.

Any quadratic expression can be written in the **completed-square form** $k(x + p)^2 + q$.
The process of writing a quadratic in this form is called **completing the square**.

Example 9

Write $2x^2 + 12x - 1$ in completed-square form.

Solution

Write the first two terms as a product of two factors where one factor is the coefficient of x^2.	$2x^2 + 12x = 2[x^2 + 6x]$
Write the expression in square brackets in completed-square form.	$= 2[(x + 3)^2 - 9]$
Multiply out the square brackets.	$= 2(x + 3)^2 - 18$
Adjust.	$2x^2 + 12x - 1 = 2(x + 3)^2 - 18 - 1$
	$= 2(x + 3)^2 - 19$

D14 (a) Write $3x^2 - 12x - 4$ in completed-square form.

(b) Sketch the graph of $y = 3x^2 - 12x - 4$, showing clearly the vertex and the y-intercept.

D15 Write the following in completed-square form.

(a) $2x^2 + 16x + 40$ (b) $3x^2 - 18x - 1$ (c) $2x^2 + 10x - 8$

Example 10

Write $-3x^2 - 6x + 5$ in completed-square form.
Hence find the maximum value of $-3x^2 - 6x + 5$.

Solution

$$-3x^2 - 6x = -3[x^2 + 2x]$$
$$= -3[(x + 1)^2 - 1]$$
$$= -3(x + 1)^2 + 3$$
$$\Rightarrow \quad -3x^2 - 6x + 5 = -3(x + 1)^2 + 3 + 5$$
$$= -3(x + 1)^2 + 8$$

$-3(x + 1)^2 \leq 0$ for all values of x, so the expression $-3x^2 - 6x + 5$ has a **maximum** value of 8.

Exercise D (answers p 163)

1 Write each of these expressions in completed-square form.

(a) $x^2 + 6x + 10$ (b) $x^2 - 10x + 3$ (c) $x^2 + 18x - 2$

(d) $x^2 - 4x + 13$ (e) $x^2 + 3x - 1$ (f) $x^2 - 5x + 9$

2 (a) Show that $x^2 - 12x + 41$ is equivalent to $(x - 6)^2 + 5$.

(b) Which of these points is the vertex of the graph of $y = x^2 - 12x + 41$?

$(6, 41)$ $(-6, 5)$ $(-6, 41)$ $(6, 5)$ $(6, -5)$ $(-12, 41)$

(c) Show that the graph of $y = x^2 - 12x + 41$ crosses the y-axis at $(0, 41)$.

3 For each equation below,

(i) write the quadratic in completed-square form

(ii) sketch the corresponding graph, indicating clearly the vertex and y-intercept

(a) $y = x^2 + 6x + 15$ **(b)** $y = x^2 + 8x - 2$ **(c)** $y = x^2 - 2x + 5$

(d) $y = x^2 - 4x - 3$ **(e)** $y = x^2 + 3x + 7$ **(f)** $y = x^2 - 7x - 2$

4 By completing the square, show that the graph of $y = x^2 - 6x + 13$ does not cross the x-axis.

5 (a) Express $x^2 + 2x + 5$ in completed-square form.

(b) (i) Show that $x^2 + 2x + 5$ has a minimum value of 4.

(ii) State the value of x that gives this minimum value.

6 Show that the graph of $y = x^2 + 4x + 1$ crosses the x-axis twice.

7 (a) Express $x^2 + 12x + 11$ in the form $(x + a)^2 + b$, finding the values of a and b.

(b) State the minimum value of the expression $x^2 + 12x + 11$.   AQA 2001

8 By completing the square, show that the graph of $y = x^2 + 4x + 4$ touches the x-axis at just one point.

9 Write each of these expressions in completed-square form.

(a) $2x^2 + 4x - 1$ **(b)** $3x^2 - 12x + 13$ **(c)** $5x^2 - 10x - 1$

(d) $2x^2 + 16x + 32$ **(e)** $3x^2 + 3x + 5$ **(f)** $4x^2 - 12x - 5$

10 (a) Show that $3x^2 + 12x - 7$ is equivalent to $3(x + 2)^2 - 19$.

(b) Write down the vertex of the graph of $y = 3x^2 + 12x - 7$.

(c) Show that the graph of $y = 3x^2 + 12x - 7$ crosses the y-axis at $(0, -7)$.

(d) Write down the equation of the line of symmetry of the curve $y = 3x^2 + 12x - 7$.

11 For each equation below,

(i) write the quadratic in completed-square form

(ii) sketch the graph, indicating clearly the vertex and y-intercept

(a) $y = 2x^2 - 12x + 21$ **(b)** $y = 3x^2 + 6x + 3$ **(c)** $y = 4x^2 + 4x + 3$

12 By completing the square, show that the graph of $y = 5x^2 - 20x + 24$ does not cross the x-axis.

13 For each expression below,

      (i) write it in completed-square form

      (ii) write down the minimum value of the expression

      (iii) state the value of x which gives this minimum value

    (a) $3x^2 + 18x + 25$ **(b)** $2x^2 - 4x + 5$ **(c)** $2x^2 + 14x + 1$

14 (a) Express $2x^2 + 8x + 7$ in the form $A(x + B)^2 + C$, where A, B and C are constants.

    (b) (i) State the minimum value of $2x^2 + 8x + 7$.

       (ii) State the value of x which gives this minimum value.   AQA 2002

15 Two ships set off from different harbours at the same time.

The distance between the ships is given by the formula $d = t^2 - 8t + 19$, where d is the distance in kilometres and t is the time in hours.

    (a) Write the formula in completed-square form.

    (b) Hence find the distance between the ships when they are nearest to each other.

    (c) How many hours have they been sailing when they are nearest to each other?

16 Write each of these expressions in completed-square form.

    (a) $2x^2 + 3x + 1$ **(b)** $3x^2 - 3x - 2$ **(c)** $4x^2 - 3x - 1$

17 (a) By multiplying out the brackets, show that $-2(x + 1)^2 + 5$ is equivalent to $-2x^2 - 4x + 3$.

    (b) Write down the vertex of the graph of $y = -2x^2 - 4x + 3$.

    (c) State the y-intercept of the graph of $y = -2x^2 - 4x + 3$.

    (d) Sketch the graph of $y = -2x^2 - 4x + 3$.

18 For each equation below,

      (i) write the quadratic in completed-square form

      (ii) sketch the corresponding graph, indicating clearly the vertex and y-intercept

    (a) $y = -x^2 - 6x + 1$ **(b)** $y = 3 + 8x - x^2$ **(c)** $y = -2x^2 - 12x - 25$

19 (a) Find the maximum value of the expression $-3x^2 + 30x - 74$.

    (b) What value of x gives this maximum value?

20 The height of a particular golf ball is given by the formula $h = 30t - 5t^2$, where h is the height in metres and t is the time in seconds.

    (a) Write the formula in completed-square form.

    (b) Hence find the maximum height of the ball.

    (c) After how many seconds does the ball reach its maximum?

E Zeros of quadratics

The line of symmetry, the vertex and the y-intercept are important features of a parabolic graph. Also useful are the points at which the graph crosses the x-axis, if it does. The graphs of all quadratic functions of x must cross the y-axis but some graphs do not cross the x-axis.

The values of x at the points of intersection with the x-axis are called the **zeros** of the function because they make the function equal to zero.

Example 11

Find where the graph of $y = 2x^2 + 3x - 2$ crosses the x-axis.

Solution

On the x-axis the value of y is 0.

$$2x^2 + 3x - 2 = 0$$
$$\Rightarrow \quad (2x - 1)(x + 2) = 0$$

Either $(2x - 1) = 0$ or $(x + 2) = 0$.

giving $x = \frac{1}{2}$ and $x = -2$

So the graph crosses the x-axis at $(\frac{1}{2}, 0)$ and $(-2, 0)$.

Example 12

Solve the equation $3x^2 + 15x + 18 = 0$.

Solution

$$3x^2 + 15x + 18 = 0$$

3 is a common factor of each term so divide each side of the equation by 3. $\Rightarrow \quad x^2 + 5x + 6 = 0$

The quadratic factorises. $\Rightarrow \quad (x + 3)(x + 2) = 0$

Either $(x + 3) = 0$ or $(x + 2) = 0$.

giving $x = -3$ and $x = -2$

So the solutions are $x = -3$ and $x = -2$.

Example 13

Show that the graph of $y = 12x - 4 - 9x^2$ just touches the x-axis at one point.

Solution

On the x-axis the value of y is 0.

$$12x - 4 - 9x^2 = 0$$

Multiply each side of the equation by -1 to make the coefficient of x^2 positive. $\Rightarrow \quad 9x^2 - 12x + 4 = 0$

The quadratic factorises. $\Rightarrow \quad (3x - 2)(3x - 2) = 0$

There is only one zero, that is when $(3x - 2) = 0$. giving $x = \frac{2}{3}$

The parabola cannot cross the x-axis at just one point, so the graph just touches it at $(\frac{2}{3}, 0)$.

Exercise E (answers p 164)

1 Solve each equation.

(a) $x^2 - 4x = 0$ (b) $x^2 + 2x = 0$ (c) $x^2 + 7x + 6 = 0$

(d) $x^2 - 6x + 9 = 0$ (e) $2x^2 - 12x - 32 = 0$ (f) $x^2 - 9x + 18 = 0$

(g) $2x^2 + 5x - 3 = 0$ (h) $3x^2 - x - 2 = 0$ (i) $6x^2 + 33x - 63 = 0$

(j) $5x^2 - 16x + 12 = 0$ (k) $12 - 35x - 3x^2 = 0$ (l) $4x^2 - 20x + 25 = 0$

2 Find out where the graph of each equation crosses or meets the x-axis.

(a) $y = x^2 + x - 12$ (b) $y = x^2 - 9x + 8$ (c) $y = 2x^2 + 13x + 6$

(d) $y = 3x^2 + 19x - 14$ (e) $y = x^2 - 7x$ (f) $y = x^2 - 9$

(g) $y = 2x^2 - 8x + 6$ (h) $y = 3x^2 + 30x + 75$ (i) $y = -2x^2 + 4x + 16$

3 The graph of $y = x^2$ has been translated to produce each graph below.
Find the equation of each graph in the form $y = ax^2 + bx + c$.

(a)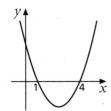

(b)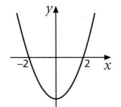

(c)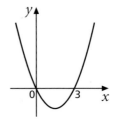

4 A graph has equation $y = x^2 + 4x - 5$.

(a) Work out where the graph crosses the x-axis.

(b) Where does the graph cross the y-axis?

(c) (i) Write $x^2 + 4x - 5$ in completed-square form.

     (ii) Hence, or otherwise, write down the coordinates of the vertex.

(d) Sketch the graph, showing the points where it crosses the x- and y-axes and the vertex.

5 Draw the graph of each equation below.
Clearly mark the points where each graph crosses the x- and y-axes and the vertex.

(a) $y = x^2 - 10x + 16$ (b) $y = x^2 + 14x + 40$ (c) $y = x^2 - 7x + 10$

(d) $y = 3x^2 + 18x - 21$ (e) $y = 2x^2 + 6x - 8$ (f) $y = 20 - x - x^2$

*6 Each graph below is a parabola.
Find the equation of each one in the form $y = ax^2 + bx + c$.

(a)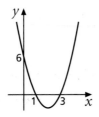

(b)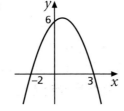

(c)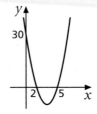

F Solving quadratic equations by completing the square

This is a sketch of the graph with equation $y = x^2 + 2x - 5$.

To find where it cuts the x-axis we need to solve the equation $x^2 + 2x - 5 = 0$.

We cannot factorise $x^2 + 2x - 5$ but we can complete the square to try to solve the equation.

$$x^2 + 2x - 5 = (x + 1)^2 - 1 - 5$$
$$= (x + 1)^2 - 6$$

So the equation $x^2 + 2x - 5 = 0$ is equivalent to

$$(x + 1)^2 - 6 = 0$$
$$\Rightarrow \quad (x + 1)^2 = 6$$
$$\Rightarrow \quad x + 1 = \pm\sqrt{6}$$
$$\text{giving } x = -1 + \sqrt{6} \text{ and } x = -1 - \sqrt{6}$$

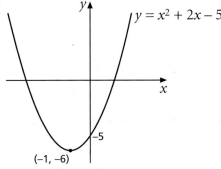

These are the exact values in surd form, giving the coordinates $(-1 + \sqrt{6}, 0)$ and $(-1 - \sqrt{6}, 0)$.

If we try to solve the equation $4x^2 - 24x - 7 = 0$, we find that the expression $4x^2 - 24x - 7$ does not factorise.

We can try solving it by completing the square.

$$4x^2 - 24x - 7 = 0 \qquad \textit{We can divide both sides by 4.}$$
$$\Rightarrow \qquad x^2 - 6x - \tfrac{7}{4} = 0$$
$$\Rightarrow \qquad (x - 3)^2 - 9 - \tfrac{7}{4} = 0$$
$$\Rightarrow \qquad (x - 3)^2 - \tfrac{43}{4} = 0 \qquad \tfrac{43}{4} \textit{ is easier to deal with than } 10\tfrac{3}{4}.$$
$$\Rightarrow \qquad (x - 3)^2 = \tfrac{43}{4}$$
$$\Rightarrow \qquad x - 3 = \pm\sqrt{\tfrac{43}{4}} = \pm\frac{\sqrt{43}}{2} = \pm\tfrac{1}{2}\sqrt{43}$$

giving $x = 3 + \tfrac{1}{2}\sqrt{43}$ and $x = 3 - \tfrac{1}{2}\sqrt{43}$

Exercise F (answers p 165)

1 Solve each equation and give your answers in surd form.

(a) $(x - 3)^2 = 2$ (b) $(x + 5)^2 - 11 = 0$ (c) $(x - 6)^2 - 6 = 0$

2 (a) Write $x^2 + 10x + 23$ in completed-square form.

    (b) Hence solve $x^2 + 10x + 23 = 0$, giving your solutions exactly in surd form.

3 Solve each equation by completing the square, giving your solutions exactly in surd form.

    (a) $x^2 + 4x + 1 = 0$ **(b)** $x^2 + 2x - 7 = 0$ **(c)** $x^2 - 6x - 2 = 0$

    (d) $x^2 - 5x - 1 = 0$ **(e)** $2x^2 + 12x + 6 = 0$ **(f)** $2x^2 - 10x + 5 = 0$

4 Work out the exact coordinates where the graph of each equation crosses the x-axis.

    (a) $y = x^2 + 2x - 4$ **(b)** $y = x^2 - 4x + 1$ **(c)** $y = 2x^2 - 14x + 9$

5 (a) Write $x^2 + 4x + 10$ in completed-square form.

    (b) What happens when you try to solve the equation $x^2 + 4x + 10 = 0$?
        How does this relate to the graph of $y = x^2 + 4x + 10$?

G Solving quadratic equations by using the formula

Completing the square can be used to establish a general formula for solving quadratic equations.

$$ax^2 + bx + c = 0$$

Divide by a to make 1 the coefficient of x^2. $$x^2 + \frac{b}{a}x + \frac{c}{a} = 0$$

Complete the square. $$\left(x + \frac{b}{2a}\right)^2 - \frac{b^2}{4a^2} + \frac{c}{a} = 0$$

Rearrange the equation. $$\left(x + \frac{b}{2a}\right)^2 = \frac{b^2}{4a^2} - \frac{c}{a}$$

$$\frac{c}{a} = \frac{c \times 4a}{a \times 4a} = \frac{4ac}{4a^2}$$ $$\left(x + \frac{b}{2a}\right)^2 = \frac{b^2 - 4ac}{4a^2}$$

Remember the positive and negative square roots. $$x + \frac{b}{2a} = \pm\sqrt{\frac{b^2 - 4ac}{4a^2}}$$

Simplify the square root. $$x = -\frac{b}{2a} \pm \frac{\sqrt{b^2 - 4ac}}{\sqrt{4a^2}}$$

$$\Rightarrow \qquad x = -\frac{b}{2a} \pm \frac{\sqrt{b^2 - 4ac}}{2a}$$

$$\Rightarrow \qquad x = \frac{-b \pm \sqrt{b^2 - 4ac}}{2a}$$

The solutions of the equation are also called the **roots** of the equation.

Example 14

Find the roots of $2x^2 + 4x - 1 = 0$.
Give the exact roots in surd form and their decimal values correct to two decimal places.

Solution

Using $x = \dfrac{-b \pm \sqrt{b^2 - 4ac}}{2a}$, where $a = 2, b = 4, c = -1$,

$$x = \frac{-4 \pm \sqrt{4^2 - 4 \times 2 \times (-1)}}{2 \times 2}$$

$$= \frac{-4 \pm \sqrt{24}}{4}$$

$$= \frac{-4 \pm 2\sqrt{6}}{4}$$

giving $x = -1 + \frac{1}{2}\sqrt{6}$ and $x = -1 - \frac{1}{2}\sqrt{6}$ *These are the **exact** solutions.*
or $x = 0.22$ and $x = -2.22$ (correct to 2 d.p.)   *These are **approximate** solutions.*

Exercise G (answers p 165)

1 Use the formula to find the exact solutions to each equation in terms of the simplest possible surds.

   (a) $3x^2 + 5x + 1 = 0$ **(b)** $x^2 - 2x - 2 = 0$ **(c)** $2x^2 - 8x + 3 = 0$

2 Use the formula to find the solutions to each equation, correct to three decimal places.

   (a) $x^2 + 5x - 3 = 0$ **(b)** $2x^2 - 6x + 3 = 0$ **(c)** $-5x^2 + x + 2 = 0$

3 Work out where the graph of $y = \frac{1}{2}x^2 - 4x + 5$ crosses the x-axis.
Give the coordinates correct to two decimal places.

4 (a) What happens when you use the formula to solve the equation $x^2 + 2x + 5 = 0$?

   (b) What does this tell you about the graph of the equation $y = x^2 + 2x + 5$?

5 (a) What happens when you use the formula to solve the equation $4x^2 - 12x + 9 = 0$?

   (b) What does this tell you about the graph of the equation $y = 4x^2 - 12x + 9$?

6 The graph of $y = x^2 + 6x + c$ cuts the x-axis in two places.
Work out the range of possible values of c.

7 The graph of $y = x^2 + 2x + c$ just touches the x-axis.
Work out the range of possible values of c.

*8 The graph of $y = 2x^2 + bx + 8$ does not cut the x-axis.
Work out the range of possible values of b.

H Using the discriminant (answers p 165)

The expression $b^2 - 4ac$ is called the **discriminant** of the equation $ax^2 + bx + c = 0$.

- If the value of the discriminant is less than zero, the equation has no real roots.
- If the value of the discriminant is zero, the equation has one real root, sometimes called a **repeated root**, as both factors of the quadratic give rise to it.

  It is sometimes helpful to think of the equation as having two roots that are the same and call them **equal roots**.

- If the value of the discriminant is greater than zero, the equation has two different (**distinct**) real roots.

H1 What can you say about the expression $ax^2 + bx + c$ if the value of the discriminant is the square of a whole number or a fraction? What about the equation $ax^2 + bx + c = 0$?

Exercise H (answers p 165)

1 What is the value of the discriminant for the equation $x^2 + 8x + 3 = 0$? Hence state if the equation has real roots.

2 By working out the value of the discriminant, decide which of these equations have two distinct real roots.

A $\quad 2x^2 - 3x + 2 = 0$ B $\quad x^2 + 5x + 3 = 0$ C $\quad 3x^2 + 4x - 2 = 0$

D $\quad x^2 - 12x + 36 = 0$ E $\quad -3x^2 - 7x - 6 = 0$ F $\quad 5 - x - x^2 = 0$

3 By working out the value of the discriminant, decide which of these equations can be solved by factorising.

A $\quad 5x^2 + 3x - 2 = 0$ B $\quad 6x^2 + 5x - 6 = 0$ C $\quad 4x^2 - 6x + 1 = 0$

4 Solve these equations, where possible, by any method. Where appropriate, write your solutions in surd form, in terms of the simplest possible surds.

(a) $x^2 - 9x + 14 = 0$ (b) $x^2 - 8x + 14 = 0$ (c) $9x^2 - 6x + 1 = 0$

(d) $9x^2 - 5x + 1 = 0$ (e) $2x^2 - 5x + 2 = 0$ (f) $x^2 + 10x + 3 = 0$

5 Use the value of the discriminant to decide which of these equations have a graph that

    (i) crosses the x-axis at two points

    (ii) just touches the x-axis at one point

    (iii) does not cross the x-axis

(a) $y = x^2 + 9x + 1$ (b) $y = 25 + 20x + 4x^2$ (c) $y = -3x^2 + 7x - 2$

(d) $y = 6x - 9x^2 - 1$ (e) $y = x^2 + x + 1$ (f) $y = \frac{1}{2}x^2 - 2x + \frac{1}{4}$

6 For each equation, work out the values of k that give an equation with equal roots.

(a) $4x^2 + kx + 25 = 0$ (b) $kx^2 + kx + 9 = 0$ (c) $x^2 + 2kx + 16 = 0$

7 Determine the values of k for which the equation $x^2 + kx + (2k - 3) = 0$ has equal roots.

8 Prove that for all real values of k the roots of the equation $x^2 + 2kx - 3 = 0$ are real and different.

9 (a) Show that $(2(a - 3))^2$ is equivalent to $4a^2 - 24a + 36$.

(b) Determine the values of k for which the equation $x^2 + 2(k - 3)x + (5k - 1) = 0$ has equal roots.

Key points

- A **quadratic** expression can sometimes be **factorised** into two **linear factors**.
  An example is $x^2 + 4x + 3 = (x + 1)(x + 3)$.   (p 33)

- The graph of any quadratic expression in x is a **parabola**.
  The graph of $y - q = k(x - p)^2$ is a **translation** of the graph of $y = kx^2$.

  Using **vector notation**, this translation can be described as $\begin{bmatrix} p \\ q \end{bmatrix}$.

  The equation can also be written as $y = k(x - p)^2 + q$.
  The vertex of the graph is (p, q) and its line of symmetry is $x = p$.   (pp 36–38)

- A quadratic expression can always be written in **completed-square form**,
  i.e. in the form $k(x + p)^2 + q$, where k, p and q are constants.
  An example is $2x^2 + 4x + 5 = 2(x + 1)^2 + 3$.   (pp 41–42)

- In the completed-square form of $x^2 + bx + c$, the constant inside the brackets is found by halving the coefficient of x.
  For example $x^2 - 6x + 5 = (x - 3)^2 - (-3)^2 + 5$
  $$= (x - 3)^2 - 9 + 5$$
  $$= (x - 3)^2 - 4$$ (p 41)

- A quadratic equation can sometimes be solved by factorising.
  An example is $x^2 - 3x - 4 = 0$
  $$\Rightarrow (x + 1)(x - 4) = 0$$
  $$\Rightarrow x = -1 \text{ and } x = 4$$ (p 45)

- Any quadratic equation with real solutions can be solved by completing the square.
  An example is $x^2 - 4x - 3 = 0$
  $$\Rightarrow (x - 2)^2 - 7 = 0$$
  $$\Rightarrow (x - 2)^2 = 7$$
  $$\Rightarrow x - 2 = \pm\sqrt{7}$$
  $$\Rightarrow x = 2 + \sqrt{7} \text{ and } x = 2 - \sqrt{7}$$ (p 47)

- Any quadratic equation $ax^2 + bx + c = 0$ with real solutions

  can be solved by using the formula $x = \dfrac{-b \pm \sqrt{b^2 - 4ac}}{2a}$.

  An example is $x^2 - 4x - 3 = 0$

  $$\Rightarrow \quad x = \frac{-(-4) \pm \sqrt{(-4)^2 - 4 \times 1 \times (-3)}}{2 \times 1}$$

  $$= \frac{4 \pm \sqrt{28}}{2}$$

  $$= \frac{4 \pm 2\sqrt{7}}{2}$$

  $$= 2 \pm \sqrt{7} \qquad \qquad \text{(p 48)}$$

- The graph of $y = ax^2 + bx + c$ crosses the y-axis when $x = 0$, i.e. when $y = c$.
  It crosses or touches the x-axis if the equation $ax^2 + bx + c = 0$ has real solutions.

- The discriminant of $ax^2 + bx + c$ is the expression $b^2 - 4ac$.
  The value of the discriminant tells you the number of real solutions (roots)
  of the equation $ax^2 + bx + c = 0$. $\qquad \qquad$ (p 50)

Test yourself (answers p 166)

None of these questions requires a calculator.

1 (a) Express $x^2 - 12x + 40$ in the form $(x - p)^2 + q$.

(b) Hence, or otherwise, find the least value of $x^2 - 12x + 40$. $\qquad$ AQA 2003

2 (a) Express $x^2 + 10x + 20$ in the form $(x + p)^2 + q$.

(b) Sketch the graph of $y = x^2 + 10x + 20$, stating the coordinates of the vertex.

3 (a) Find the constants a, b and c such that, for all values of x,
$$3x^2 - 6x + 10 = a(x + b)^2 + c$$

(b) Hence write down the equation of the line of symmetry
of the curve $y = 3x^2 - 6x + 10$.

4 (a) Express $x^2 + 5x + 1$ in the form $(x + p)^2 + q$.

(b) Hence give the translation that maps the graph of $y = x^2$ to $y = x^2 + 5x + 1$.

5 (a) Express $x^2 - 8x + 4$ in the form $(x + p)^2 + q$.

(b) Hence, or otherwise, solve the equation $x^2 - 8x + 4 = 0$.
Write your answers in the form $a + b\sqrt{c}$, where c is as small as possible.

6 Solve the equation $2x^2 + 7x + 4 = 0$, giving your answers in surd form.

7 Each of these graphs is a translation of $y = x^2$.
Determine the equation of each one in the form $y = ax^2 + bx + c$.

(a)

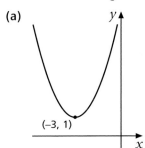

$(-3, 1)$

(b)

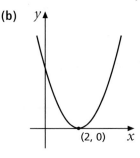

$(2, 0)$

(c)

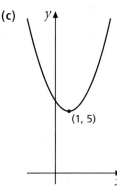

$(1, 5)$

8 (a) Solve the equation $2x^2 + 32x + 119 = 0$.
Write your answers in the form $p + q\sqrt{2}$, where p and q are rational numbers.

(b) (i) Express $\qquad\qquad 2x^2 + 32x + 119$

in the form $\qquad\quad 2(x + m)^2 + n$

where m and n are integers.

(ii) Hence write down the minimum value of $2x^2 + 32x + 119$. $\hfill$ AQA 2002

9 (a) Express $4x^2 - 32x + 4$ in the form $a(x + b)^2 + c$.

(b) Hence find the coordinates of the vertex of the graph of $y = 4x^2 - 32x + 4$.

(c) Sketch the graph of $y = 4x^2 - 32x + 4$, giving the x-coordinates of the points where the graph meets the x-axis.

10 (a) Calculate the discriminant of $2x^2 - 3x + 5$.

(b) Hence state the number of real roots of the equation $2x^2 - 3x + 5 = 0$.

11 When $y = 8 - (x - 3)^2$, write down the maximum value of y.

12 Determine the values of k for which the quadratic equation
$x^2 + 3(k - 2)x + (k + 5) = 0$ has equal roots. $\hfill$ AQA 2001

*13 A parabola has a vertex with coordinates $(-4, 1)$ and goes through the point with coordinates $(2, -17)$.
Find the equation of the parabola in the form $y = ax^2 + bx + c$.

4 Further equations

In this chapter you will learn how to
- solve equations where rearrangement is involved
- form and solve quadratic equations to solve problems
- solve simultaneous equations where one is linear and one is quadratic
- use the discriminant to find the relationship between two graphs

A Rearranging to solve equations: revision

Sometimes it is necessary to rearrange an equation to make it easier to solve.

Example 1

Solve the equation $2(x - 1) = x(5 - x)$, giving your solutions in surd form.

Solution

$$2(x - 1) = x(5 - x)$$

Expand the brackets. $\qquad 2x - 2 = 5x - x^2$

Add x^2 to both sides. $\qquad x^2 + 2x - 2 = 5x$

Subtract $5x$ from both sides. $\qquad x^2 - 3x - 2 = 0$

The quadratic expression does not factorise,
so use the formula to solve the equation.
$$x = \frac{-(-3) \pm \sqrt{(-3)^2 - 4 \times 1 \times (-2)}}{2 \times 1}$$

$$= \frac{3 \pm \sqrt{17}}{2}$$

These are the exact solutions in surd form. $\qquad x = \dfrac{3 - \sqrt{17}}{2} \text{ or } \dfrac{3 + \sqrt{17}}{2}$

As decimals, these solutions are −0.562 and 3.562 (to 3 d.p.).
You can check these solutions by substituting back into the original equation.

Example 2

Solve $\dfrac{2}{x} = \dfrac{4}{x + 2}$.

Solution

$$\frac{2}{x} = \frac{4}{x + 2}$$

Multiply each side by $x(x + 2)$, the 'LCM'
of the denominators.
$$\frac{2x(x + 2)}{x} = \frac{4x(x + 2)}{x + 2}$$

Cancel. $\qquad 2(x + 2) = 4x$

Multiply out the brackets. $\qquad 2x + 4 = 4x$

Rearrange. $\qquad 2x = 4$

$\Rightarrow \qquad x = 2$

Example 3

Solve $\dfrac{2}{x} = \dfrac{x+2}{4}$.

Solution

$$\dfrac{2}{x} = \dfrac{x+2}{4}$$

Multiply each side by 4x, the 'LCM' of the denominators.

$$\dfrac{8x}{x} = \dfrac{4x(x+2)}{4}$$

Cancel.

$$8 = x(x+2)$$

Multiply out the brackets.

$$8 = x^2 + 2x$$

Subtract 8 from both sides.

$$x^2 + 2x - 8 = 0$$

The quadratic expression factorises.

$$(x+4)(x-2) = 0$$

$$\Rightarrow \qquad x = -4 \text{ or } 2$$

Exercise A (answers p 166)

1 Solve each equation.
Give exact solutions, using surd form where appropriate.

(a) $x^2 = 8x$ (b) $x^2 + 2x = 15$ (c) $x^2 = 4(x+3)$

(d) $4(x-6) = 3(2-x)$ (e) $x(x-3) = 2(x-3)$ (f) $5x^2 + 12 = 23x$

(g) $3x^2 + x = 5$ (h) $2x(6x+1) = 5(1-x)$ (i) $2x^2 + x = 6x + 1$

2 Solve each equation.
Give exact solutions, using surd form where appropriate.

(a) $x + 1 = \dfrac{6}{x}$ (b) $\dfrac{x}{5} = \dfrac{1}{x+6}$ (c) $\dfrac{x+8}{3} = \dfrac{3}{x}$

(d) $\dfrac{x}{5} = \dfrac{3}{2x+7}$ (e) $\dfrac{x}{2+x} = \dfrac{1}{x-3}$ (f) $\dfrac{4x}{x-3} = \dfrac{3}{x+10}$

(g) $\dfrac{x+5}{6} = \dfrac{x-1}{3}$ (h) $\dfrac{5}{x} = \dfrac{10-x}{5}$ (i) $x = \dfrac{x-7}{x+7}$

(j) $2x = \dfrac{45}{x} - 1$ (k) $\dfrac{x+2}{x} = \dfrac{3}{4}$ (l) $\dfrac{4x}{x-1} = \dfrac{6}{x-3}$

3 Solve each equation.
Give solutions correct to three decimal places.

(a) $x = \dfrac{3}{x}$ (b) $x(5x+1) = 1 + x(x-3)$

(c) $3x - 1 = \dfrac{1}{x}$ (d) $(2x+3)^2 + x^2 = 7$

(e) $\dfrac{4x-1}{5} = \dfrac{x}{6}$ (f) $\dfrac{x}{2} = \dfrac{1}{8+x}$

B Solving problems

Some problems can be solved by forming an equation, solving it and interpreting the solution.

Example 4

The path round a square lawn is 1 metre wide and made from rectangular slabs.
If the area of the path and the area of the lawn are equal, find the area of the lawn, to 2 d.p.

Solution

Let x be the length of the lawn.

It's often a good idea to draw a diagram.

*Here the path is shown split into
four equal rectangles, each $x + 1$ by 1.*

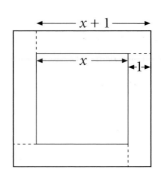

Area of lawn $= x^2$
Area of path $= 4(x + 1)$

The areas of the path and lawn are the same.

$$x^2 = 4(x + 1)$$
$$\Rightarrow x^2 - 4x - 4 = 0$$

*The quadratic expression does not factorise,
so use formula to solve the equation.*

$$x = \frac{-(-4) \pm \sqrt{(-4)^2 - 4 \times 1 \times (-4)}}{2 \times 1}$$

$$= \frac{4 \pm \sqrt{32}}{2}$$

$$\Rightarrow x = 4.828\ldots \text{ or } -0.828\ldots$$

We ignore the negative root as the length is positive.

Hence the area of the lawn is $(4.828\ldots)^2 = 23.31 \, \text{m}^2$ (to 2 d.p.)

Example 5

Find the coordinates of the points of intersection
of the graphs of $y = x + 1$ and $y = x^2 + 3x - 2$.

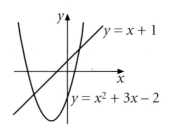

Solution

Where the graphs intersect it is true that

$$x^2 + 3x - 2 = x + 1$$
$$\Rightarrow \quad x^2 + 2x - 3 = 0$$

The quadratic expression factorises.

$$(x + 3)(x - 1) = 0$$

$$\Rightarrow \qquad\qquad x = -3 \text{ or } 1$$

Substitute into $y = x + 1$ for each value of x.

When $x = -3$, $y = -3 + 1 = -2$
When $x = 1$, $y = 1 + 1 = 2$

So the points of intersection are $(-3, -2)$ and $(1, 2)$.

Exercise B (answers p 166)

1 The path round a square lawn is 2 metres wide.
If the area of the path is equal to the area of the lawn
find the perimeter of the lawn, correct to 3 d.p.

2 The diagram shows a sketch of the
graphs of $y = \dfrac{x-2}{2}$ and $y = \dfrac{6}{x-3}$.
They intersect at two points.

Find the coordinates of both points of intersection.

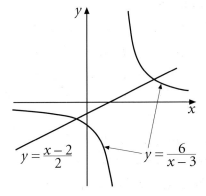

3 Work out the coordinates of the points of intersection for
the graphs of $y = 2x^2 + x$ and $y = 2(2 - 3x)$.

4 The sketch shows the graphs of
$y = x^2 - x - 1$ and $y = x + 1$.
They intersect at two points.

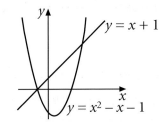

(a) Show that one of the points of intersection is
$(1 - \sqrt{3}, 2 - \sqrt{3})$.

(b) Find the coordinates of the other point of intersection in surd form.

5 A rectangle has width 1 unit and length x units.
A square is cut off it as shown.

The rectangle left behind is similar to
the original rectangle.

Find the value of x in surd form.

The value of x is called the Golden Ratio.
You may like to find out more about this fascinating number.

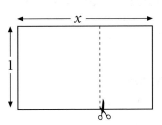

6 A market trader sells radios. She finds that the number of radios she sells each week depends on the profit she makes per radio.

She uses a formula to estimate the approximate number she will sell each week. It is

$$N = 60 - 6p$$

where N is the number of radios sold per week and £p is the profit per radio.

(a) Write an expression, in terms of p, for the total profit per week from these radios.

(b) One week she wants to make a profit of £80 from her radios.
What profit per radio should she choose?
Show carefully how you decided.

(c) Could she make of profit of £200 per week?
Explain your answer carefully.

C Solving simultaneous equations by substitution

Example 6

The difference between two positive numbers is 2.
Their product is 4.
What are the two numbers?

Solution

Let x and y be the two numbers.

Form a pair of simultaneous equations.
$$x - y = 2$$
$$xy = 4$$

Rearrange the first equation.
$$x = y + 2 \qquad \textit{It could be rearranged as } y = x - 2.$$

Substitute in the second equation.
$$(y + 2)y = 4$$
$$\Rightarrow y^2 + 2y - 4 = 0$$

The quadratic expression does not factorise so use completing the square.
$$(y + 1)^2 - 5 = 0$$
$$\Rightarrow \quad (y + 1)^2 = 5$$
$$\Rightarrow \quad y + 1 = \pm\sqrt{5}$$
$$\Rightarrow \quad y = -1 + \sqrt{5} \text{ or } -1 - \sqrt{5}$$

We reject $-1 - \sqrt{5}$ as we know the numbers are positive.

One number must be $\sqrt{5} - 1$.

Substitute into $x = y + 2$.

The other is $\sqrt{5} - 1 + 2 = \sqrt{5} + 1$.
So the two numbers are $\sqrt{5} - 1$ and $\sqrt{5} + 1$.

Example 7

Solve the simultaneous equations

$$y - 2x = 7$$
$$x^2 + xy + 2 = 0$$

Solution

Rearrange the first equation.	$y = 7 + 2x$
Substitute in the second equation.	$x^2 + x(7 + 2x) + 2 = 0$
Multiply out the brackets and rearrange.	$3x^2 + 7x + 2 = 0$
The quadratic expression factorises.	$(3x + 1)(x + 2) = 0$
	$\Rightarrow \qquad x = -\frac{1}{3}$ or -2

Substitute into $y = 7 + 2x$ to find the corresponding values of y.

When $x = -\frac{1}{3}$, $y = 7 + 2 \times -\frac{1}{3} = 6\frac{1}{3}$
When $x = -2$, $y = 7 + 2 \times -2 = 3$

So the two solutions are

$x = -\frac{1}{3}, y = 6\frac{1}{3}$ and $x = -2, y = 3$

*Each solution is a **pair** of values so $x = -\frac{1}{3}, y = 6\frac{1}{3}$ is **one** solution.*

Exercise C (answers p 167)

1 Solve each pair of simultaneous equations.

(a) $y = x^2$
 $6x + y = 7$

(b) $y = x + 1$
 $xy - 4x = 10$

(c) $y = x^2 + 5$
 $x + 4y = 23$

(d) $x = y - 2$
 $x^2 + y^2 = 10$

(e) $y = x - 3$
 $\dfrac{y}{x} = x + 5$

(f) $x = 3 - 2y$
 $2xy - y^2 + 8 = 0$

2 The graphs of $y = x + 9$ and $xy = 5(x + 1)$ intersect.
Work out the coordinates of both points of intersection.

3 Solve the simultaneous equations

$$y = 6 - 2x$$
$$xy + x = 3$$

AQA 2002

4 Two functions are given by $y = \frac{1}{2}x^2 - 2x + 1$ and $y = 4 - x$, where $-2 \le x \le 5$.

(a) On graph paper, draw accurate graphs of the functions on the same set of axes.

(b) Use your graphs to estimate to 1 d.p. the coordinates of each point of intersection.

(c) Use algebra to find these coordinates correct to 3 d.p.

5 Solve each pair of simultaneous equations.

(a) $x + y = 6$

$x^2 = 16 - 3y$

(b) $y - x = 3$

$x^2 + xy + y^2 = 21$

(c) $2y + x = 5$

$3y^2 + 4xy = 0$

6 Solve each pair of simultaneous equations.
Where appropriate, give your answer using the simplest possible surds.

(a) $y = x + 5$

$y = x^2 - 3x + 1$

(b) $y + 2x = 3$

$x^2 - xy = 9$

(c) $x^2 - 2y = 1$

$\dfrac{y}{x} + 2 = x$

7 Two positive numbers differ by 2 and have a product of 10.
Find the two numbers exactly.

8 The perimeter of a rectangle is 20 cm.
The length of one of its diagonals is $3\sqrt{6}$ cm.
Work out the dimensions of the rectangle in surd form.

*9 The graphs of $y = x^2 - 4$ and $x^2 + y^2 = 9$ intersect.
Work out the coordinates of all the points of intersection, correct to 3 d.p.

D Counting points of intersection

In a plane, two distinct straight lines either intersect at one point or are parallel.

A line and a curve can intersect any number of times depending on the 'wiggliness' of the curve and the position of the line.

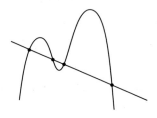 

The line meets the curve at three points of intersection.

The line does not meet the curve.

The line meets the curve at four points of intersection.

The line meets the curve at one point. It is a tangent to the curve.

Consider the parabola $y = x^2 + 1$ and the straight line $y = 4x - 3$.

Where they intersect, the x-values will satisfy the equation

$$x^2 + 1 = 4x - 3$$

which rearranges to give $\qquad x^2 - 4x + 4 = 0$

$$\Rightarrow \quad (x - 2)^2 = 0$$

so $x = 2$ is the only solution.

When $x = 2$, $y = 2^2 + 1 = 5$.

So the only point that lies on the curve and the straight line is $(2, 5)$.

This means that the straight line just
touches the curve at one point.
So it is a tangent to the curve.

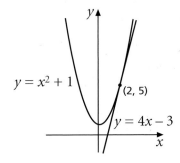

We can see that the straight line is a tangent to the curve just by looking at
the value of the discriminant of $x^2 - 4x + 4 = 0$.

The value of the discriminant is $(-4)^2 - 4 \times 1 \times 4 = 0$ so the solution is $x = \dfrac{4 \pm \sqrt{0}}{2} = \dfrac{4}{2} = 2.$

Whenever the discriminant is 0, the equation has just one real root.

Hence the straight line meets the curve at just one point and is a tangent to the curve.

Consider the parabola $y = 2x^2 - 4x + 5$ and the straight line $y + x = 3$.

The equation $y + x = 3$ rearranges to give $y = 3 - x$.

So, where the graphs intersect, the x-values will satisfy the equation

$$2x^2 - 4x + 5 = 3 - x$$

which rearranges to give $\qquad 2x^2 - 3x + 2 = 0$

The value of the discriminant is $(-3)^2 - 4 \times 2 \times 2 = 9 - 16 = -7$.

The value is negative so we know that the equation has no real roots.

Hence the straight line does not intersect the curve.
This is confirmed by a sketch.

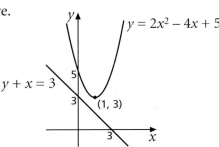

Exercise D (answers p 167)

1 Show that the straight line $y = 3x + 2$ and the curve $y = x^2 + 2x + 4$ do not intersect.

2 Show that the straight line $y = 1 - 2x$ is a tangent to the curve $y = x^2 - 6x + 5$.

3 (a) Show that $y - x = 5$ is a tangent to the curve $y = 2x^2 + 13x + 23$.

(b) Find the coordinates of the point where the straight line meets the curve.

4 Determine the relationship between the graphs of the following pairs of equations.
Each pair of graphs is a straight line and a parabola.
Do they intersect at two points, meet at one point, or fail to meet at all?

(a) $y + x = 10$ (b) $y = 2x - 9$ (c) $y = 5 - 4x^2$

     $y = 3x^2 - 2x - 3$ $y = (x - 4)^2$ $y + 3x = 6$

5 Show that the line $x = -1$ does not intersect the curve $y^2 = 4x$.

6 The graph of $y = 2x + k$ meets the graph of $y = x^2 - 4x + 2$ at only one point.
Find the value of k.

7 The line $y = 3x - 5$ is a tangent to the curve $y = 2x^2 + 9x + k$.
Find the value of k.

8 Show that it is impossible to find two real numbers with a product of 5 and a sum of 4.

9 The line $y = 1 + kx$ is a tangent to the curve $y = 3x^2 + 5x + 13$.
Find two possible values for k.

Key points

- Some problems can be solved by forming an equation and solving it.
  The solution needs to be interpreted in the context of the original problem.
  For example, a length cannot be negative.   (p 56)

- A pair of simultaneous equations can be represented as graphs and the solutions
  interpreted as points of intersection.

- A pair of simultaneous equations can be solved by substituting
  to eliminate one of the unknowns.   (pp 58–59)

- If a pair of simultaneous equations leads to a quadratic equation then
  the discriminant tells you the geometrical relationship between
  the graphs of the equations.

  If the value of the discriminant is negative, the graphs do not intersect.

  If the value of the discriminant is positive, the graphs intersect at two points.

  If the value of the discriminant is zero, the graphs meet at just one point.   (pp 60–61)

Test yourself (answers p 168)

None of these questions requires a calculator.

1 The area of the rectangle below is 2 square units.

$\frac{x}{2} + 4$ (top edge), x (left edge)

Find the length of each edge in surd form.

2 (a) Solve the simultaneous equations

$$y = 2x + 10$$
$$y = 3x^2 - 4x + 1$$

(b) Hence write down the coordinates of the points of intersection of the graphs of $y = 2x + 10$ and $y = 3x^2 - 4x + 1$.

3 Solve the simultaneous equations

$$y = 2 - x$$
$$x^2 + 2xy = 3$$

AQA 2003

4 Find the values of x and y that satisfy the simultaneous equations

$$y = 2 - x^2$$
$$x + 2y = 1$$

AQA 2003

5 (a) Solve the simultaneous equations

$$y = 3x - 5$$
$$y = x^2 - 5x + 11$$

(b) Hence describe the geometrical relationship between the straight line with equation $y = 3x - 5$ and the parabola with equation $y = x^2 - 5x + 11$, giving a reason for your answer.

6 Solve the simultaneous equations

$$x + 2y = 1$$
$$2y^2 + 3xy + 1 = 0$$

7 Show that the straight line with equation $x + y = 2$ and the curve with equation $y^2 + 7x = 0$ do not intersect.

5 Inequalities

In this chapter, you will learn how to
• solve linear and quadratic inequalities
• solve problems by forming and solving inequalities

A Linear inequalities: revision (answers p 168)

A1 (a) Decide whether the inequality $3t > t + 6$ is true or false when

      (i) $t = 5$ **(ii)** $t = 0$ **(iii)** $t = 4\frac{1}{2}$ **(iv)** $t = -2$ **(v)** $t = 3$

    (b) Which of these inequalities describes **all** the values of t for which $3t > t + 6$?

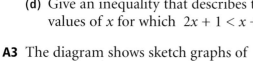

         $t > 6$ $t < 3$ $t \geq 3$ $t > 3$ $t \geq 6$

A2 The diagram shows sketch graphs of $y = 2x + 1$ and $y = x + 6$.

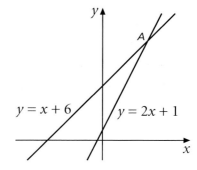

(a) Work out the x-coordinate of A, the point of intersection.

(b) How can you tell from the graph that $2x + 1 < x + 6$ when $x = 2$?

(c) Give an inequality that describes the values of x for which $2x + 1 \geq x + 6$.

(d) Give an inequality that describes the values of x for which $2x + 1 < x + 6$.

A3 The diagram shows sketch graphs of $y = -2x - 1$ and $y = x + 5$.

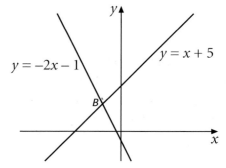

(a) Work out the x-coordinate of B, the point of intersection.

(b) Give an inequality that describes the values of x for which $-2x - 1 > x + 5$.

(c) Give an inequality that describes the values of x for which $-2x - 1 < x + 5$.

A4 (a) Decide if the inequality $-p + 3 \geq p - 2$ is satisfied when

      (i) $p = 3$ **(ii)** $p = 2$ **(iii)** $p = 0$ **(iv)** $p = 1.4$ **(v)** $p = 2.5$

    (b) Which of these inequalities describes **all** the values of p for which $-p + 3 \geq p - 2$?

         $p > 2.5$ $p < 2.5$ $p \leq 2.5$ $p \geq 2.5$

The complete set of values that satisfies an equation or inequality is called the **solution set**.

We can see from the diagram that $2x - 1 > x + 2$ has the solution set $x > 3$.

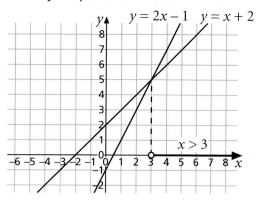

The empty circle on 3 means it is not included in the solution set.

Will the solution set change if we operate on each side of the inequality in the same way?

For example, subtracting 7 from each side gives

$$2x - 1 - 7 > x + 2 - 7$$

which is $2x - 8 > x - 5$

We can see from the diagram that $2x - 8 > x - 5$ also has the solution set $x > 3$.

So subtracting 7 from both sides of the inequality has not changed the solution set.

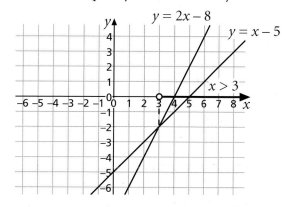

Multiplying each side by -1 gives

$$-1(2x - 1) > -1(x + 2)$$

which is $-2x + 1 > -x - 2$

We can see from the diagram that $-2x + 1 > -x - 2$ has the solution set $x < 3$.

So multiplying both sides by -1 has changed the solution set by **reversing** the direction of the inequality.

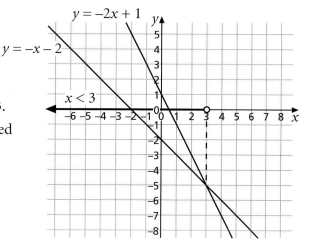

A5 What symbol, $>$ or $<$, must be used in the inequality $-2x + 1 \;\square\; -x - 2$ so that it has the same solution set as $2x - 1 > x + 2$?

A6 What happens to the solution set if a positive or negative number is added to or subtracted from both sides of the inequality?
What if you multiply or divide both sides by a positive or negative number?

Finding the solution set of an inequality is called **solving** an inequality.

An inequality such as $2x + 1 \geq x - 7$ is called a **linear inequality** as each expression $2x + 1$ and $x - 7$ is linear.

A linear inequality can be solved like a linear equation except that **multiplying or dividing each side by a negative number reverses the direction of the inequality sign.**

Example 1

Solve $1 - (x + 4) > 2(2x + 1)$.

Solution

$$1 - (x + 4) > 2(2x + 1)$$
$$\Rightarrow \quad 1 - x - 4 > 4x + 2$$
$$\Rightarrow \quad -x - 3 > 4x + 2$$
$$\Rightarrow \quad -3 > 5x + 2$$
$$\Rightarrow \quad -5 > 5x$$
$$\Rightarrow \quad -1 > x$$

that is $\quad x < -1$ *We usually write the variable on the left.*

Example 2

Solve $-3x + 10 \leq 4$.

Solution

$$-3x + 10 \leq 4$$

We could add $3x$ to both sides but we choose to subtract 10 from each side. $\quad -3x \leq -6$

Divide each side by -3 (remembering to reverse the inequality sign). $\quad x \geq 2$

Exercise A (answers p 168)

1 Solve the following inequalities.

(a) $5x - 9 \geq 6$ (b) $6y + 1 < 3y + 7$ (c) $3 > 1 + 2z$

(d) $6p - 3 < 10p - 15$ (e) $7 - 2q \leq 1$ (f) $-4a + 5 > 13$

(g) $5b + 3 \geq 2b - 3$ (h) $3 - 2x > 2 - 3x$ (i) $1 - \frac{1}{3}y < 4$

(j) $7z + 1 \leq 4z + 9$ (k) $6 + w < 9 - 5w$ (l) $5 - d \geq 7 + 6d$

2 Solve the following inequalities.

(a) $2(3x - 1) < 3x + 1$ (b) $3(x + 2) > 11(x - 2)$ (c) $15 - (1 + 2x) \geq 3(3x - 10)$

(d) $4(2y - 1) > 3(y - 2)$ (e) $2y + 1 \leq 7 - 2(y - 3)$ (f) $8 + \frac{1}{2}(y - 6) > y + 9$

3 Solve the following inequalities.

(a) $\dfrac{x + 6}{5} < 2(x - 3)$ (b) $\dfrac{2(x + 1)}{3} > \dfrac{x - 4}{5}$ (c) $\dfrac{2x + 1}{2} - \dfrac{x - 1}{3} \leq 5$

B Linear inequalities: solving problems

Some problems can be solved by forming an inequality, solving it and interpreting the solution.

Example 3

The *Toneway Times* charges a flat rate of £3.25 plus an extra 10p per word to place an advertisement in the 'For Sale' column.

The *Somerlea Gazette* charges 20p per word.

Form and solve an inequality to find when it is cheaper to advertise in the *Toneway Times*.

Solution

Let n be the number of words in the advertisement.

Then the cost of the ad (in pence) in the *Toneway Times* is	$325 + 10n$
and the cost of the same ad in the *Somerlea Gazette* is	$20n$
It is less expensive in the *Toneway Times* when	$325 + 10n < 20n$
$\Rightarrow$	$325 < 10n$
$\Rightarrow$	$n > 32.5$

So it is cheaper to use the *Toneway Times* when the advertisement uses 33 words or more.

Exercise B (answers p 168)

1 Eve employs a part-time gardener. She pays him a 'retainer' of £11.00 per week plus £8.00 for every hour she asks him to work. A National Insurance contribution must be paid if the total weekly payment is greater than £73.00.

Form and solve an inequality to find the length of time worked beyond which National Insurance must be paid.

2 Cutting Edge hire out tools.
For chain saws, they charge a fixed fee of £10.00 plus £2.00 per day.
A rival company, Helping Hands, charges a fixed fee of £5.00 plus £3.50 per day.

Form and solve an inequality to find when it is less expensive to hire a chain saw from Cutting Edge.

3 A piece of wire is to be bent to make an isosceles triangle.
The base is to be 6 cm longer than each of the other two sides.
Let l cm be the length of the base.

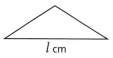
l cm

(a) (i) Show that l must be greater than 12.

(ii) Show that the total length of wire used must be greater than 24 cm.

(b) The maximum length of wire available is 1 metre.
Show that l must satisfy $l \leq 37\frac{1}{3}$ cm.

4 Jamie is fencing off part of his garden.
It is to be a rectangular area with a wall
along one side and the other three sides
fenced as shown in the diagram.

He wants to use 40 metres of fencing.

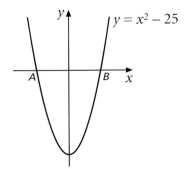

Wall

w metres

(a) Explain why the width, w, must satisfy the inequality $w < 20$.

(b) Write down the length of the rectangle in terms of w.

(c) Jamie wants to plant bushes round the edge of the whole rectangle.
He will not have enough bushes if the perimeter is more than $60\,\text{m}$.

    (i) Show that w must satisfy the inequality $80 - 2w \le 60$.

    (ii) Solve this inequality and hence find the minimum possible value of w.

C Quadratic inequalities (answers p 169)

C1 (a) Decide whether the inequality $x^2 < 9$ is true or false if

    (i) $x = 5$ **(ii)** $x = 2.5$ **(iii)** $x = -2$ **(iv)** $x = -4$ **(v)** $x = -3$

  (b) Which of these inequalities describes **all** the values of t for which $x^2 < 9$?

$x < 3$	$-3 \le x \le 3$	$x \le 3$	$-3 < x < 3$

C2 The diagram shows a sketch graph of $y = x^2 - 25$.

  (a) Work out the coordinates of points A and B.

  (b) Write down a pair of inequalities that describe
the values of x for which $x^2 - 25 \ge 0$.

$y = x^2 - 25$

A B x

C3 The diagram shows sketch graphs of
$y = x^2 + 2x + 3$ and $y = x + 5$.

  (a) Work out the coordinates of the
points of intersection, P and Q.

  (b) Write down an inequality that
describes the values of x for which
$x^2 + 2x + 3 < x + 5$.

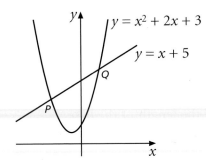

$y = x^2 + 2x + 3$

$y = x + 5$

Q

P

x

A graphical approach can be used in solving quadratic inequalities.

Example 4

Solve the inequality $x^2 + x - 6 > 0$.

Solution

Find where the graph of $y = x^2 + x - 6$ cuts the x-axis.

The quadratic expression factorises.

$$x^2 + x - 6 > 0$$
$$x^2 + x - 6 = 0$$
$$(x + 3)(x - 2) = 0$$
$$\Rightarrow \quad x = -3 \text{ or } x = 2$$

So a sketch graph of $y = x^2 + x - 6$ is

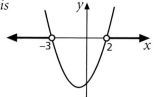

The heavy lines on the x-axis show where the inequality $x^2 + x - 6 > 0$ is satisfied.

The solution is the set of values given by $x < -3$ and $x > 2$.

Example 5

Solve the inequality $x(x + 2) \leq 1$.

Solution

$$x(x + 2) \leq 1$$

Expand the brackets.

$$x^2 + 2x \leq 1$$

Rearrange the inequality to get zero on one side.

$$x^2 + 2x - 1 \leq 0$$

Find where the graph of $y = x^2 + 2x - 1$ cuts the x-axis.

$$x^2 + 2x - 1 = 0$$

The quadratic does not factorise so use the formula.

$$x = \frac{-2 \pm \sqrt{2^2 - 4 \times (-1)}}{2}$$

$$= \frac{-2 \pm \sqrt{8}}{2}$$

$$= \frac{-2 \pm 2\sqrt{2}}{2}$$

$$= -1 \pm \sqrt{2}$$

So a sketch graph of $y = x^2 + 2x - 1$ is

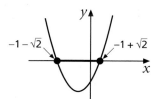

The solution is the set of values given by $-1 - \sqrt{2} \leq x \leq -1 + \sqrt{2}$.

An approach that uses number lines is useful when the quadratic factorises. It involves looking at each factor separately and then looking at the product.

For example, to solve the inequality $2x^2 - 5x - 3 < 0$, first factorise to give $(2x + 1)(x - 3) < 0$.

So we need to find where the product of $(2x + 1)$ and $(x - 3)$ is negative.

A sign diagram is

$2x + 1$ This line shows $2x + 1$ is positive when $x > -\frac{1}{2}$ and negative when $x < -\frac{1}{2}$.

$x - 3$ This line shows $x - 3$ is positive when $x > 3$ and negative when $x < 3$.

$(2x + 1)(x - 3)$ This line shows the product $(2x + 1)(x - 3)$ is negative when $-\frac{1}{2} < x < 3$.

The product is positive as both factors are negative.

The product is negative as one factor is negative and one is positive.

The product is positive as both factors are positive.

So the solution set is the range of values given by $-\frac{1}{2} < x < 3$.

This method of using number lines has the advantage that you don't have to sketch a graph in order to solve an inequality. This is especially useful in harder examples where a graph might be hard to visualise.

C4 Use the number line method to solve the inequality $(x + 4)(x - 7) \geq 0$.

D

C5 Use the number line method to solve the inequality $(x + 5)(3 - x) \geq 0$. (Be careful with the factor $(3 - x)$.)

C6 Show that the solution of $x^2 < 5$ is the set of values given by $-\sqrt{5} < x < \sqrt{5}$.

C7 Show that the solution of $x^2 > 5$ is the set of values given by $x < -\sqrt{5}$ and $x > \sqrt{5}$.

K

The solution of an inequality of the form $x^2 < k$ is the set of values $-\sqrt{k} < x < \sqrt{k}$.

The solution of an inequality of the form $x^2 > k$ is the set of values $x < -\sqrt{k}$ and $x > \sqrt{k}$.

Exercise C (answers p 169)

1 Solve these inequalities.

(a) $x^2 + 3x - 10 < 0$ (b) $x^2 + 11x + 18 \geq 0$ (c) $x^2 - 9x + 18 > 0$

(d) $x^2 - 5x - 14 \leq 0$ (e) $x^2 - 3x \geq 0$ (f) $x^2 - 4 > 0$

2 Solve these inequalities.

   (a) $2q^2 + 9q - 5 < 0$ (b) $3k^2 - 11k - 4 > 0$ (c) $3y^2 + 12y \geq 0$

   (d) $2p^2 + 5p - 3 \leq 0$ (e) $3a^2 - a < 0$ (f) $6t^2 + 5t - 6 \geq 0$

3 Solve these inequalities, leaving all values in surd form.

   (a) $x^2 - 2 < 0$ (b) $x^2 - 2x - 1 \geq 0$ (c) $2x^2 + 4x - 1 < 0$

4 Solve these inequalities.

   (a) $k^2 > 25$ (b) $k^2 - 2k < 3$ (c) $k^2 + 3k \geq 10$

   (d) $2k^2 + 8k > k + 4$ (e) $k^2 < 5k$ (f) $3k^2 < 15$

   (g) $k^2 > 2k + 2$ (h) $k^2 + 3k > 1 - 3k^2$ (i) $4k^2 < 9$

5 (a) Show that the inequality $6x - x^2 < 5$ is equivalent to $x^2 - 6x + 5 > 0$.

   (b) Hence solve $6x - x^2 < 5$.

6 (a) Show that the inequality $5x - x^2 > 6$ is equivalent to $(2 - x)(x - 3) > 0$.

   (b) Hence solve $5x - x^2 > 6$.

7 Solve these inequalities.

   (a) $9 - x^2 > 0$ (b) $-x^2 + 3x + 4 < 0$ (c) $14 - x^2 < 5x$

8 (a) Show that the inequality $y(y + 2) < 8$ is equivalent to $y^2 + 2y - 8 < 0$.

   (b) Hence solve $y(y + 2) < 8$.

9 Solve these inequalities.

   (a) $x(x - 6) < x - 12$ (b) $(y + 5)(y + 1) < 12$ (c) $2(k^2 - 1) > k(1 - k)$

10 (a) Write $x^2 + 2x - 15$ in completed square form.

   (b) Hence solve $x^2 + 2x < 15$.

*11 Solve each inequality, explaining your answers carefully.

   (a) $x^2 + 4x + 5 > 0$ (b) $x^2 + 2x + 1 < 0$

*12 Solve the inequality $\dfrac{x - 4}{x - 1} \leq 0$ using the number line method.

*13 Solve these inequalities.

   (a) $\dfrac{x + 3}{x + 5} > 0$ (b) $(x + 2)(x - 1)(x + 4) \geq 0$ (c) $\dfrac{x^2 + 4x - 5}{x - 6} < 0$

*14 Solve these inequalities.

   (a) $\dfrac{2x - 5}{x + 1} < 1$ (b) $\dfrac{2x - 7}{x + 5} > 4$

D Inequalities and the discriminant (answers p 170)

You know that the discriminant of the equation $ax^2 + bx + c = 0$ is the expression $b^2 - 4ac$.

- If the value of the discriminant is less than zero, the equation has no real roots.
- If the value of the discriminant is greater than or equal to zero, the equation has real roots.

D1 (a) What is the value of the discriminant of the equation $x^2 + 3x + 1 = 0$?

(b) How does this tell you that the equation has real roots?

D2 (a) What is the value of the discriminant of the equation $x^2 + x + 1 = 0$?

(b) How does this tell you that the equation has no real roots?

D3 (a) Write down the discriminant of the equation $x^2 + kx + 1 = 0$.

(b) Find the values of k for which the equation has real roots.

D4 (a) Write down the discriminant of the equation $x^2 + kx + k = 0$.

(b) Find the values of k for which the equation has no real roots.

Example 6

The equation $x^2 + kx + 2k = 0$ has real roots.
Find the set of possible values of k.

Solution

The discriminant is $\qquad\qquad k^2 - 4 \times 2k = k^2 - 8k$

The discriminant cannot be negative so $\quad k^2 - 8k \geq 0$

$$k(k - 8) \geq 0$$

A sign diagram is

With practice, you may be able to omit the first two lines.

Alternatively, use a graphical approach.

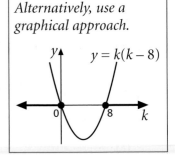

The possible values for k are given by $k \leq 0$ and $k \geq 8$.

Example 7

Find the values of k for which the equation $kx^2 + kx + \frac{1}{2}(k-1) = 0$ has no real roots.

Solution

The discriminant is

$$k^2 - 4 \times k \times \tfrac{1}{2}(k-1) = k^2 - 2k(k-1)$$
$$= k^2 - 2k^2 + 2k$$
$$= 2k - k^2$$

The discriminant must be less than zero so

$$2k - k^2 < 0$$
$$k(2-k) < 0$$

A sign diagram is

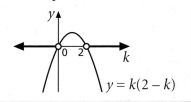

Take care with this factor.

If you use a graphical approach here, note that the graph is an inverted parabola.

Hence the values for k are given by $k < 0$ and $k > 2$.

Exercise D (answers p 170)

1 The equation $x^2 + kx + 16 = 0$, where k is a constant, has real roots.
 (a) Show that $k^2 - 64 \geq 0$.
 (b) Hence find the set of possible values for k.

2 Work out the values for k for which each equation has real roots.
 (a) $5x^2 + kx + 5 = 0$ (b) $x^2 + 3kx + k = 0$ (c) $x^2 + (k+3)x - k = 0$

3 The equation $x^2 + 4kx + 5k = 0$, where k is a constant, has **distinct** real roots.
 Find the set of possible values for k.

4 Work out the values for k for which each equation has distinct real roots.
 (a) $x^2 + kx + 4k = 0$ (b) $kx^2 - 3x + k = 0$ (c) $(2k-3)x^2 + kx + (k-1) = 0$

5 Show that $x^2 - kx + 2 = 0$ does not have real roots when $-2\sqrt{2} < k < 2\sqrt{2}$.

6 Work out the values for k for which each equation has no real roots.
 (a) $x^2 + 2kx + 3 = 0$ (b) $x^2 - kx + 3 - k = 0$ (c) $(2k-1)x^2 + (k+1)x + k = 0$

7 Show that $kx^2 - (k + 4)x + 4 = 0$ has real roots for all possible real values of k.

8 A parabola has equation $y = x^2 + 6x + 2$.
A line has equation $y = 3x + k$, where k is a constant.
Find the possible values for k so that the line intersects the parabola at two points.

9 A parabola has equation $y = -x^2 + 5x - 5$.
A line has equation $y = kx - 1$, where k is a constant.
Find the possible values for k so that the line does not intersect the parabola.

E Quadratic inequalities: solving problems

Example 8

Harry is digging a rectangular flower bed.
The perimeter of the bed is to be 60 m and the area is to be at least 200 m².
Work out the range of possible values for the width of the flower bed.

Solution

Let w be the width of the rectangle.
A diagram is

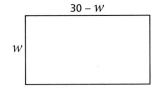

30 – w

w

The perimeter is 60 m so the sum of the width and length is 30 m

The area is at least 200 m² so we have the inequality

$$w(30 - w) \geq 200$$
$$\Rightarrow \quad 30w - w^2 \geq 200$$

Rearrange the inequality and get zero on one side.

$$-w^2 + 30w - 200 \geq 0$$

Multiplying each side by –1 reverses the direction of the inequality.

$$w^2 - 30w + 200 \leq 0$$

The quadratic factorises so we can use number lines.

$$(w - 10)(w - 20) \leq 0$$

A sign diagram is

$$
\begin{array}{ll}
w - 10 & - - - \ 0 + + + + + + + \\
& \qquad\quad 10
\end{array}
$$

$$
\begin{array}{ll}
w - 20 & - - - - - - - - \ 0 + + + \\
& \qquad\qquad\qquad 20
\end{array}
$$

$$
\begin{array}{ll}
(w - 10)(w - 20) & + + + \ 0 - - - - \ 0 + + + \\
& \qquad\quad 10 \qquad\quad 20
\end{array}
$$

The solution set is the range of values given by $10 \leq w \leq 20$.

So the width of the flower bed can be between 10 m and 20 m.

Example 9

The diagrams on the right show the
first four pentagonal numbers   1, 5, 12, 22, ...

The nth pentagonal number is $\dfrac{n(3n-1)}{2}$.

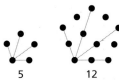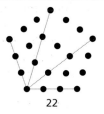

1   5   12   22

Work out the first pentagonal number that is greater than 100.

Solution

We have the inequality $\dfrac{n(3n-1)}{2} > 100$

Multiply both sides by 2. $n(3n-1) > 200$

$\Rightarrow$ $3n^2 - n > 200$

Rearrange the inequality to get zero on one side. $3n^2 - n - 200 > 0$

The quadratic factorises so we can use number lines. $(3n - 25)(n + 8) > 0$

A sign diagram is

$3n - 25$ $-\ -\ -\ -\ -\ -\ -\ 0\ +\ +\ +$
                          $8\frac{1}{3}$

$n + 8$ $-\ -\ -\ 0\ +\ +\ +\ +\ +\ +\ +$
                  -8

$(3n - 25)(n + 8)$ $+\ +\ +\ 0\ -\ -\ -\ 0\ +\ +\ +$
                            -8 $8\frac{1}{3}$

The solution set is the range of values given by $n < -8$ and $n > 8\frac{1}{3}$.

In this context, n cannot be negative or fractional so the first value of n that
satisfies these inequalities here is 9.

This gives the pentagonal number $\dfrac{9(27-1)}{2} = 117$

Exercise E (answers p 170)

1 The diagrams on the right show the
first three hexagonal numbers 1, 6, 15, ...

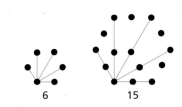

1   6   15

The nth hexagonal number is $n(2n - 1)$.

(a) By writing an inequality and solving it, find the value of n that gives the first
hexagonal number greater than 465.

(b) What is the first hexagonal number that is greater than 465?

2 Susie is designing a stand for an exhibition.
It is to have display screens round three sides and to be open on the other side.
40 m of screens are available for the stand and the owners want a rectangular
floor space of at least 150 square metres.

What limits must Susie work within for the lengths of the sides of the stand?

3 The nth triangle number is $\dfrac{n(n+1)}{2}$.

    (a) By writing an inequality and solving it, find the value of n that gives
the first triangle number greater than 100.

    (b) What is the first triangle number greater than 100?

    (c) What value of n gives the first triangle number greater than 1000?

*4 Zane is designing a viewing area for a seal sanctuary.
The area is to be rectangular and surrounded by metal railings.
The total length of the railings must be 50 m and the enclosed area must be
no more than 150 m².

    (a) If w is the width of the viewing area, explain why w must satisfy
the inequality $0 < w < 25$.

    (b) Work out the complete range of possible values for the width of the viewing area.

Key points

- A linear inequality can be solved like a linear equation except that **multiplying or dividing each side by a negative number reverses the direction of the inequality sign.**
  For example, multiplying both sides of $4 - \frac{1}{2}x > 5$ by -2 gives $-8 + x < -10$.   (p 66)

- A quadratic inequality can be solved using a graphical or an algebraic approach.
  For example, the inequality $x^2 + 4x - 5 < 0$ factorises to give $(x + 5)(x - 1) < 0$.

Graphical approach	Algebraic approach (using a sign diagram)

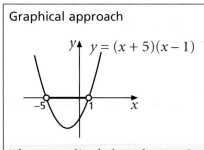 $y = (x + 5)(x - 1)$	$x + 5$ $-\ -\ -\ -\ 0\ +\ +\ +\ +\ +\ +\ +$
	         -5
	
	$x - 1$ $-\ -\ -\ -\ -\ -\ -\ -\ 0\ +\ +\ +$
	           1
	
	$(x + 5)(x - 1)$ $+\ +\ +\ 0\ -\ -\ -\ 0\ +\ +\ +$
	           -5 1

The curve lies below the x-axis for $-5 < x < 1$. (p 69)	The product is negative for $-5 < x < 1$. (p 70)

- If the equation $ax^2 + bx + c = 0$ has real roots, then $b^2 - 4ac \geq 0$.
  If the equation $ax^2 + bx + c = 0$ does not have real roots, then $b^2 - 4ac < 0$.   (p 72)

Test yourself (answers p 170)

None of these questions requires a calculator.

1 Solve the following inequalities.

(a) $5x - 2 > 3x + 11$ (b) $3(3x - 1) \leq 5x + 6$

2 The *Hambridge Advertiser* charges £5.00 plus an extra 20p per word to publish a Valentine's Day message.

The *Cadzow Times* charges £2.50 plus an extra 50p per word.

Form and solve an inequality to find when it is cheaper to use the *Cadzow Times* for a Valentine's Day message.

3 Solve the following inequalities.

(a) $5(y + 5) < 7 - 3(y + 2)$ (b) $x^2 + 4x - 12 > 0$ AQA 2002

4 Solve the inequality $2x^2 + 17x < 9$.

5 (a) Solve $2x^2 + 8x + 7 = 0$, giving your answers in surd form.

(b) Hence solve $2x^2 + 8x + 7 > 0$.   AQA 2002

6 The equation $x^2 - 5kx + k = 0$, where k is a constant, has distinct real roots.

(a) Prove that $k(25k - 4) > 0$.

(b) Hence find the set of possible values for k.

7 The height of a particular ball is given by the formula $h = 12t - 5t^2$, where h is the height above the ground in metres and t is the time in seconds.

Form and solve an inequality to find when the height of the ball above the ground is less than 4 metres.

8 Jo is designing a rectangular pool.
The perimeter is to be 100 m and the area is to be at least 525 m^2.
Work out the possible values for the width of the pool.

9 A parabola has equation $y = x^2 + 1$.
A line has equation $y = kx - 3$, where k is a constant.
Find the possible values for k so that the line intersects the parabola at two points.

*10 A circle has equation $x^2 + y^2 = 20$.
A line has a gradient of 2 and intersects the circle at two points.
Find the possible values for the y-intercept of the line.

6 Polynomials

In this chapter you will learn how to
- evaluate and manipulate powers of the form kx^n where n is a positive integer
- sketch cubic graphs and consider the effect of translations on their equations
- multiply out brackets to give a polynomial expression
- relate the roots of a polynomial to where its graph crosses the x-axis
- use function notation
- divide a polynomial expression by a linear one
- use the remainder and factor theorems to factorise polynomial expressions

A Indices: revision

In an expression such as x^5, the 5 is called the **index** (the plural is **indices**).
The expression x^5 is defined as $x \times x \times x \times x \times x$.

Example 1

Evaluate $5x^3$ when $x = 2$.

Solution

When $x = 2$, $\quad 5x^3 = 5 \times 2^3 \qquad$ *This is not the same as $(5 \times 2)^3$.*
$\qquad\qquad\qquad\quad = 5 \times 8$
$\qquad\qquad\qquad\quad = 40$

Example 2

Simplify $2x \times 3x^2$.

Solution

$2x \times 3x^2 = 2 \times x \times 3 \times x \times x$
$\qquad\qquad = 2 \times 3 \times x \times x \times x$
$\qquad\qquad = 6x^3$

Exercise A (answers p 171)

1 Evaluate these when $n = 3$.

   (a) n^4 (b) $n^2 + n^3$ (c) $2n^2$ (d) $(n + 2)^3$ (e) $3(n + 1)^2$

   (f) $3n^2 - 5n$ (g) $2n^5 - 3n$ (h) $\frac{1}{3}n^4 + 1$ (i) $2(n^3 - 7)$ (j) $(n - 1)^3 + n^3$

2 Evaluate these when $x = \frac{1}{2}$.

   (a) $6x^2$ (b) $5x(2x - 1)$ (c) $(x - 1)^3$

3 Evaluate these when $a = -1$.

   (a) $10a^4$ (b) a^9 (c) $4(a + 3)^3$

4 Simplify each of these.

   (a) $5x \times x^2$ (b) $4x^2 \times 3x$ (c) $2x^2 \times 5x^3$ (d) $\frac{1}{4}x^3 \times 8x$

   (e) $5x^2 \times \frac{1}{3}x$ (f) $(2x)^3$ (g) $(3x^2)^2$ (h) $(\frac{1}{2}x^3)^2$

B Cubic graphs (answers p 171)

B1 Use a graph plotter on a computer or graphic calculator to draw some graphs of the form $y = ax^3 + bx^2 + cx + d$, where a, b, c and d are constants.
Include some where the value of a is negative.
What do you notice about the shapes of your graphs?

B2 Use a graph plotter to draw each graph below.
How many times does each one cross or touch the x-axis?

$$y = x^3 + 3x^2 + 4x + 5 \qquad y = x^3 - 2x^2 - x + 2 \qquad y = x^3 - x^2 - x + 1$$

B3 Use a graph plotter to draw graphs of the three equations below.

$$y = x^3 \qquad\qquad y = x^3 - x \qquad\qquad y = x^3 + x$$

Describe the shape of each graph as fully as you can.
Make sketches that show clearly the shape of each graph for $-1 \le x \le 1$.

B4 For each equation below,

    (i) make a sketch to show what you think the graph will look like

    (ii) check by graphing on a graph plotter

(a) $y = -x^3$ **(b)** $y = x^3 + 2$ **(c)** $y = -x^3 - 5$

B5 **(a)** Make a sketch of $y = x^3$.

    (b) Sketch what you think the graph of $y = (x - 2)^3$ will look like.

    (c) Check on a graph plotter.

B6 For each equation below, sketch what you think the graph will look like and then check on a graph plotter.

(a) $y = (x + 4)^3$ **(b)** $y = (x - 2)^3 + 5$ **(c)** $y = (x + 6)^3 - 7$

B7 The graph of $y = x^3$ is translated
by $\begin{bmatrix} 3 \\ -1 \end{bmatrix}$ as shown in the diagram.

    (a) Which do you think is the correct
equation for the new graph?

        A $y = (x - 3)^3 + 1$ **B** $y = (x - 3)^3 - 1$

        C $y = (x + 3)^3 + 1$ **D** $y = (x + 3)^3 - 1$

    (b) Check on a graph plotter.

    (c) Work out where the new graph crosses the y-axis.

B8 The graph of $y = x^3$ is translated by $\begin{bmatrix} -2 \\ 4 \end{bmatrix}$.

    (a) Write down what you think is the correct equation for the translated graph.

    (b) Work out where the translated graph crosses the y-axis.

We can work algebraically when translating curves.

In the diagram below, the graph of $y = x^3$ has been translated 3 units to the right and 1 unit up.

Using vector notation this translation is represented by $\begin{bmatrix} 3 \\ 1 \end{bmatrix}$.

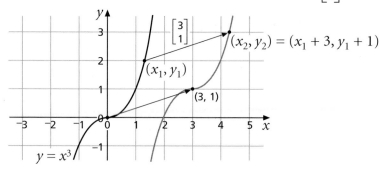

Let (x_1, y_1) be a point on $y = x^3$ and let (x_2, y_2) be its image on the translated curve.

Then $(x_2, y_2) = (x_1 + 3, \ y_1 + 1)$ giving

$$x_1 = x_2 - 3 \qquad \textit{from rearranging } x_2 = x_1 + 3$$

and $\qquad y_1 = y_2 - 1 \qquad \textit{from rearranging } y_2 = y_1 + 1$

We know that $y_1 = x_1{}^3$, so it must be true that

$$y_2 - 1 = (x_2 - 3)^3$$

and so $\qquad y - 1 = (x - 3)^3 \qquad$ is the equation of the transformed curve.

This can be written as $y = (x - 3)^3 + 1$.

> So to find the equation of the curve that is the result of translating $y = x^3$ by $\begin{bmatrix} 3 \\ 1 \end{bmatrix}$ you can replace x by $(x - 3)$ and y by $(y - 1)$.

B9 Which translation will transform the curve $y = x^3$ to $y = (x - 5)^3 + 3$?

B10 The graph of $y = x^3 + x$ is translated by $\begin{bmatrix} 2 \\ -9 \end{bmatrix}$.

(a) Which do you think is the correct equation for the new graph?

A $\ y = (x + 2)^3 + (x + 2) + 9$ B $\ y = (x + 2)^3 + (x + 2) - 9$

C $\ y = (x - 2)^3 + (x - 2) + 9$ D $\ y = (x - 2)^3 + (x - 2) - 9$

(b) Check by graphing on a graph plotter.

(c) Work out where the new graph crosses the y-axis.

K   To find the equation of any curve after it has been translated by $\begin{bmatrix} p \\ q \end{bmatrix}$, replace x by $(x - p)$ and replace y by $(y - q)$.

Example 3

Sketch the graph of $y = (x + 2)^3 + 5$.

Solution

The equation can be written as $y - 5 = (x + 2)^3$.

This is $y = x^3$ with x replaced by $(x + 2)$ and y replaced by $(y - 5)$.

So the curve $y = x^3$ is translated by $\begin{bmatrix} -2 \\ 5 \end{bmatrix}$.

A sketch is shown on the right.

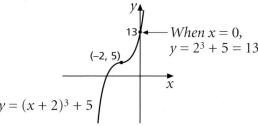

When $x = 0$,
$y = 2^3 + 5 = 13$

$(-2, 5)$

$y = (x + 2)^3 + 5$

Example 4

The graph is a translation of $y = x^3 + x$ by $\begin{bmatrix} 5 \\ 0 \end{bmatrix}$.

Find an equation for the graph.

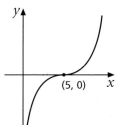

$(5, 0)$

Solution

The translation is $\begin{bmatrix} 5 \\ 0 \end{bmatrix}$ so we replace x by $(x - 5)$, giving $y = (x - 5)^3 + (x - 5)$.

Exercise B (answers p 172)

1 Which translation will transform the curve $y = x^3$ to each of these?

(a) $y - 2 = (x - 1)^3$ (b) $y + 5 = (x - 3)^3$ (c) $y - 1 = (x + 7)^3$

2 Which translation will transform the curve $y = x^3$ to each of these?

(a) $y = (x - 4)^3 + 5$ (b) $y = (x + 2)^3 - 1$ (c) $y = (x + 6)^3 + 3$

3 The curve $y = x^3$ is translated by $\begin{bmatrix} 3 \\ 0 \end{bmatrix}$.

(a) Write an equation for the translated curve.

(b) Sketch the curve, showing where it crosses each axis.

4 The curve $y = x^3$ is translated by $\begin{bmatrix} 5 \\ -3 \end{bmatrix}$.

Write the equation of the translated curve in the form $y = (x + a)^3 + b$.

5 Find the equation of the curve $y = x^3 + x$ after a translation of $\begin{bmatrix} 2 \\ 0 \end{bmatrix}$.

6 The curve $y = x^3 + x$ is translated by $\begin{bmatrix} 1 \\ 3 \end{bmatrix}$.

    (a) Write the equation for the translated curve in the form $y = (x + p)^3 + x + q$.

    (b) Work out where the curve crosses the y-axis.

7 The curve $y = x^3 - x$ is translated by $\begin{bmatrix} -3 \\ -2 \end{bmatrix}$.

    Write the equation for the translated curve in the form $y = (x + p)^3 - x + q$.

C Further graphs and manipulation (answers p 173)

A **cubic** expression is one that can be written in the form $ax^3 + bx^2 + cx + d$ $(a \neq 0)$ where a, b, c and d are constants.

Graphs of the form $y = ax^3 + bx^2 + cx + d$ have one of these basic shapes:

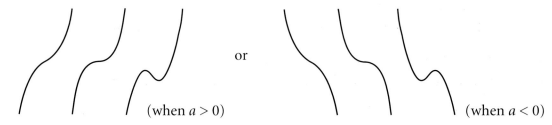

         (when $a > 0$)   or   (when $a < 0$)

Here is a sketch of $y = (x - 4)^3$.

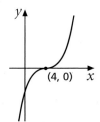

(4, 0)

We can multiply out the brackets to write $y = (x - 4)^3$ in the form $y = ax^3 + bx^2 + cx + d$.

$(x - 4)^3 = (x - 4)(x - 4)(x - 4)$

$\qquad = (x - 4)(x^2 - 4x - 4x + 16)$

$\qquad = (x - 4)(x^2 - 8x + 16)$

×	x	-4
x	x^2	$-4x$
-4	$-4x$	16

$\qquad = x^3 - 8x^2 + 16x - 4x^2 + 32x - 64$

$\qquad = x^3 - 12x^2 + 48x - 64$

×	x^2	$-8x$	16
x	x^3	$-8x^2$	$16x$
-4	$-4x^2$	$32x$	-64

So the equation of the graph can also be written as $y = x^3 - 12x^2 + 48x - 64$.

The constant multipliers in an expression such as $x^3 - 12x^2 + 48x - 64$ are called **coefficients**. In this example, the coefficient of x^2 is -12.

C1 Write $y = (x + 3)^3$ in the form $y = ax^3 + bx^2 + cx + d$.

D

C2 Each expression below is a product of three different linear expressions. Multiply out the brackets in each one.

    (a) $(x + 1)(x + 3)(x + 5)$ **(b)** $(2x + 1)(x + 2)(x - 3)$

C3 (a) Solve the equation $(x + 3)(x + 2)(x - 1) = 0$.

    (b) What does this tell you about the graph of $y = (x + 3)(x + 2)(x - 1)$?

    (c) Where will the graph cross the y-axis?

    (d) Sketch the graph of $y = (x + 3)(x + 2)(x - 1)$.

    (e) Write the equation of the graph in the form $y = ax^3 + bx^2 + cx + d$.

C4 (a) (i) Where will the graph of $y = (2x - 1)(x - 3)(x + 1)$ cross the x-axis?

      (ii) Where will it cross the y-axis?

    (b) Sketch the graph of $y = (2x - 1)(x - 3)(x + 1)$.

    (c) Write the equation of the graph in the form $y = ax^3 + bx^2 + cx + d$.

C5 (a) Sketch the graph of $y = (2x + 1)(3x - 1)(x + 4)$.

    (b) Write the equation of the graph in the form $y = ax^3 + bx^2 + cx + d$.

D

C6 (a) Solve the equation $(x + 3)(x - 1)^2 = 0$.

    (b) What does this tell you about the graph of $y = (x + 3)(x - 1)^2$?

    (c) Where will the graph cross the y-axis?

    (d) Sketch the graph of $y = (x + 3)(x - 1)^2$.

    (e) Write the equation of the graph in the form $y = ax^3 + bx^2 + cx + d$.

C7 (a) Show that $(x + 3)^3 + 1$ is equivalent to $x^3 + 9x^2 + 27x + 28$.

    (b) Sketch the graph of $y = x^3 + 9x^2 + 27x + 28$.

C8 (a) Show that $(x + 4)(x - 5)(2 - x)$ is equivalent to $-x^3 + 3x^2 + 18x - 40$.

    (b) Decide which of the graphs below is a sketch of $y = -x^3 + 3x^2 + 18x - 40$.

A 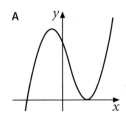 B 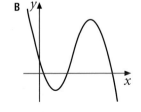 C 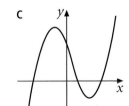 D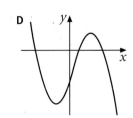

K The product of three linear expressions can always be written in the form $ax^3 + bx^2 + cx + d$.

Example 5

Sketch the graph of $y = (2x - 1)(x - 3)(x + 2)$.

Solution

The expression is the product of three linear factors so the graph is a cubic shape.

The graph cuts the x-axis when $(2x - 1)(x - 3)(x + 2) = 0$.

The equation has three solutions when

$2x - 1 = 0$ gives $x = \frac{1}{2}$,

$x - 3 = 0$ gives $x = 3$,

and $x + 2 = 0$ gives $x = -2$.

When $x = 0$, $y = -1 \times -3 \times 2 = 6$.

Hence, a sketch of the graph is

$$y = (2x - 1)(x - 3)(x + 2)$$

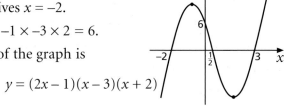

In chapter 9, you will learn how to find the coordinates of the points marked with dots. Concentrate on the x- and y-intercepts for now.

Example 6

Write $(2x - 1)(x - 3)(x + 2)$ in the form $ax^3 + bx^2 + cx + d$.

Solution

$(2x - 1)(x - 3)(x + 2)$

$= (2x - 1)(x^2 + 2x - 3x - 6)$

×	x	2
x	x^2	$2x$
-3	$-3x$	-6

$= (2x - 1)(x^2 - x - 6)$

$= 2x^3 - 2x^2 - 12x - x^2 + x + 6$

$= 2x^3 - 3x^2 - 11x + 6$

×	x^2	$-x$	-6
$2x$	$2x^3$	$-2x^2$	$-12x$
-1	$-x^2$	x	6

Exercise C (answers p 173)

1 For each equation below

    (i) sketch a graph showing clearly where it crosses the x- and y-axes

    (ii) write the equation in the form $y = ax^3 + bx^2 + cx + d$

  (a) $y = (x + 1)(x + 3)(x + 4)$ **(b)** $y = (x + 2)^3$

  (c) $y = (x + 4)(x - 1)(x + 2)$ **(d)** $y = x(x + 3)(x - 2)$

  (e) $y = (x - 5)^3$ **(f)** $y = (2x + 1)(x - 2)(x + 2)$

  (g) $y = \frac{1}{2}x(2x + 3)(x - 2)$ **(h)** $y = (x + 4)^3 + 1$

2 (a) Solve the equation $(x + 1)(x - 3)^2 = 0$.

(b) Sketch the graph of $y = (x + 1)(x - 3)^2$, showing clearly where it meets both axes.

(c) Write the equation of the graph in the form $y = ax^3 + bx^2 + cx + d$.

3 (a) Sketch the graph of $y = (2x - 3)(x + 1)(3 - x)$.

(b) Write the equation of the graph in the form $y = ax^3 + bx^2 + cx + d$.

4 Sketch the graph of $y = (2x + 3)^2(x - 1)$, showing clearly where it meets both axes.

D Polynomial functions

A **polynomial** is an expression that can be written in the form
$a + bx + cx^2 + dx^3 + ex^4 + fx^5 + \ldots$ where $a, b, c, d, e, f, \ldots$ are constants.

Some examples of polynomials are $7x^4 + x - 10$ and $6 + 5x^2 - x^3 - 5x^7$.

Expressions such as $\sqrt{x} + 3x^2 - 5$ and $\dfrac{1}{x} + 7x$ are not polynomials as they involve terms in x that cannot be written in the form x^n where n is a positive integer ($\sqrt{x}$ and $\dfrac{1}{x}$).

The **degree** of a polynomial is the value of its highest index.
For example, $6 + 5x^2 - x^3 - 5x^7$ is a polynomial of degree 7.

The sum, difference or product of two polynomials is also a polynomial.

For example, $(x^4 - 5x)(3x^3 + x - 10)$

$\times$	$3x^3$	x	-10
x^4	$3x^7$	x^5	$-10x^4$
$-5x$	$-15x^4$	$-5x^2$	$50x$

$\quad = 3x^7 + x^5 - 10x^4 - 15x^4 - 5x^2 + 50x$

$\quad = 3x^7 + x^5 - 25x^4 - 5x^2 + 50x$

Function notation is useful when dealing with polynomials.

For example, if a polynomial function is defined by $f(x) = x^3 + 4x^2 - 1$,
then $f(3)$ is the value of the polynomial at $x = 3$.

$$\text{So } f(3) = 3^3 + 4 \times 3^2 - 1 = 27 + 36 - 1 = 62$$

Example 7

Polynomials are given by $f(x) = x^4 - 2x^3 + 5$ and $g(x) = x^3 + 7x^2 - 3$.
Expand and simplify $2f(x) - g(x)$.

Solution

$2f(x) - g(x) = 2(x^4 - 2x^3 + 5) - (x^3 + 7x^2 - 3)$

$\qquad\qquad = 2x^4 - 4x^3 + 10 - x^3 - 7x^2 + 3$

$\qquad\qquad = 2x^4 - 5x^3 - 7x^2 + 13$

Example 8

Polynomials are given by $p(x) = x^3 - 2$ and $q(x) = 2x^3 + 3x - 5$.

Expand and simplify $p(x)q(x)$.

Solution

$$p(x)q(x) = (x^3 - 2)(2x^3 + 3x - 5)$$
$$= 2x^6 + 3x^4 - 5x^3 - 4x^3 - 6x + 10$$
$$= 2x^6 + 3x^4 - 9x^3 - 6x + 10$$

$\times$	$2x^3$	$3x$	-5
x^3	$2x^6$	$3x^4$	$-5x^3$
-2	$-4x^3$	$-6x$	10

Exercise D (answers p 174)

1 Expand and simplify $2(x^3 + 3x - 1) - x(x^2 + x - 5)$.

2 Work out the value of each polynomial when $x = 2$.

   (a) $x^5 - x^3 + 6$ **(b)** $4x^3 + 5x^2 - 9$ **(c)** $2x^5 - 4x^3 - 5x^2 - 7x + 2$

3 Expand and simplify each of these.

   (a) $(x + 2)(x^4 + 3x + 1)$ **(b)** $(x^2 + 6)^2$

   (c) $(x^2 + 3x - 1)(2x^3 + x + 5)$ **(d)** $(1 - x)(x^3 - 1) + 6x$

   (e) $(3x^2 - x)(x^2 + 3) + x^2$ **(f)** $(x^2 - 1)^3$

   (g) $(x + 1)(x + 4)(x - 2)(x - 3)$ **(h)** $(1 - 2x)(x + 6)(3x - 2) + x(2x + 1)$

4 A polynomial is given by $f(x) = 2x^4 - x^3 - 2x + 6$.
Evaluate each of these.

   (a) $f(1)$ **(b)** $f(0)$ **(c)** $f(2)$ **(d)** $f(-1)$ **(e)** $f(-2)$

5 A polynomial is given by $g(x) = x^3 + 2x^2 - 25x - 50$.

   (a) Evaluate $g(5)$, $g(-5)$ and $g(-2)$.

   (b) Hence, write down the coordinates of the points where
       the graph of $y = g(x)$ crosses the x-axis.

6 Polynomials are given by $p(x) = x^2 + 1$ and $q(x) = x^5 - 2x^2 - 2$.
Expand and simplify each of these.

   (a) $2p(x) + q(x)$ **(b)** $3p(x) - q(x)$ **(c)** $p(x)q(x)$ **(d)** $(q(x))^2$

7 A polynomial is given by $f(x) = -2x^3 + 7x^2 - 3x$.

   (a) Evaluate each of these.

      (i) $f(0)$ **(ii)** $f(-1)$ **(iii)** $f(3)$ **(iv)** $f(\frac{1}{2})$ **(v)** $f(1)$

   (b) Sketch the graph of $y = f(x)$.

8 A function is given by $f(x) = (2x - 3)(x + 4)^2$.

    (a) Write the function in the form $f(x) = ax^3 + bx^2 + cx + d$.

    (b) Sketch the graph of $y = f(x)$.

E Division (answers p 175)

The sum, difference or product of any two integers is always another integer.
We know that this isn't true for dividing two integers – sometimes there is a remainder.

A statement such as $57 = 4 \times 16 + 1$ tells us that dividing 57 by 4 leaves a remainder of 1.

We know that the sum, difference or product of any two polynomials is also a polynomial.
Now we will consider whether or not dividing polynomials will work in the same way as
dividing two integers. Will there sometimes be a remainder here too?

E1 (a) Work out the missing polynomial in the statement
$$x^2 + 7x + 12 = (x + 3)(\qquad).$$

    (b) Hence, write down the expression equivalent to
$$(x^2 + 7x + 12) \div (x + 3).$$

E2 Find the missing polynomial in each statement below.

    (a) $3x^2 + 10x + 3 = (x + 3)(\qquad)$

    (b) $2x^2 + x - 3 = (x - 1)(\qquad)$

E3 Can you find the missing polynomials in the statements below?

    (a) $x^3 + 3x^2 + 7x + 5 = (x + 1)(\qquad)$

    (b) $x^3 - 2x^2 - 17x - 6 = (x + 3)(\qquad)$

    (c) $x^3 - 3x^2 - 7x - 15 = (x - 5)(\qquad)$

E4 Find the missing polynomial in each statement below.

    (a) $x^2 + 2x + 1 = x(\qquad) + 1$

    (b) $x^2 + 4x + 7 = (x + 1)(\qquad) + 4$

    (c) $x^2 - 8x + 13 = (x - 3)(\qquad) - 2$

E5 (a) Can you complete the statement below so that R is an integer?
$$x^2 + 6x + 7 = (x + 5)(\qquad) + R$$

    (b) What is the remainder after dividing $(x^2 + 6x + 7)$ by $(x + 5)$?

E6 (a) Can you complete the statement below so that R is an integer?
$$x^2 - 10x + 31 = (x - 3)(\qquad) + R$$

    (b) What is the remainder after dividing $(x^2 - 10x + 31)$ by $(x - 3)$?

E7 (a) Can you complete the statement below so that R is an integer?
$$x^2 - 10x + 11 = (x - 3)(\qquad) + R$$

    (b) What is the remainder after dividing $(x^2 - 10x + 11)$ by $(x - 3)$?

To divide $(x^3 - x^2 + x + 15)$ by $(x + 2)$, we need to find the missing polynomial and the value for R in the statement

$$x^3 - x^2 + x + 15 = (x + 2)(\qquad) + R$$

We can use a 'reverse table' method to find the missing expressions.

$\left(x^3 - x^2 + x + 15\right)$

×	
x	x^3
2	

This must be x^3 as it's the term with the highest power of x ...

... *so this is x^2* ...

×	x^2
x	x^3
2	

×	x^2
x	x^3
2	$2x^2$

... *and this is $2x^2$.*

$\left(x^3 - x^2 + x + 15\right)$

×	x^2
x	x^3
2	$2x^2$

The sum of the circled expressions must be $-x^2$ ...

... *so this is $-3x^2$* ...

×	x^2
x	x^3 $-3x^2$
2	$2x^2$

... *this is $-3x$* ...

×	x^2 $-3x$
x	x^3 $-3x^2$
2	$2x^2$

×	x^2 $-3x$
x	x^3 $-3x^2$
2	$2x^2$ $-6x$

... *and this is $-6x$.*

$\left(x^3 - x^2 + x + 15\right)$

×	x^2 $-3x$
x	x^3 $-3x^2$
2	$2x^2$ $-6x$

The sum of the circled expressions must be x ...

... *so this is $7x$* ...

×	x^2 $-3x$
x	x^3 $-3x^2$ $7x$
2	$2x^2$ $-6x$

... *this is 7* ...

×	x^2 $-3x$ 7
x	x^3 $-3x^2$ $7x$
2	$2x^2$ $-6x$ 14

... *and finally this is 14.*

So $x^3 - x^2 + x + 14 = (x + 2)(x^2 - 3x + 7)$

We need to add 1 to each side to obtain the correct polynomial so

$$x^3 - x^2 + x + 15 = (x + 2)(x^2 - 3x + 7) + 1$$

Hence $(x^3 - x^2 + x + 15) \div (x + 2) = (x^2 - 3x + 7)$ with a remainder of 1.

Alternatively, we can use a 'long division' method and work as in numerical long division.

$$
\begin{array}{r}
x^2 - 3x + 7 \\
x + 2 \overline{)\ x^3 - x^2 + x + 15} \\
x^3 + 2x^2 \\
\overline{\quad -3x^2 + x} \\
-3x^2 - 6x \\
\overline{\quad\quad 7x + 15} \\
7x + 14 \\
\overline{\quad\quad\quad 1}
\end{array}
$$

This also shows that $(x^3 - x^2 + x + 15) \div (x + 2) = (x^2 - 3x + 7)$ with a remainder of 1.

Exercise E (answers p 175)

1 Find the result of each of these.
Some have remainders and some divide exactly.

(a) $x^3 + 4x^2 + 7x + 9$ divided by $x + 1$

(b) $x^3 + 2x^2 - 9x + 2$ divided by $x - 2$

(c) $x^3 - 6x^2 + 11x - 31$ divided by $x - 5$

(d) $2x^3 + 5x^2 + 5x + 9$ divided by $x + 2$

(e) $3x^3 - x^2 - 7x + 5$ divided by $x - 1$

(f) $5x^3 + 13x^2 - 7x - 5$ divided by $x + 3$

(g) $x^3 + 2x^2 - x - 2$ divided by $x + 2$

2 Find the result when $x^3 - 2x - 1$ is divided by $x + 1$.
(It might help to think of the cubic expression as $x^3 + 0x^2 - 2x - 1$.)

3 Find the result of each of these.

(a) $x^3 - 13x + 12$ divided by $x - 1$

(b) $x^3 + x + 12$ divided by $x + 2$

(c) $2x^3 + 7x^2 - 9$ divided by $x + 3$

(d) $3x^3 - 5x + 1$ divided by $x - 2$

(e) $4x^3 - x^2 + 3$ divided by $x + 1$

4 Find the result when $x^3 - 1$ is divided by $x - 1$.

5 A polynomial is defined by $f(x) = x^3 + 7x^2 + 7x - 15$.

(a) Show that f(x) divides by $x + 5$ exactly.

(b) Hence write f(x) as a product of two expressions, one linear and one quadratic.

(c) Factorise the quadratic expression.
Hence write the polynomial f(x) as the product of three linear expressions.

6 A polynomial is defined by $p(x) = x^3 - 6x^2 + 5x + 12$.

  (a) Find the remainder when $p(x)$ is divided by

  (i) $x - 2$ **(ii)** $x - 1$ **(iii)** x **(iv)** $x + 1$ **(v)** $x + 2$

  (b) Which of the expressions in (a) is a factor of $p(x)$?

  (c) Hence write $p(x)$ as a product of two expressions, one linear and one quadratic.

  (d) Factorise the quadratic expression.
  Hence write the polynomial $p(x)$ as the product of three linear expressions.

  (e) Solve $p(x) = 0$.

*7 Find the result of each of these.

  (a) $6x^3 - 20x^2 - 21x + 10$ divided by $3x - 1$

  (b) $4x^3 + x^2 - 12x - 3$ divided by $4x + 1$

  (c) $2x^3 + 13$ divided by $2x + 1$

F Remainders and factors (answers p 175)

A division results in a **quotient** and a remainder.

For example, $39 \div 7 = 5$ remainder 4
                 In this case, the quotient is 5 and the remainder is 4.

Another example is $48 \div 6 = 8$ remainder 0
                       Here the quotient is 8.
                       As the remainder is 0 we know that 6 is a factor of 48.

F1 A polynomial is defined by $p(x) = x^3 + 2x^2 - 9x + 10$.

  (a) (i) Divide $p(x)$ by $x - 2$ and write down the remainder.

      (ii) Calculate $p(2)$.

      (iii) What do you notice?

  (b) (i) Divide $p(x)$ by $x + 1$ and write down the remainder.

      (ii) Calculate $p(-1)$.

      (iii) What do you notice?

  (c) For various values of a

      (i) Divide $p(x)$ by $x - a$ and write down the remainder.

      (ii) Calculate $p(a)$.

      (iii) What do you notice?

      (iv) Can you explain this?

When $p(x) = x^3 + 2x^2 - 9x + 10$ is divided by $x - 2$,
there is a quotient of $x^2 + 4x - 1$ and a remainder of 8.

Hence we can write $p(x) = (x - 2)(x^2 + 4x - 1) + 8$.

If $x = 2$ is substituted, then $(x - 2) = 0$.
So the quotient is multiplied by 0, leaving $p(2) = 8$ which is the remainder.

In general, suppose that $p(x)$ is a polynomial in x and that
dividing $p(x)$ by $(x - a)$ gives a quotient of $q(x)$ and a remainder R.

Then we can write $p(x) = (x - a)q(x) + R$

This gives us $p(a) = 0 \times q(a) + R = R$

That is, $p(a) = R$

K This result is called the **remainder theorem** and can be summarised:

When $p(x)$ is divided by $(x - a)$, the remainder is $p(a)$.

F2 A polynomial is defined by $p(x) = x^3 + 5x^2 - 2x - 2$.

    (a) Use the remainder theorem to work out the remainder when $p(x)$ is divided by $x - 1$.

    (b) Confirm your result by dividing $p(x)$ by $x - 1$.

D **F3** A polynomial is defined by $f(x) = x^3 - x^2 - 7x + 3$.
    Find the value of $f(3)$. What does this tell you?

F4 A polynomial is defined by $p(x) = x^3 + 3x^2 - 10x - 24$.

    (a) Use the remainder theorem to work out the remainder when $p(x)$ is divided by

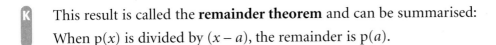

        (i) $x - 1$ **(ii)** x **(iii)** $x + 1$ **(iv)** $x + 2$ **(v)** $x + 3$

    (b) Use your results to write down a factor of $p(x)$.

    (c) Write $p(x)$ as the product of a linear and a quadratic expression.

    (d) Factorise the quadratic and write $p(x)$ as the product of three linear factors.

    (e) Hence solve the equation $x^3 + 3x^2 - 10x - 24 = 0$.

    (f) Sketch the graph of $y = x^3 + 3x^2 - 10x - 24$.

K For a given polynomial $p(x)$, if $p(a) = 0$ then $(x - a)$ is a factor of $p(x)$.
The converse is also true: if $(x - a)$ is a factor of $p(x)$, then $p(a) = 0$.

This result is called the **factor theorem**.

D **F5** A polynomial is defined by $p(x) = 2x^3 - 5x^2 + x - 12$.
    Use the factor theorem to find one linear factor of $p(x)$.

Example 9

A polynomial is given by $p(x) = x^3 + 4x^2 + x - 6$.
Show that $(x + 3)$ is a factor of $p(x)$ and express $p(x)$ as a product of three linear factors.

Solution

To show that $(x + 3)$ is a factor, evaluate $p(-3)$.
$$p(-3) = (-3)^3 + 4(-3)^2 + (-3) - 6$$
$$= -27 + 36 - 3 - 6$$
$$= 0$$

So $(x + 3)$ is a factor of $p(x)$.

Now write $p(x)$ as the product of $(x + 3)$ and a quadratic factor.

$p(x) = (x + 3)(x^2 + x - 2)$ *With practice, you will be able to write down the quadratic factor straight away by realising that the coefficient of x^2 must be 1, the constant term must be –2 and hence the coefficient of x must be 1 (to achieve $4x^2 + x$ in the expansion).*

$\quad = (x + 3)(x + 2)(x - 1)$ *The quadratic factorises. This will not always be the case.*

Example 10

Factorise $p(x) = x^3 - 5x^2 + 5x + 3$ completely.
Hence solve $p(x) = 0$, giving all solutions as exact values.

Solution

In any linear factor of the form $(x - c)$, the value of c must be a factor of 3 (the constant term in $p(x)$).
So first evaluate $p(1)$, $p(3)$, $p(-1)$ and $p(-3)$ to look for linear factors.

$p(1) = 1 - 5 + 5 + 3 = 4$ so $(x - 1)$ is not a factor.
$p(3) = 27 - 45 + 15 + 3 = 0$ so $(x - 3)$ is a factor.

Now write $p(x)$ as the product of $(x - 3)$ and a quadratic factor.

$p(x) = (x - 3)(x^2 - 2x - 1)$ *The quadratic expression does not factorise so we have now factorised $p(x)$ completely. It has only one linear factor.*

So $p(x) = 0 \implies (x - 3)(x^2 - 2x - 1) = 0$

$\qquad\qquad \implies (x - 3) = 0$ which gives $x = 3$ or

$\qquad\qquad (x^2 - 2x - 1) = 0$ which gives $x = \dfrac{2 \pm \sqrt{8}}{2} = \dfrac{2 \pm 2\sqrt{2}}{2} = 1 \pm \sqrt{2}$

So the equation $p(x) = 0$ has solutions $x = 3, 1 + \sqrt{2}, 1 - \sqrt{2}$.

When factorising a cubic polynomial, once you have found a linear factor, then the quadratic factor can be found by comparing coefficients.

Exercise F (answers p 176)

1 Use the remainder theorem to find the remainder when $x^3 - 3x^2 + x - 10$ is divided by $x - 4$.

2 A polynomial is given by $p(x) = x^3 + 5x^2 - 17x - 21$.

  (a) By finding the value of $p(3)$, show that $(x - 3)$ is a factor of $p(x)$.

  (b) Express $p(x)$ as a product of three linear factors.

3 A polynomial is given by $f(x) = x^3 - 4x^2 - 7x + 10$.

  (a) By finding the value of $f(-2)$, show that $(x + 2)$ is a factor of $f(x)$.

  (b) Factorise $f(x)$ into the product of three linear factors.

4 Given that $f(x) = x^3 + 4x^2 + x - 6$:

  (a) find $f(1)$ and $f(-1)$;

  (b) factorise $f(x)$ into the product of three linear factors.   AQA 2002

5 A polynomial is given by $q(x) = x^3 + 6x^2 - 13x - 42$.

  (a) Show that $(x + 7)$ is a factor of $q(x)$.

  (b) Express $q(x)$ as a product of three linear factors.

  (c) Hence solve the equation $q(x) = 0$.

6 A function is defined as $f(x) = x^3 + 4x^2 - 11x + 6$.

  (a) Factorise $f(x)$ completely.

  (b) Hence solve the equation $x^3 + 4x^2 - 11x + 6 = 0$.

  (c) Sketch the graph of $y = x^3 + 4x^2 - 11x + 6$.

7 A polynomial is given by $p(x) = x^3 + x^2 + 3x - 5$.

  (a) Show that $(x - 1)$ is a factor of $p(x)$.

  (b) Express $p(x)$ as a product of one linear and one quadratic expression.

  (c) (i) Find the value of the discriminant of the quadratic expression.

     (ii) Hence show that the equation $p(x) = 0$ has only one real solution.

8 A polynomial is given by $p(x) = x^3 + x^2 - 7x - 7$.

  (a) Show that $(x + 1)$ is a factor of $p(x)$.

  (b) Express $p(x)$ as a product of one linear and one quadratic expression.

  (c) Hence, solve the equation $p(x) = 0$.
    (Give any non-integer solutions as exact values.)

9 Factorise these cubics completely. (Some have only one linear factor.)

  (a) $x^3 + 4x^2 - 7x - 10$ **(b)** $2x^3 + 5x^2 - x - 6$ **(c)** $x^3 - x^2 - 3x + 2$

  (d) $x^3 + 7x^2 + 14x + 8$ **(e)** $2x^3 + 2x^2 - 5x - 5$ **(f)** $x^3 + 8x^2 + 21x + 18$

G Further problems

Example 11

A polynomial is given by $f(x) = 2x^3 + ax^2 + 6x + 3$, where a is a constant.
When $f(x)$ is divided by $(x - 2)$, there is a remainder of 7.
Find the value of a.

Solution

Dividing $f(x)$ by $(x - 2)$ gives a remainder of 7 so $f(2) = 7$

$$\Rightarrow \quad 2 \times 2^3 + a \times 2^2 + 6 \times 2 + 3 = 7$$
$$\Rightarrow \quad 16 + 4a + 12 + 3 = 7$$
$$\Rightarrow \quad 31 + 4a = 7$$
$$\Rightarrow \quad a = -6$$

Example 12

The polynomial $f(x) = x^3 + ax^2 - 4x + b$ has a factor $(x + 2)$.
When $f(x)$ is divided by $(x - 3)$, there is a remainder of 30.
Find the values of a and b.

Solution

$(x + 2)$ is a factor so $f(-2) = 0$

$$\Rightarrow \quad (-2)^3 + a \times (-2)^2 - 4 \times (-2) + b = 0$$
$$\Rightarrow \quad -8 + 4a + 8 + b = 0$$
$$\Rightarrow \quad 4a + b = 0$$

Dividing by $(x - 3)$ gives a remainder of 30 so $f(3) = 30$

$$\Rightarrow \quad 3^3 + a \times 3^2 - 4 \times 3 + b = 30$$
$$\Rightarrow \quad 27 + 9a - 12 + b = 30$$
$$\Rightarrow \quad 9a + b = 15$$

We now have two equations in a and b that we can solve simultaneously.

$$9a + b = 15$$
$$4a + b = 0$$

Subtracting gives
$$5a = 15$$
$$\Rightarrow \quad a = 3$$

Substituting in the second equation gives
$$12 + b = 0$$
$$\Rightarrow \quad b = -12$$

Exercise G (answers p 176)

1 The polynomial $f(x)$ is given by $f(x) = x^3 + 2x^2 + kx - 1$, where k is a constant.
When $f(x)$ is divided by $(x - 2)$, there is a remainder of 17.
Find the value of k.

2 Given that $(x + 1)$ is a factor of $p(x) = x^3 + ax^2 - 6x + 5$, find the value of
the constant a.

3 When the polynomial $x^3 + bx^2 + bx + 5$ is divided by $x + 2$, there is a remainder of 5.
Find the value of b.

4 Given that $x - 3$ is a factor of $ax^3 + 2ax^2 + 3ax - 54$, find the value of the constant a.

5 The polynomial $x^3 + px^2 + qx - 40$ has factors $(x - 5)$ and $(x + 1)$.
Find the values of p and q.

6 The polynomial $q(x) = x^3 + ax^2 + bx - 6$ has factors $(x - 3)$ and $(x + 2)$.
Find the values of a and b.

7 The polynomial $f(x) = x^3 + px^2 - 4x + q$ has a factor of $(x + 3)$.
When $f(x)$ is divided by $(x - 1)$, there is a remainder of 4.
Find the values of p and q.

8 The polynomial $p(x) = x^3 + ax^2 + bx + 2$ has a factor of $(x + 2)$.
When $p(x)$ is divided by $(x - 2)$, there is a remainder of 60.
Find the values of a and b.

9 The polynomial $hx^3 - 10x^2 + kx + 26$ has a factor of $(x - 2)$.
When the polynomial is divided by $(x + 1)$, there is a remainder of 15.
Find the values of h and k.

Key points

- To find the equation of a curve after a translation of $\begin{bmatrix} p \\ q \end{bmatrix}$,
  replace x with $(x - p)$ and replace y with $(y - q)$. (pp 80–81)

- The graph of a cubic polynomial meets the x-axis one, two or three times,
  depending on its shape and position. (p 82)

- The x-coordinates of the points where the graph of $y = p(x)$ meets the x-axis
  can be found by solving the equation $p(x) = 0$. (p 84)

- A **polynomial** is an expression that can be written in the form
  $a + bx + cx^2 + dx^3 + ex^4 + fx^5 + \ldots$, where $a, b, c, d, e, f, \ldots$ are constants. (p 85)

- The **remainder theorem** says that when a polynomial $p(x)$ is
  divided by $(x - a)$ the remainder is $p(a)$. (p 91)

The **factor theorem** says that

if p(a) = 0 then the polynomial p(x) has a factor (x − a) and
if the polynomial p(x) has a factor (x − a) then p(a) = 0.   (p 91)

- When factorising a cubic polynomial, once you have found a linear factor,
  then the quadratic factor can be found by comparing coefficients.   (p 92)

Mixed questions (answers p 176)

1 The graph of $y = x^3$ is translated by $\begin{bmatrix} 4 \\ 1 \end{bmatrix}$.

   (a) Which is the correct equation for the new graph?

      A $y = (x + 4)^3 + 1$ **B** $y = (x + 4)^3 - 1$

      C $y = (x - 4)^3 + 1$ **D** $y = (x - 4)^3 - 1$

   (b) Write the correct equation in the form $y = ax^3 + bx^2 + cx + d$.

2 A polynomial is given by $f(x) = (2x + 1)(x + 2)(x - 3)$.

   (a) Evaluate f(0).

   (b) Sketch the graph of $y = f(x)$, showing clearly where the graph crosses
      both axes.

   (c) Write the polynomial in the form $f(x) = ax^3 + bx^2 + cx + d$.

3 Divide $x^3 + 2x^2 - 5x - 6$ by $x + 1$.   AQA 2002

4 (a) Express $6x^3 + 17x^2 + 14x + 3$ in the form $(x + 1)(ax^2 + bx + c)$, stating
      the values of a, b and c.

   (b) Hence solve the equation $6x^3 + 17x^2 + 14x + 3 = 0$.   AQA 2002

5 A polynomial is given by $p(x) = x^3 - 3x + 2$.

   (a) Use the factor theorem to show that $(x + 2)$ is a factor of $p(x)$.

   (b) Express $p(x)$ as a product of linear factors.

   (c) Sketch the graph of $y = p(x)$.
      Indicate the coordinates of the points where the graph intersects the
      coordinate axes.   AQA 2003

6 The polynomial $x^3 + px^2 + qx - 45$ has factors $(x + 3)$ and $(x - 3)$.
   Find the values of p and q.

7 (a) Show that the polynomial $p(x) = x^3 - 2x^2 - 3x + 6$ has only one linear factor.

   (b) Solve p(x) = 0.

*8 A function is defined as $f(x) = x^3 + 6x^2 + 11x + 6$.

   (a) Factorise f(x) completely.

   (b) Hence show that the value of $f(a)$ is a multiple of 3 for any integer a.

Test yourself (answers p 177)

None of these questions requires a calculator.

1 The graph of $y = x^3 + x$ is translated by $\begin{bmatrix} 2 \\ -1 \end{bmatrix}$.

(a) Find the equation of the new graph in the form $y = ax^3 + bx^2 + cx + d$.

(b) Where does this graph cross the y-axis?

2 It is given that $f(x) = x^3 + 3x^2 - 6x - 8$.

(a) Find the value of $f(2)$.

(b) Use the factor theorem to write down a factor of $f(x)$.

(c) Hence express $f(x)$ as a product of three linear factors.   AQA 2002

3 (a) Show that $(x + 2)$ is a factor of $p(x) = 2x^3 - x^2 - 8x + 4$.

(b) Hence factorise $p(x)$ completely into linear factors.   AQA 2001

4 (a) Factorise $p(x) = x^3 - 7x^2 + 14x - 8$ completely into linear factors.

(b) Sketch the graph of $y = p(x)$.

5 The polynomial $f(x)$ is given by $f(x) = x^3 + px^2 + x + 54$, where p is a real number. When $f(x)$ is divided by $x + 3$, the remainder is -3.

Use the remainder theorem to find the value of p.   AQA 2003

6 Given that $(x - 2)$ is a factor of $p(x) = 4x^3 - kx + 10$, show that $k = 21$.   AQA 2003

7 The cubic polynomial $x^3 + ax^2 + bx + 4$, where a and b are constants, has factors $x - 2$ and $x + 1$.

Use the factor theorem to find the values of a and b.   AQA 2001

8 The polynomial $f(x) = x^3 + px^2 + qx + 6$ has a factor $(x - 1)$. When $f(x)$ is divided by $x + 1$, there is a remainder of 8.

Find the values of p and q.   AQA 2001

9 The polynomial $f(x)$ is given by $f(x) = x^3 + x^2 - 7x + k$, where k is a real number. $(x - 3)$ is a factor of $f(x)$.

(a) Find the value of k.

(b) Factorise $f(x)$ as the product of a linear factor and a quadratic factor.

(c) Show that there is only one real value of x for which $f(x) = 0$.

7 Equation of a circle

In this chapter you will learn how to
- form and interpret the equation of a circle
- find the tangent and normal to a circle
- decide whether a straight line intersects a circle and find points of intersection

A A circle as a graph (answers p 178)

A1 Use Pythagoras's theorem to find the distance of each of these points from the origin $(0, 0)$.

(a) $(15, 8)$ (b) $(-6, -8)$ (c) $(12, -3.5)$ (d) $(-10, 10.5)$

A2 The diagram shows a circle with centre $(0, 0)$ and radius 13 units.

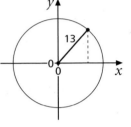

(a) Use Pythagoras to decide whether each of the following points lies inside the circle, on the circle or outside the circle.

(i) $(6.6, 11.2)$ (ii) $(-12, 5)$ (iii) $(9, 9)$

(iv) $(-11, -7)$ (v) $(3.2, -12.6)$

(b) Write an equation connecting x and y that is satisfied by all points (x, y) that lie on the circle.

A3 Use a graph plotter to draw the graph of your equation from A2 (b). (With some graph plotters you may need to rearrange the equation to give y in terms of x. This form of the equation will contain a square root, so the graph will need to be drawn in two sections, one using the positive square root and the other using the negative square root.)

A4 A circle has the equation $x^2 + y^2 = 49$. Give its centre and radius.

> **K** A circle with radius r and centre $(0, 0)$ has the equation $x^2 + y^2 = r^2$.
> Notice that this formula still works if x or y is negative.

A5 Use Pythagoras to find the distance of the point $(5, 5)$ from the point $(2, 1)$.

A6 A circle is drawn with centre $(2, 1)$ and radius 5.

(a) Use Pythagoras to decide whether each of the following points lies inside the circle, on the circle or outside the circle.

(i) $(-2, 4)$ (ii) $(5, -3)$ (iii) $(2, -4)$ (iv) $(6.8, 2.4)$

(v) $(-2, -3)$ (vi) $(7, 1)$ (vii) $(-2, -1)$

(b) Give three other points that lie on this circle.

If (x, y) is a general point on the circle in question A6, the right-angled triangle shown has width $(x - 2)$ and height $(y - 1)$.

From Pythagoras, $(x - 2)^2 + (y - 1)^2 = 5^2$. This is the equation of this circle.

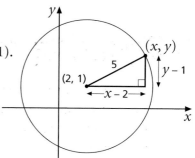

 A7 Show that $(x - 2)^2 + (y - 1)^2 = 5^2$ still works as the equation for the circle, even if the point (x, y) is to the left of the circle's centre or below it.

A8 If your graph plotter will accept an equation in the form $(x - 2)^2 + (y - 1)^2 = 5^2$, use it to draw the graph of the equation.

Here, (x, y) is a point on a general circle with centre (a, b) and radius r.
The right-angled triangle has width $(x - a)$ and height $(y - b)$.
From Pythagoras's theorem, $(x - a)^2 + (y - b)^2 = r^2$.
The following is true in general:

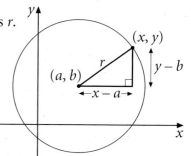

A circle with radius r and centre (a, b) has the equation
$(x - a)^2 + (y - b)^2 = r^2$.

This is sometimes called the 'cartesian equation' of a circle, after the French mathematician and philosopher René Descartes (1596–1650) who pioneered coordinate geometry of the kind you are doing in this chapter.

A9 Give the cartesian equation for a circle with radius 4 and centre $(5, -2)$.

A10 Give the centre and radius of a circle with the equation $(x + 4)^2 + (y - 7)^2 = 6^2$.

Notice that circle C' with centre (a, b) is the image of circle C with centre $(0, 0)$ after a translation by $\begin{bmatrix} a \\ b \end{bmatrix}$.

Notice too that the equation for C' results from replacing x by $(x - a)$ and y by $(y - b)$ in the equation for C.

This corresponds with work you did earlier on translating quadratic graphs.

An equation of a circle can have its brackets expanded and its numerical terms gathered together. So, for example, the equation of A10 becomes
$$x^2 + 8x + 16 + y^2 - 14y + 49 = 36$$
which becomes $\quad x^2 + 8x + y^2 - 14y + 29 = 0$.

A11 In the same way, expand your answer to A9 and then gather its numerical terms together.

The expanded equation for a circle generally takes the form $x^2 + y^2 + cx + dy + e = 0$, when c, d and e are numerical values. The order of terms can of course vary. Note the following:

- The x^2 and y^2 terms must have the same coefficient and the same sign (so in practice you usually see x^2 and $+ y^2$).
- There are no terms such as xy.
- The x and y terms and the constant term (e above) may be absent.

You can experiment on a graph plotter to see what curves you get if you break the first two conditions.

If you are given the equation of a circle in expanded form you can use 'completing the square' (see pp 40–41) to 'put the brackets back' and so find the centre and radius of the circle. This is shown in the following example.

Example 1

Write the circle equation $x^2 - 2x + y^2 + 4y + 1 = 0$ in the form $(x - a)^2 + (y - b)^2 = r^2$ and hence give the coordinates of its centre and its radius.

Solution

Complete the square for the x^2 and x terms. $\qquad x^2 - 2x = (x - 1)^2 - 1$

Complete the square for the y^2 and y terms. $\qquad y^2 + 4y = (y + 2)^2 - 4$

So the original circle equation is $\qquad (x - 1)^2 - 1 + (y + 2)^2 - 4 + 1 = 0$

Tidy the numerical values. $\qquad (x - 1)^2 + (y + 2)^2 - 4 = 0$

Rearrange so the radius term is visible. $\qquad (x - 1)^2 + (y + 2)^2 = 2^2$

So the centre is at $(1, -2)$ and the radius is 2 units.

Exercise A (answers p 178)

1 Write an equation for each of these circles in the form $(x - a)^2 + (y - b)^2 = r^2$.

    (a) Centre $(6, 3)$, radius 4   **(b)** Centre $(-2, 0)$, radius 5

    (c) Centre $(1, -6)$, radius 3   **(d)** Centre $(-2, -2)$, radius 7

2 For each of these circle equations

    (i) give the coordinates of the centre and the radius

    (ii) expand and simplify the equation

    (a) $(x - 2)^2 + (y - 6)^2 = 16$ **(b)** $(x + 3)^2 + (y - 4)^2 = 25$

    (c) $(x - 4)^2 + y^2 = 7$ **(d)** $(x + 1.5)^2 + (y - 0.5)^2 = 4$

3 Find the equation of a circle that has its centre at $(-2, -3)$ and passes through the point $(1, 1)$. (Hint: first find the radius.)

4 A circle has the line segment from $(-10, 0)$ to $(16, -10)$ as a diameter. Find the equation of the circle.

5 Find the equation of a circle that has the line segment from $(-7, -1)$ to $(-1, -3)$ as a diameter.

6 State, with reasons, whether the point $(-1, 2)$ lies inside, on or outside the circle $(x - 1)^2 + (y - 4)^2 = 9$.

7 Find the radius and the coordinates of the centre of the circle given by each of these equations.

(a) $x^2 - 4x + y^2 - 2y + 1 = 0$ (b) $x^2 - 2x + y^2 + 6y + 1 = 0$

(c) $x^2 + 10x + y^2 - 4y + 18 = 0$ (d) $x^2 + y^2 - 10y - 24 = 0$

(e) $x^2 + y^2 + 8x - 6y - 11 = 0$ (f) $x^2 - x + y^2 - 7y + 8\frac{1}{2} = 0$

8 Which of these could not be the equation of a circle?

A $x^2 + y^2 - 6y = 0$ B $x^2 + 8x + 2y^2 + 4y - 16 = 0$

C $y^2 - 12y = 4x - x^2$ D $x^2 - 16x + y^2 - 2y + 15 = 0$

9 Find the equation of the circle that has a radius of 4 units and the same centre as the circle $x^2 - 12x + y^2 + 29 = 0$.

10 (a) Show that the circle $x^2 + 6x + y^2 - 4y = 0$ goes through the origin $(0, 0)$.

    (b) A diameter has one end at the origin. Where is its other end?

*11 $P(9, 2)$ and $Q(-5, 4)$ are points on the circle $x^2 - 4x + y^2 - 6y - 37 = 0$.

    (a) Show that P and Q are the ends of a diameter of the circle.

    (b) Point $R(a, 8)$, where a is positive, is a third point on the circle. Find a.

    (c) Calculate the gradients of PR and RQ. What do these values show?

    (d) What general property of a circle accounts for your result in (c)?

*12 Show that the equation $x^2 + 2x + y^2 - 6y + 14 = 0$ does not represent a circle.

B Tangent and normal to a circle

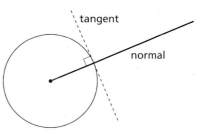

A **tangent** to a circle is a straight line that just touches it.

A radius from the centre to where the tangent touches the circle is perpendicular to the tangent.

The **normal** to a circle (or any other curve) is a line drawn at right angles to the tangent where it touches.

A normal to a circle always goes through the centre of the circle so a diameter (and hence two radii) are part of it.

Example 2

A circle has its centre at C $(3, 3)$ and has a radius of 2 units.
From the point P $(10, -3)$ a tangent is drawn that touches the circle at Q.
Find the length of PQ.

Solution

Draw and label a sketch.

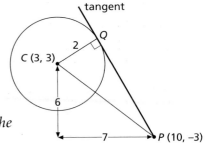

Using Pythagoras, $CP = \sqrt{7^2 + 6^2} = \sqrt{85}$.

*Notice that triangle CPQ is right-angled and
has two of its sides given and one to be found.*

Using Pythagoras, $PQ = \sqrt{CP^2 - CQ^2} = \sqrt{85 - 4} = 9$ units.

*Note that another tangent, the same length, could be drawn on the
other side of the circle.*

Example 3

C $(-2, 1)$ is the centre of a circle and S $(-4, 5)$ is a point on the circumference.
Find the equations of the normal and tangent to the circle at S.

Solution

The gradient of SC is $\dfrac{1-5}{-2-(-4)} = \dfrac{-4}{2} = -2$

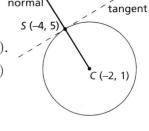

The line through (x_1, y_1) with gradient m has equation $y - y_1 = m(x - x_1)$.

The equation of SC (and therefore of the normal) is

$$y - 5 = -2(x + 4)$$
$$\Rightarrow \quad y - 5 = -2x - 8$$
$$\Rightarrow \quad y = -2x - 3$$

If the gradient of the normal is m, the gradient of the tangent is $-\dfrac{1}{m}$.

The gradient of the tangent is $-\dfrac{1}{-2} = \dfrac{1}{2}$.

Use $y - y_1 = m(x - x_1)$ again.

The equation of the tangent is

$$y - 5 = \tfrac{1}{2}(x + 4)$$
$$\Rightarrow \quad y - 5 = \tfrac{1}{2}x + 2$$
$$\Rightarrow \quad y = \tfrac{1}{2}x + 7$$

Exercise B (answers p 179)

1 P $(6, 7)$ is a point on a circle with its centre at $(-3, 1)$.

   (a) Find the equation of the normal to the circle at P.

   (b) Find the equation of the tangent to the circle at P.

2 A circle has the equation $x^2 + y^2 + 2x - 6y = 0$.

(a) Find the radius of the circle, and the coordinates of its centre.

(b) Find the equation of the tangent to the circle at the point $(2, 4)$.   AQA 2002

3 A circle has the equation $x^2 + y^2 - 2x - 16y + 49 = 0$.

(a) Find the position of its centre and its radius.

(b) Sketch the circle.

(c) Find the length of a tangent drawn from the origin to the circle, showing your method on your sketch.

4 The line joining the points A $(0, 5)$ and B $(4, 1)$ is a tangent to a circle whose centre, C, is at the point $(5, 4)$.

(a) Find the equation of the line AB.

(b) Find the equation of the line through C which is perpendicular to AB.

(c) Find the coordinates of the point of contact of the line AB with the circle.

(d) Find the equation of the circle.   AQA 2002

5 The line with equation $y = \frac{1}{3}x + 5$ is a tangent to a circle with centre $(-2, 1)$. Find the equation of the circle.

*6 A circle has the equation $x^2 - 8x + y^2 - 4y + 3 = 0$.

(a) Find the coordinates of its centre.

(b) The point P (a, b) lies on the circle. Express, in terms of a and b,

    (i) the gradient of the normal at P

    (ii) the gradient of the tangent at P

*7 Circle A has its centre at $(2, 1)$ and passes through the point T $(6, 4)$. Circle B has twice the radius of circle A and touches it externally at T.

(a) Draw a sketch. What can you say about the two line segments from T to the centres of the circles?

(b) Give the coordinates of the centre of circle B.

(c) Write the equation of each circle.

C Intersection of a straight line and a circle (answers p 179)

C1 A circle has the equation $x^2 - 16x + y^2 - 2y + 15 = 0$.
A straight line has the equation $y = x + 1$.

Solve these as a pair of simultaneous equations to find where the circle and the line cross. First substitute $x + 1$ for y in the equation of the circle.

C2 Using the same approach, try to find where these lines cross the circle given in C1.

(a) $y = x + 3$ (b) $y = x + 5$

C1 gives a quadratic equation in x and hence two solutions, $x = 1$ and $x = 7$. The corresponding solutions for y are $y = 2$ and $y = 8$. Drawing on paper or with a graph plotter shows that these solutions represent the points $(1, 2)$ and $(7, 8)$ where the line intersects the circle.

C2 (a) gives a quadratic that has one solution, $x = 3$, from which $y = 6$. Drawing shows that the point $(3, 6)$ is where the line just touches the circle. The line is a tangent to the circle.

Notice the factorised quadratic has two brackets the same, so the result $x = 3$ can come from either of them. We sometimes say the equation has a 'repeated' solution (or 'root').

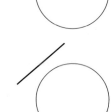

In C2 (b) the quadratic does not factorise; and it cannot be solved by the formula because its **discriminant** is negative. We say it has 'no real roots'. (Reminder: the discriminant of the quadratic equation $ax^2 + bx + c = 0$ is the expression $b^2 - 4ac$.) Drawing shows that the line fails to intersect or touch the circle.

The discriminant is also useful for distinguishing between the intersecting and touching cases, as the following summary indicates.

- Two different (distinct) real roots (solutions) $\Leftrightarrow$ line intersects circle
  In this case the discriminant of the equation is positive.

- One real root (or a 'repeated root') $\Leftrightarrow$ line is a tangent to circle
  Here the discriminant is zero.

- No real roots $\Leftrightarrow$ line fails to meet circle
  The discriminant is negative.

(The symbol $\Leftrightarrow$ means 'implies and is implied by'; so in each of these three cases the geometrical fact follows from the algebraic fact and the algebraic fact follows from the geometrical fact.)

Example 4

A line has the equation $x - y + 1 = 0$.
A circle has the equation $x^2 - 6x + y^2 = 0$.
Determine whether the line intersects the circle, is a tangent to it or fails to meet it.

Solution

Rearrange the equation for the line. $y = x + 1$

Substitute for y in the circle equation. $x^2 - 6x + (x + 1)^2 = 0$

$\Rightarrow \quad x^2 - 6x + x^2 + 2x + 1 = 0$

$\Rightarrow \quad 2x^2 - 4x + 1 = 0$

The discriminant is $(-4)^2 - 4 \times 2 \times 1 = 8$
As this is greater than zero the line intersects the circle.

When a line intersects a circle, the line segment between the points of intersection is called a **chord**.

The perpendicular from the centre of the circle to a chord bisects the chord.

Conversely, the perpendicular bisector of a chord goes through the centre of the circle. This fact can be useful if you are given points on the circle and are required to find its centre, as the following example shows.

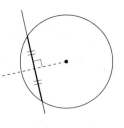

Example 5

A circle has its centre on the y-axis and passes through the points $P\,(-3, 3)$ and $Q\,(-1, -1)$. Find its equation.

Solution

Draw a sketch.
Mark in the perpendicular bisector of the chord PQ.
It will pass through the centre of the circle.

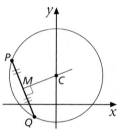

Label some points so you can refer to them.

Let M be the mid-point of PQ.
Let C be the centre of the circle (on the y-axis).

Find what you need to get the equation of MC.

M is $\left(\dfrac{-3+-1}{2}, \dfrac{3+-1}{2}\right)$, which is $(-2, 1)$.

$$\text{gradient of } PQ = \frac{-4}{2} = -2$$

$$\Rightarrow \text{gradient of } MC = \tfrac{1}{2}$$

The equation of MC is given by

Use $y - y_1 = m(x - x_1)$ with the point M.

$$y - 1 = \tfrac{1}{2}(x + 2)$$

$$\Rightarrow y - 1 = \tfrac{1}{2}x + 1$$

$$\Rightarrow y = \tfrac{1}{2}x + 2$$

The y-intercept of a line with this equation is 2.
So the centre of the circle is at $(0, 2)$.

Find the radius using Pythagoras.

$$r = PC = \sqrt{3^2 + 1^2} = \sqrt{10}$$

So the equation of the circle is $x^2 + (y - 2)^2 = 10$.

Exercise C (answers p 179)

1 In each of the following the equation of a line and of a circle is given. Without solving for points of intersection or contact, determine whether the line intersects the circle, is a tangent to it or fails to meet it.

(a) $x + y = 3$
$x^2 + y^2 - 6 = 0$

(b) $y = 5 - 2x$
$x^2 + y^2 - 8x - 4y + 15 = 0$

(c) $y = x + 1$
$x^2 + y^2 - 6x - 4y + 4 = 0$

(d) $x + y = 4$
$x^2 + y^2 + 4x + 2y - 12 = 0$

2 In each of the following the equations of a line and a circle are given. Find the coordinates of any points of intersection or tangential contact, or if the line fails to meet the curve state this fact.

(a) $y = 2x + 1$
$x^2 - 8x + y^2 - 8y + 22 = 0$

(b) $2x + y = 4$
$x^2 + 4x + y^2 - 8 = 0$

(c) $y = 20 - 3x$
$x^2 - 6x + y^2 - 2y = 0$

(d) $x + y = 4$
$x^2 - 2x + y^2 - 4y + 4 = 0$

3 A circle has the equation $x^2 - 10x + y^2 + 2y - 24 = 0$.

(a) Find the position of its centre.

(b) Find where the circle cuts the axes.

(c) Sketch the circle.

4 (a) Solve the following pair of simultaneous equations.
$$y = x - 1$$
$$x^2 + 8x + y^2 + 2y + 9 = 0$$

(b) Hence describe with reasons how the straight line with equation $y = x - 1$ and the circle with equation $x^2 + 8x + y^2 + 2y + 9 = 0$ are related geometrically.

5 (a) A circle has centre $(1, 0)$ and radius $\sqrt{10}$.
Write down the equation of the circle.

(b) The circle is intersected by the two straight lines $y = 2x + 3$ and $y = 2x - 7$.
Show that the points of intersection of these straight lines with the circle are the vertices of a square.

6 A circle cuts the x-axis at $(4, 0)$ and $(14, 0)$, and cuts the y-axis at $(0, 6)$ and $(0, 8)$.
Find its equation.

7 A circle has centre $(0, 1)$ and radius $\sqrt{85}$.
$P(9, a)$ and $Q(b, 8)$, where a and b are positive, are points on the circle.

(a) Find the values of a and b.

(b) Find the equation of the line through the centre of the circle, perpendicular to the chord PQ, and verify that this line passes through the mid-point of PQ.

*8 A circle has the equation $x^2 + 8x + y^2 + a = 0$.
A straight line has the equation $y = \sqrt{3}x$
Find the value of a for which the line is a tangent to the circle.

*9 Find the centre, radius and equation of the circle passing through the points $(5, 1)$, $(-3, 9)$ and $(-7, -3)$.

*10 Two circles, C and D, have the same centre but different radii.
$P(3, 3)$ and $Q(1, -3)$ are points on C.
$R(-3, 7)$ and $S(1, 3)$ are points on D.
Find the centre of the two circles.

Key points

- A circle with centre $(0, 0)$ and radius r has the equation $x^2 + y^2 = r^2$.

  A circle with centre (a, b) and radius r has the equation $(x - a)^2 + (y - b)^2 = r^2$.

  The second equation is obtained from the first by replacing x by $(x - a)$ and y by $(y - b)$; the second circle is the image of the first after translation by $\begin{bmatrix} a \\ b \end{bmatrix}$.   (p 99)

- A line from the centre of a circle to where a tangent touches the circle is perpendicular to the tangent. A perpendicular to a tangent is called a normal.   (p 101)

- Solving simultaneously the equations for a line and a circle results in a quadratic equation. The number of roots of this equation is related to the geometrical situation as follows:

  two distinct real roots (discriminant > 0) $\Leftrightarrow$ line intersects circle

  a repeated root (discriminant $= 0$) $\Leftrightarrow$ line is a tangent to circle

  no real roots (discriminant < 0) $\Leftrightarrow$ line fails to meet circle   (p 104)

Test yourself (answers p 180)

1 Write an equation for each of these circles in the form $x^2 + y^2 + cx + dy + e = 0$.

   (a) Centre $(4, 1)$, radius 2   (b) Centre $(-2, -3)$, diameter 6

   (c) Centre $(2.5, 4)$, diameter 4   (d) Centre $(1, -7)$, radius $\sqrt{7}$

2 Find the radius and coordinates of the centre of the circle given by each of these.

   (a) $x^2 - 4x + y^2 - 2y - 31 = 0$ (b) $x^2 + y^2 + 6y - 16 = 0$

   (c) $x^2 + 4x + y^2 + 8y + 17 = 0$ (d) $x^2 + y^2 - 3x - 5y - \frac{1}{2} = 0$

3 A circle has centre $(-1, -2)$ and radius $\sqrt{13}$.

   (a) Verify that the point $P(1, 1)$ lies on the circle.

   (b) Find the equation of the normal to the circle at P.

4 A circle has the equation $x^2 + y^2 + 4x - 14y + 4 = 0$.

   (a) Find the radius of the circle and the coordinates of its centre.

   (b) Sketch the circle.

   (c) Find the length of a tangent from the point $P(6, 8)$ to the circle.   AQA 2003

5 (a) Solve the simultaneous equations
$$y = x + 1$$
$$x^2 - 8x + y^2 - 2y + 9 = 0$$

   (b) Hence describe the geometrical relationship between the straight line with equation $y = x + 1$ and the circle with equation $x^2 - 8x + y^2 - 2y + 9 = 0$, giving a reason for your answer.   AQA 2001

8 Rates of change

In this chapter you will learn
- that the gradient of a graph gives the rate of change
- how to find the gradient of a curved graph
- how to find the equations of a tangent and a normal to a graph

A Gradient as rate of change (answers p 180)

The Earth's crust gets hotter as you go deeper.

The graph below shows the relationship between temperature and depth in a mine.
The graph is a straight line, showing that temperature increases at a steady rate with depth.

The **rate of change** of temperature with respect to depth can be measured in °C per metre.

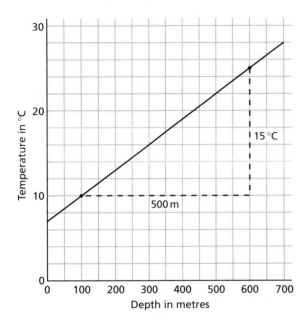

Two points on the graph have been chosen.
The difference in depth between these points is 500 m.
The difference in temperature is 15 °C.

The rate of change of temperature with depth

$$= \frac{\text{difference in temperature}}{\text{difference in depth}}$$

$$= \frac{15\,°C}{500\,m}$$

$$= \mathbf{0.03\,°C\ per\ m}$$

Notice that this is also the **gradient** of the graph.

A1 (a) Use the value of the rate of change to calculate by how much the temperature increases when the depth increases by 100 m.

(b) Read from the graph the temperature at the surface.

(c) Calculate the temperature at a depth of

(i) 1000 m   (ii) 1300 m   (iii) 2500 m

(d) At what depth will the temperature be 67 °C?

A2 This graph shows the relationship between temperature and height on a mountain.

(Note that the scale on the horizontal axis is different from the previous one.)

(a) Find the rate of change of temperature with height in °C per metre. How do you show that it is a rate of **decrease**?

(b) By how much does the temperature decrease for every extra 100 m climbed?

(c) What will the temperature be at a height of 6000 m?

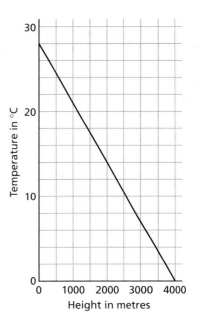

If y is a linear function of x, the rate of change of y with respect to x can be found by choosing any two points (x_1, y_1) and (x_2, y_2) on the line and calculating

the difference between the y-coordinates
———————————————————————— , which is $\dfrac{y_2 - y_1}{x_2 - x_1}$.
the difference between the x-coordinates

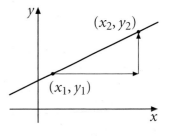

The symbol $\dfrac{dy}{dx}$ is used for the rate of change of y with respect to x.
For a linear graph the rate of change is equal to the gradient.

A3 (a) The sketch on the right shows the graph of $y = 2x + 1$.
What is the value of $\dfrac{dy}{dx}$?

(b) What is the value of $\dfrac{dy}{dx}$ for each of these linear functions?

(i) $y = 2x + 3$ (ii) $y = 5x - 1$

(iii) $y = \frac{1}{2}x + 9$ (iv) $y = 6 + 4x$

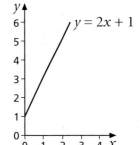

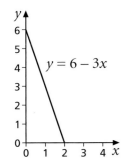

A4 (a) The sketch on the left shows the graph of $y = 6 - 3x$.
What is the value of $\dfrac{dy}{dx}$?

(b) Find $\dfrac{dy}{dx}$ for each of these linear functions.

(i) $y = -2x + 5$ (ii) $y = -x - 7$

(iii) $y = 12 - \frac{1}{2}x$ (iv) $y = \dfrac{4 + 7x}{2}$

D **A5** A model vehicle moves along a straight track.
Its position is given by the equation $s = 4t + 5$, where s is its distance in metres from a fixed point and t is the time in seconds.

(a) Sketch a graph of s against t.

(b) What is the value of $\dfrac{ds}{dt}$?

(c) What does $\dfrac{ds}{dt}$ represent in this case?

A6 You are told that a straight-line graph has gradient given by $\dfrac{dy}{dx} = 3$.

(a) What can you deduce about the equation of the line?

(b) You are given the additional information that the line goes through $(2, 5)$. What is the equation of the line?

A7 $y = 5$ is an example of a constant function (y has the value 5 whatever the value of x). Sketch the graph of $y = 5$. What is the value of $\dfrac{dy}{dx}$ for a constant function?

Exercise A (answers p 180)

1 Find the value of $\dfrac{dy}{dx}$ for each of these linear functions.

(a) $y = 3x - 2$ (b) $y = 5 - 7x$ (c) $y = 4 + x$ (d) $y = -2$ (e) $y = \frac{1}{2}(3x - 1)$

2 The cost of electricity consists of a standing charge of 900p and a charge of 5p for each unit of electricity used.

(a) Write a formula for the total cost, C pence, in terms of the number of units, n.

(b) What is the value of $\dfrac{dC}{dn}$? Explain what it means.

3 A linear graph has $\dfrac{dy}{dx} = 5$ and passes through the point $(-1, 2)$. Find its equation.

4 Find the equation of the line through $(3, 2)$ with $\dfrac{dy}{dx} = -2$.

5 A line passes through the points $(1, 5)$ and $(4, 11)$. Find $\dfrac{dy}{dx}$ and the equation of the line.

6 A line passes through $(4, 7)$ and $(10, 4)$. Find $\dfrac{dy}{dx}$ and the equation of the line.

7 (a) A plumber charges £30 for a call-out plus £20 per hour for labour.

(i) Write a formula for the charge £C in terms of t, the number of hours taken.

(ii) What is the value of $\dfrac{dC}{dt}$?

(b) Another plumber charges £70 for a 2-hour job and £145 for a 5-hour job.

Find $\dfrac{dC}{dt}$ in this case and say what it means.

B Gradient of a curve (answers p 181)

This is the distance–time graph of
a train passing through a station.

The gradient is $\frac{40}{5} = 8$.

This represents the speed of the train in m/s.

The gradient is the same at every point of
the graph.

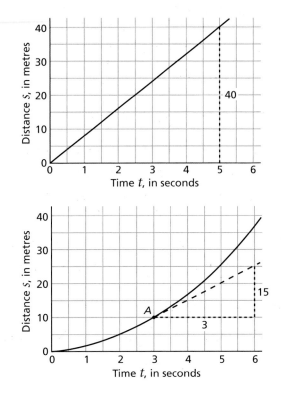

This is the distance–time graph of
a train setting out from a station.

The graph is a curve, getting steeper. This
shows that the train's speed is increasing.

Imagine that the speed stops increasing at
point A and that the train continues at
a constant speed from then on.

The dashed line shows how the graph would
continue. It is the **tangent** at point A.

The gradient of the curve at A is defined
as the gradient of the tangent at A.

The gradient at A is 5.
So the speed of the train at A is 5 m/s.

B1 This is the distance–time graph for a
tube train leaving a station.

The tangent to the graph has been drawn
at the point where $t = 3$.

(a) Find the gradient of this tangent.

(b) What does the gradient represent?

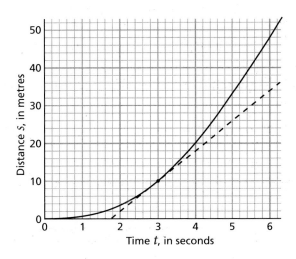

B2 Use the tangents drawn here to find the gradient of the curve

$$y = -\tfrac{1}{4}x^2 + 2x - 1$$

at the points (2, 2) and (5, 2.75).

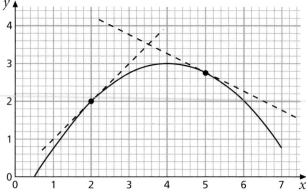

K The notation $\dfrac{\mathrm{d}y}{\mathrm{d}x}$ is still used for curved graphs, but now it means the gradient of the tangent to the curve.

D **B3** On graph paper, draw accurately the graph of $y = x^2$ for values of x from −3 to 3, using the same scale for both axes.

(a) Draw, as accurately as possible, the tangent at (1.5, 2.25) and hence find the gradient $\dfrac{\mathrm{d}y}{\mathrm{d}x}$ of the curve at this point.

(b) By repeating this process as necessary, and using the symmetry of the graph, copy and complete this table.

x	−2	−1.5	−1	0	1	1.5	2
$\dfrac{\mathrm{d}y}{\mathrm{d}x}$							

(c) Plot all the points $\left(x, \dfrac{\mathrm{d}y}{\mathrm{d}x} \right)$ to obtain the gradient graph for $y = x^2$.

(d) What do these points suggest for the equation of the gradient graph? Write its equation $\dfrac{\mathrm{d}y}{\mathrm{d}x} = \ldots$

Questions B4 and B5 can be done either by accurate drawing on graph paper or by using a graph plotter.

B4 Draw the graph of $y = 4x - x^2$ for values of x from −2 to 4, using the same scale for both axes.

(a) Find the gradients of tangents at several points and record your results in a table as in question B3.

(b) Plot the points $\left(x, \dfrac{\mathrm{d}y}{\mathrm{d}x} \right)$.

(c) Suggest an equation for the gradient graph.

B5 Draw the graph of $y = 0.1x^3 - x$ for values of x from −4 to 5, using the same scale for both axes.

(a) Find the gradients of tangents at several points and record your results in a table as in question B3.

(b) Plot the points $\left(x, \dfrac{\mathrm{d}y}{\mathrm{d}x} \right)$.

(c) What type of equation does the gradient graph appear to have?

In questions B3 to B5 you drew a graph of a function (y) together with a graph of $\dfrac{dy}{dx}$. The latter graph shows the **gradient function** of the original function.

Here, for example, is a typical curved graph.

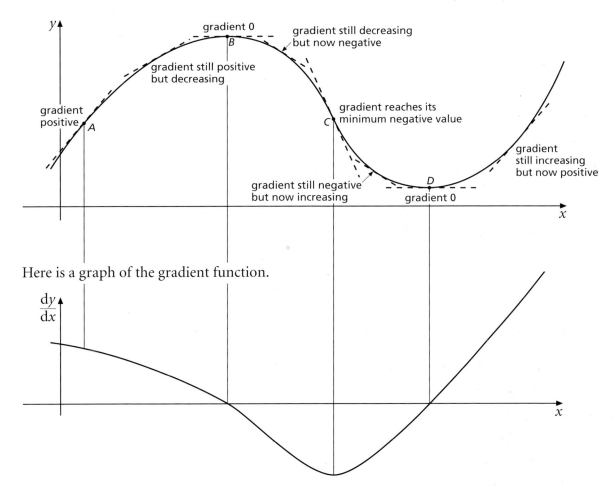

Here is a graph of the gradient function.

At points B and D on the original graph, the value of $\dfrac{dy}{dx}$ is 0. These are called **stationary points**.

B is called a **local maximum** and D a **local minimum**.

B and D are also called **turning points** because the gradient changes from positive to negative or vice versa.

Exercise B (answers p 181)

1 Copy this graph.

Directly beneath it, sketch the graph of its gradient function, using the same scale for x.

Mark any points you think are special and describe them.

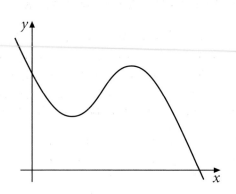

2 Repeat question 1 for each of these graphs.

(a)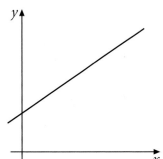

(b)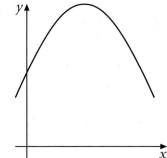

(c)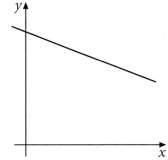

(d)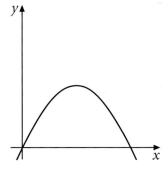

(e)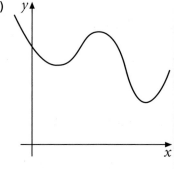

(f)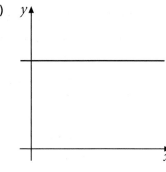

*3 Sketch each of these graphs and its gradient graph. Start by deciding what happens to each gradient graph when x is near zero and when x is numerically large (either positive or negative).

(a)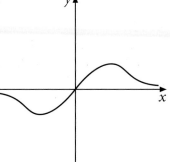

(b)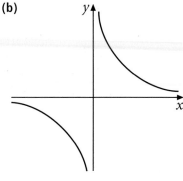

C Calculating the gradient of a curved graph (answers p 182)

The problem of finding the gradient function $\dfrac{dy}{dx}$ for a given function y
was crucial for the advance of mechanics, the branch of theoretical physics that
deals with the laws of motion. The problem belongs to a part of mathematics
called 'calculus' which was developed independently by Newton (1642–1727)
in England and Leibniz (1646–1716) in Germany.

Here we start with a specific example:
how to find the gradient of the graph
of $y = x^2$ at the point $(3, 9)$.

Near the point $(3, 9)$ the graph
itself and the tangent are very
close together. (You can see this by
zooming in on a graph plotter.)

A is the point $(3, 9)$ and B is a
point on the graph very close to A.

The gradient of AB will be very
close to the gradient of the tangent.

Also, the gradient of AB gets closer
to the gradient of the tangent as
B gets closer to A.

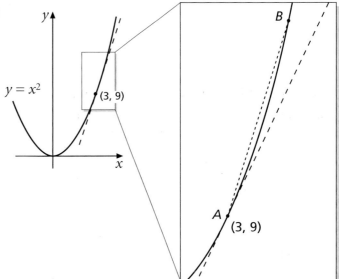

Suppose, for example, that the x-coordinate of B is 3.1.
Because B is on the graph $y = x^2$, its y-coordinate will be $3.1^2 = 9.61$.

The gradient of AB $\dfrac{\text{difference in } y}{\text{difference in } x} = \dfrac{9.61 - 9}{3.1 - 3} = \dfrac{0.61}{0.1} = 6.1.$

To get a better approximation, move B closer to A.

Let the x-coordinate of B be 3.01, so that the y-coordinate is $3.01^2 = 9.0601$.

Now the gradient of $AB = \dfrac{9.0601 - 9}{3.01 - 3} = \dfrac{0.0601}{0.01} = 6.01.$

C1 (a) Repeat the calculation when the x-coordinate of B is 3.001.

(b) What do the results, taken together, suggest as the exact value of the
gradient of the tangent at $(3, 9)$?

C2 Now let A be the point $(4, 16)$.
Calculate approximations to the gradient of the tangent at A by letting the
x-coordinate of B be first 4.1, then 4.01 and then 4.001.

What conclusion do you draw?

The symbol δx ('delta x') is used for the difference between the x-coordinates of two points on the graph. (The δ is not a number multiplying x; δx is one complete symbol.)

Similarly, δy means the difference between the y-coordinates of the two points.

The gradient of the line joining the two points is thus $\dfrac{\delta y}{\delta x}$.

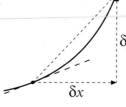

The calculation of $\dfrac{\delta y}{\delta x}$ can be done in a table or spreadsheet.

Here, for example, are the calculations that lead to the gradient of $y = x^2$ at $(5, 25)$.

x-coordinate of A	y-coordinate of A	x-coordinate of B	y-coordinate of B	δx	δy	$\dfrac{\delta y}{\delta x}$
5	25	5.1	26.01	0.1	1.01	10.1
5	25	5.01	25.1001	0.01	0.1001	10.01
5	25	5.001	25.010001	0.001	0.010001	10.001

It seems clear from this table that as δx gets smaller, $\dfrac{\delta y}{\delta x}$ gets closer to 10. So the gradient of the tangent at $(5, 25)$ is 10.

K

$\dfrac{\delta y}{\delta x}$ is the gradient of the line joining two points on the graph.

$\dfrac{dy}{dx}$ is the gradient of the tangent.

As δx gets smaller, the value of $\dfrac{\delta y}{\delta x}$ gets closer and closer to $\dfrac{dy}{dx}$.

C3 (a) Find the gradient of $y = x^2$ when $x = 1$, when $x = 2$ and when $x = 6$.
Record all the results so far in a table:

x	0	1	2	3	4	5	6
$\dfrac{dy}{dx}$							

(b) What is the equation of the gradient function for $y = x^2$?

D

C4 (The work involved in this question can be shared out, with each student calculating the gradient at one of the values of x.)

(a) For the function $y = x^2 + 5x + 3$ calculate the gradient at the points where $x = 0, 1, 2, 3, 4$ and 5.

For example, a table for $x = 3$ starts like this.

x-coordinate of A	y-coordinate of A	x-coordinate of B	y-coordinate of B	δx	δy	$\dfrac{\delta y}{\delta x}$
3	27	3.1	28.11	0.1	1.11	11.1

(b) What is the equation of the gradient function for $y = x^2 + 5x + 3$?

The process of finding the gradient function $\frac{dy}{dx}$ for a given function y is called **differentiating** the function with respect to x.

The gradient function $\frac{dy}{dx}$ is called the **derivative** of the original function.

In question C4 you should have found that if $y = x^2 + 5x + 3$, then $\frac{dy}{dx} = 2x + 5$.

Note that $x^2 + 5x + 3$ is the sum of x^2 and $5x + 3$.
We have already found that the derivative of x^2 is $2x$.
We also know that the derivative of the linear function $5x + 3$ is 5.

This illustrates a general point about derivatives:

(K) The derivative of the sum of two functions is the sum of the separate derivatives.

You could also think of $x^2 + 5x + 3$ as made up of three parts:

$$y = x^2 + 5x + 3$$
$$\frac{dy}{dx} = 2x + 5 + 0 \qquad \text{(because the gradient of a constant function is 0)}$$

C5 If you go through the gradient calculations for the function $y = 3x^2$ (or use a graph plotter), you will find that $\frac{dy}{dx} = 6x$.

In other words, the derivative of $3x^2$ is 3 times the derivative of x^2.

Can you explain why this is, possibly by using the diagrams shown here?

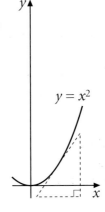
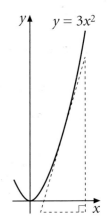

The result in question C5 illustrates another general point about derivatives:

(K) The derivative of k times a function is k times the derivative of the function.

D **C6** (The work in this question can be shared out as in C4.
Or it can be done on a graph plotter if the plotter has the facility for calculating gradients.)

(a) Find the gradient of the function $y = x^3$ when $x = 0, 1, 2, 3, 4, 5$.

(b) From the shape of the graph of $y = x^3$, deduce the gradient at $x = -1, -2, -3, -4, -5$.

(c) Draw the graph of $\frac{dy}{dx}$ against x. What kind of function does it appear to be?

(d) Find the equation of the graph in (c). This will be the derivative of $y = x^3$.

The derivatives of $y = x^4$, $y = x^5$, and so on, can also be found by the method used so far. The results are:

$$y = x^4 \qquad y = x^5 \qquad y = x^6$$

$$\frac{dy}{dx} = 4x^3 \qquad \frac{dy}{dx} = 5x^4 \qquad \frac{dy}{dx} = 6x^5$$

The general rule for positive integers n is this:

  If $y = x^n$, then $\dfrac{dy}{dx} = nx^{n-1}$

Using function notation

If a letter, such as f or g, is used to define a function, the derivative is denoted by f′ or g′.

For example, if $f(x) = x^3 - x^2$, then $f'(x) = 3x^2 - 2x$.

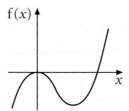

These are all ways of stating essentially the same question:

If $y = x^3 - x^2$, find $\dfrac{dy}{dx}$.

If $f(x) = x^3 - x^2$, find $f'(x)$.

Differentiate $x^3 - x^2$ with respect to x.

If $f(x) = x^3 - x^2$, find the derivative of $f(x)$.

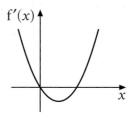

Example 1

If $f(x) = x^4 + 2x^3$, find $f'(x)$.

Solution

$f'(x) = 4x^3 + 2(3x^2) = 4x^3 + 6x^2$

Example 2

Find the gradient of the graph of $y = 2x^3 - 5x^2 + 3x + 4$ at the point P where $x = 2$.

Solution

First differentiate. $\quad \dfrac{dy}{dx} = 2(3x^2) - 5(2x) + 3 + 0 = 6x^2 - 10x + 3$

Substitute x = 2. $\quad$ When $x = 2$, $\dfrac{dy}{dx} = 24 - 20 + 3 = 7$

So the gradient at P is 7.

Example 3

If $f(x) = (x^2 + 2)(x^2 - 3)$, find $f'(x)$.

Solution

First multiply out the brackets to get the function in polynomial form.

$f(x) = x^4 - 3x^2 + 2x^2 - 6 = x^4 - x^2 - 6.$ $\qquad$ So $f'(x) = 4x^3 - 2x.$

Exercise C (answers p 182)

1 If $y = 2x^3 - 5x + 1$, find $\dfrac{dy}{dx}$.

2 Find $\dfrac{dy}{dx}$ for each of the following functions.

(a) $y = 4x^2 - x + 9$ (b) $y = 3x^4 - 5x^3 + 1$ (c) $y = 3 + 4x - 6x^2 + 7x^3$

3 Find the gradient of the graph of $y = x^3 - 6x$ at the point where $x = -1$.

4 Find the gradient of each of these graphs at the given point.

(a) $y = 4 - 2x^2$ at $(3, -14)$ (b) $y = 2x^3 + 7x$ at $(2, 30)$

5 (a) Given that $f(x) = 2x^4 - 3x + 1$, find $f'(x)$.

(b) Given that $g(x) = x^5 + 3x^3 - 2x$, find $g'(x)$.

(c) Given that $h(x) = (x^3 + 1)(x - 3)$, find $h'(x)$.

6 On the same axes, sketch the graphs of $y = x^2$, $y = x^2 + 2$ and $y = x^2 - 3$. Use the sketch graphs to explain why $\dfrac{dy}{dx}$ is the same for all three functions.

7 Given that $f(x) = 5x^4 - 6x^3$, find the value of $f'(2)$.

8 (a) What are the coordinates of the points where the graph of $y = x(x - 2)(x - 3)$ crosses the x-axis?

(b) Sketch the graph.

(c) Calculate the gradient of the graph at each point where it crosses the x-axis.

9 The gradient of the graph of $y = 2x^3 + px - 1$, at the point where $x = 1$, is 14. Find the value of p.

10 The graph of $y = 4x^3 + ax + b$ goes through the point $P(-1, 1)$. The gradient of the graph at P is 14. Find the values of a and b.

11 A stone is thrown vertically upwards. While it is in the air, its height h metres above its starting point after t seconds is given by the formula

$$h = 40t - 5t^2$$

(a) For what values of t is $h = 0$?

(b) Sketch the graph of h against t.

(c) Find the value of $\dfrac{dh}{dt}$ when $t = 3$. What does this tell you?

(d) Find the value of $\dfrac{dh}{dt}$ when $t = 6$. What does this tell you?

12 The graph of $y = ax^3 + bx$ has gradient 4 when $x = -1$ and gradient 31 when $x = 2$. Find the values of a and b.

D Tangents and normals

If A is a point on a curve, the line through A perpendicular to the tangent at A is called the **normal** to the curve at A.

If the gradient of the tangent is m, the gradient of the normal is $-\dfrac{1}{m}$ (because tangent and normal are perpendicular).

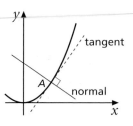

Example 4

The graph of $y = x^3 - x^2$ passes though the point $P(2, 4)$. Find

(a) the gradient of the tangent to the graph at P

(b) the equation of the tangent to the graph at P

Solution

(a) *First differentiate.* $\qquad\qquad \dfrac{dy}{dx} = 3x^2 - 2x$

    Then substitute $x = 2$. $\qquad$ When $x = 2$, $\dfrac{dy}{dx} = 12 - 4 = 8.$

                      So the gradient of the tangent at P is 8.

(b) *The line through (x_1, y_1) with gradient m has equation $y - y_1 = m(x - x_1)$.*

    Equation of tangent at P is $y - 4 = 8(x - 2)$

                        $\Rightarrow \quad y = 8x - 12$

Example 5

The graph of $y = x^2 - 6x + 9$ passes though the point $A\,(4, 1)$.
Find the equation of the normal to the graph at A.

Solution

First find the gradient of the tangent at A. $\qquad \dfrac{dy}{dx} = 2x - 6$

                                 When $x = 4$, $\dfrac{dy}{dx} = 2$

                                 So the tangent at A has gradient 2.

Then find the gradient of the normal. $\qquad$ The normal at A has gradient $-\frac{1}{2}$.

Use the fact that the normal goes through A. $\quad$ Equation of normal at A is $y - 1 = -\frac{1}{2}(x - 4)$

                                       $\Rightarrow \qquad y = -\frac{1}{2}x + 3$

Exercise D (answers p 183)

1 Find the equation of the tangent to $y = x^2$ at the point $(3, 9)$.

2 Find the equations of the tangent and the normal to $y = x^3$ at the point $(-1, -1)$.

3 Find the equations of the tangent and the normal to $y = x^3 - 10x + 1$ at the point P where $x = 2$.

4 Find the equations of the tangent and the normal to $y = x^2(x - 4)$ at $(4, 0)$.

5 Find the equation of the tangent to $y = x(x^2 - 5)$ at the point where $x = 2$.

6 Find the equation of the normal to $y = 16 - x^2$ at the point $(4, 0)$.

7 The graph of $y = (x - 3)(x + 4)$ crosses the y-axis at the point P.
Find the equation of
  (a) the tangent to the graph at P **(b)** the normal to the graph at P

*8 Prove that, for all values of k,
  (a) the tangent to $y = x^2$ at the point (k, k^2) crosses the y-axis at $(0, -k^2)$
  (b) the normal to $y = x^2$ at the point (k, k^2) crosses the y-axis at $(0, k^2 + \frac{1}{2})$

E Differentiation: algebraic approach

The diagram shows two points on the graph of a function $y = f(x)$.

A is the point (x, y).
B is the point $(x + \delta x, y + \delta y)$.

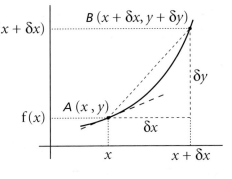

Both A and B lie on the graph, so

$$y = f(x)$$
$$\text{and } y + \delta y = f(x + \delta x)$$

Subtracting, we get $\quad \delta y = f(x + \delta x) - f(x)$

So the gradient of AB is $\quad \dfrac{\delta y}{\delta x} = \dfrac{f(x + \delta x) - f(x)}{\delta x}$

To get any further, we need to know the function $f(x)$.

Suppose $f(x) = x^2$.

In this case $\dfrac{\delta y}{\delta x} = \dfrac{(x + \delta x)^2 - x^2}{\delta x} = \dfrac{x^2 + 2x\delta x + (\delta x)^2 - x^2}{\delta x} = \dfrac{\delta x(2x + \delta x)}{\delta x} = 2x + \delta x$

As B gets closer to A, δx gets closer to 0 and $\dfrac{\delta y}{\delta x}$ gets closer to $2x$.

So $\dfrac{dy}{dx}$, the gradient of the tangent at A, is $2x$.

This method can be used to prove that the derivative of x^3 is $3x^2$, and so on.

Key points

- The gradient of a curve at a point is defined as the gradient of the tangent. (p 111)

- If y is given as a function of x (for example $y = x^2 - 3x$), the function that gives the gradient is denoted by $\dfrac{dy}{dx}$ and is called the derivative of the original function. (p 112)

- If a letter is used to denote a function, for example f(x), the derivative is denoted by a dash, f$'(x)$. (p 118)

- The process of finding the derivative of a function is called differentiating the function. (p 117)

- The derivative of x^n, where n is a positive integer, is nx^{n-1}. (pp 115–118)

- The derivative of a constant function, for example $y = 5$ or f$(x) = 3$, is zero. (p 117)

- The derivative of the sum of functions is the sum of the separate derivatives. The derivative of k times a function is k times the derivative of the function. (p 117)

- The derivative of a polynomial such as $x^3 + 4x^2 - 3x + 6$ is found by differentiating term by term. (p 117)

- The normal to a curve at a point P is the line through P perpendicular to the tangent at P. (p 120)

Mixed questions (answers p 183)

1 Given that f$(x) = x^4 - 3x^2 + 5x$, find

   (a) f$'(x)$ **(b)** the gradient of the curve $y = $ f(x) at the point where $x = 2$

2 The distance, s metres, of a model car from its starting point is given by $s = 0.1t^2 + 3t$, where t is the time in seconds from the start.

   (a) Find the value of $\dfrac{ds}{dt}$ when $t = 5$.

   (b) What does this tell you about the car?

3 Given that $y = (x^2 + 4)(x - 3)$, find $\dfrac{dy}{dx}$.

4 The function g is defined by g$(x) = (x + 2)(x^3 - 1)$. Find the value of g$'(-2)$.

5 (a) Find the equation of the tangent to the curve $y = 5x^2 - 3x$ at the point $P(1, 2)$.

   (b) Find the equation of the normal at P.

6 (a) Find the equation of the tangent to $y = \frac{1}{4}x^2(x^2 - 6)$ at the point where $x = 2$.

   (b) Find the equation of the normal at this point.

7 (a) Find the equation of the normal to the graph of $y = 5x - x^2$ at the point $(3, 6)$.

(b) This normal intersects the graph again at the point A. Find the coordinates of A.

8 The gradient of the graph of $y = x^5 + kx^2$, at the point where $x = -2$, is 12. Find the value of k.

9 The graph of $y = ax^3 + bx$ goes through $(2, 2)$ and its gradient at this point is 17. Find the values of a and b.

*10 The graph of $y = px^2 + qx + r$ goes through the points $A(-1, 13)$ and $B(1, 7)$. The gradient of the graph at A is 5. Find the values of p, q and r.

*11 If the algebraic method of differentiation in section E above is applied to the function $y = x^3$, then

$$\frac{\delta y}{\delta x} = \frac{(x + \delta x)^3 - x^3}{\delta x}$$

(a) Expand $(x + \delta x)^3$. You can think of it as $(x + \delta x)(x + \delta x)^2$.

(b) Hence show that $\dfrac{\delta y}{\delta x} = 3x^2 + 3x\delta x + (\delta x)^2$.

(c) What happens to $\dfrac{\delta y}{\delta x}$ as the value of δx gets smaller and smaller?

Test yourself (answers p 183)

None of these questions requires a calculator.

1 (a) Express $3(x + 1)^2$ in the form $px^2 + qx + r$.

(b) Find the gradient of the curve with equation $y = 3(x + 1)^2$ at the point where $x = 4$.

AQA 2002

2 (a) Given that $y = (x - 2)(x^2 + 3)$, find $\dfrac{dy}{dx}$.

(b) Hence find the equation of the tangent to the curve $y = (x - 2)(x^2 + 3)$ at the point whose x-coordinate is 1. Give your answer in the form $y = mx + c$.

3 A curve has equation $y = x^3 + 3x^2 - 7x - 1$.

(a) Find $\dfrac{dy}{dx}$ in terms of x.

Points P and Q lie on the curve. The gradient at both P and Q is 2. The x-coordinate of P is 1.

(b) Find the x-coordinate of Q.

(c) Find an equation for the tangent at P, giving your answer in the form $y = mx + c$, where m and c are constants.

This tangent intersects the coordinate axes at points R and S.

(d) Find the length of RS, giving your answer as a surd.

4 Find the equation of the normal to the graph of $y = x^2 - 10x$ at the point where $x = 4$.

9 Using differentiation

In this chapter you will learn
- how to tell whether a function is increasing or decreasing
- how to find maximum and minimum values of a function and solve optimisation problems
- what is meant by the second derivative of a function and how this can be used to distinguish between maximum and minimum values of the function

A Increasing and decreasing functions, stationary points

This is the (x, y) graph of a function.

At point A, the value of the gradient $\dfrac{dy}{dx}$ is positive.

The function is **increasing** at A.

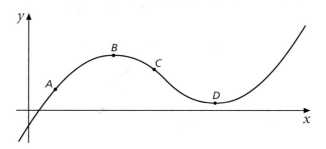

At point C, the value of $\dfrac{dy}{dx}$ is negative.
The function is **decreasing** at C.

At points B and D, $\dfrac{dy}{dx} = 0$. B and D are **stationary points**.

B is a (local) maximum and D is a (local) minimum.
(These are also called 'turning points'.)

In the absence of a graph you can still distinguish between a maximum and a minimum by considering what happens to the gradient $\dfrac{dy}{dx}$ either side of the stationary point.

At a local maximum,
the sign of $\dfrac{dy}{dx}$ goes
from positive on the left
to negative on the right.

At a local minimum,
the sign of $\dfrac{dy}{dx}$ goes
from negative on the left
to positive on the right.

Example 1

The function f is defined by $f(x) = x^3 - 5x^2 + 1$.
Is the function increasing, decreasing or stationary at the point where $x = 3$?

Solution

First differentiate to get f$'(x)$.　　$f'(x) = 3x^2 - 10x$
Substitute $x = 3$.　　　　　　$f'(3) = 27 - 30 = -3$
Look at the sign of f$'(3)$.　　　$f'(3)$ is negative, so f is decreasing at $x = 3$.

Example 2

(a) Find the stationary points on the graph of $y = x^3 - 12x + 1$ and determine their types.

(b) Hence sketch the graph of $y = x^3 - 12x + 1$.

Solution

(a) $\dfrac{dy}{dx} = 3x^2 - 12$

At stationary points, $\dfrac{dy}{dx} = 0$, so $3x^2 - 12 = 0$

$$\Rightarrow \quad 3(x^2 - 4) = 0$$
$$\Rightarrow \quad\quad x^2 = 4$$
$$\Rightarrow \quad\quad x = 2 \text{ or } -2$$

When $x = -2$, $y = (-2)^3 - 12 \times -2 + 1 = -8 + 24 + 1 = 17$
When $x = 2$, $y = 2^3 - 24 + 1 = -15$

So the stationary points are $(-2, 17)$ and $(2, -15)$.

To decide what types these points are, calculate the value of $\dfrac{dy}{dx}$ a little to the left and a little to the right of each one.

$(-2, 17)$ When $x = -2.1$, $\dfrac{dy}{dx} = 3 \times (-2.1)^2 - 12 = 1.23$

When $x = -1.9$, $\dfrac{dy}{dx} = 3 \times (-1.9)^2 - 12 = -1.17$

The gradient goes from positive to negative, so $(-2, 17)$ is a local maximum.

$(2, -15)$ When $x = 1.9$, $\dfrac{dy}{dx} = 3 \times 1.9^2 - 12 = -1.17$

When $x = 2.1$, $\dfrac{dy}{dx} = 3 \times 2.1^2 - 12 = 1.23$

The gradient goes from negative to positive, so $(2, -15)$ is a local minimum.

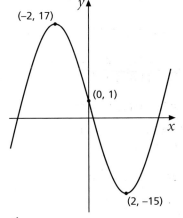

(b) When x is large and negative, $x^3 - 12x + 1$ is large and negative.
When x is large and positive, $x^3 - 12x + 1$ is large and positive.
When $x = 0$, $y = 1$. The sketch is shown above.

Exercise A (answers p 184)

1 (i) Find the stationary point on the graph of $y = 2x^2 - 12x + 15$.

(ii) Determine whether it is a local maximum or local minimum.

(iii) Sketch the graph of $y = 2x^2 - 12x + 15$.

2 Repeat question 1 for each of the following graphs.

(a) $y = -x^3 + 27x - 2$ (b) $y = 2x^3 - 9x^2 + 12x - 7$ (c) $y = x^3 - 3x^2 + 5$

(d) $y = -x^2 + 4x - 4$ (e) $y = 2x^3 - 9x^2 + 12$ (f) $y = x^4 - 8x^2 + 12$

B Increasing and decreasing functions again

Testing whether a function is increasing or decreasing at a given point is straightforward. Simply calculate the derivative and see whether it is positive or negative.

The reverse process of finding the range of points for which a given function is increasing or decreasing is not so easy. It involves solving an inequality.

Example 3

The function $f(x)$ given by $f(x) = 2x^3 - 3x^2 - 36x$ is decreasing over the interval $a < x < b$. Calculate the values of a and b.

Solution

$f'(x) = 6x^2 - 6x - 36$

For $f(x)$ to be decreasing, $f'(x) < 0$, so $6x^2 - 6x - 36 < 0$

$\Rightarrow \quad x^2 - x - 6 < 0$

$\Rightarrow \quad (x + 2)(x - 3) < 0$

Use a 'sign diagram' to solve this inequality.

$$
\begin{array}{c|cccc}
 & -2 & & 3 & \\
\hline
x + 2 & - - - & 0 + + + & + + + & + + + \\
x - 3 & - - - & - - - - & 0 + + & + \\
\hline
(x + 2)(x - 3) & + + + & 0 - - - & - - 0 & + + +
\end{array}
$$

$(x + 2)(x - 3) < 0$ for $-2 < x < 3$.

So $a = -2$ and $b = 3$.

Exercise B (answers p 184)

1 The function $f(x)$ defined by $f(x) = x^3 - 6x^2$ is decreasing over the interval $p < x < q$. Calculate the values of p and q.

2 The function $g(x)$ is given by $g(x) = x^3 - 27x + 20$.
   Find the range of values of x for which $g(x)$ is an increasing function.

3 The function $s(x)$ is defined by $s(x) = x(75 - x^2)$.
   Find the range of values of x for which $s(x)$ is an increasing function.

4 The population of an animal colony is modelled by the equation
   $$P = 500 + 150t - \tfrac{1}{2}t^3 \quad (t \geq 0)$$
   where t is the time in years since the population was first counted.
   For what range of values of t will P be increasing?

C Second derivative (answers p 184)

Here is the graph of the function

$$f(x) = \tfrac{1}{3}x^3 - 2x^2 + 3x + 1$$

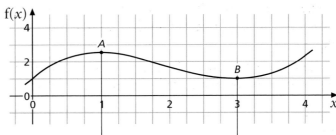

By differentiating, we get the derivative:

$$f'(x) = x^2 - 4x + 3$$

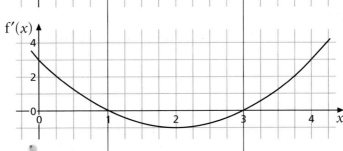

The function $f'(x)$ can also be differentiated.
The result is called the **second derivative** of $f(x)$ and is denoted by $f''(x)$:

$$f''(x) = 2x - 4$$

The second derivative gives the rate of change of the gradient of $f(x)$.

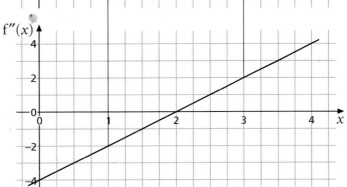

D **C1** (a) Point A, where $x = 1$, is a maximum point on the graph of $f(x)$.
Look at the graph of $f'(x)$ at the point where $x = 1$.
The value of $f'(x)$ goes from positive on the left to negative on the right.
Is $f'(x)$ increasing or decreasing at $x = 1$?

(b) What feature of the graph of $f''(x)$ at $x = 1$ tells you that $f'(x)$ must be decreasing at $x = 1$?

(c) What feature of the graph of $f''(x)$ tells you that $f'(x)$ must be increasing at $x = 3$?

The second derivative can be used to test whether a stationary point is a maximum or a minimum.

If the value of $f''(x)$ is positive at the stationary point, the point is a minimum.
If the value of $f''(x)$ is negative, the point is a maximum.

(Note. If the value of $f''(x)$ is zero, no conclusion can be drawn. In this case you will have to look at the sign of $f'(x)$ either side of the stationary point.)

In the other notation for derivatives, the second derivative of y with respect to x is denoted by $\dfrac{d^2y}{dx^2}$.

Example 4

Find the stationary points on the graph of $y = x^3 - 3x^2 - 9x + 5$ and determine their types.

Solution

$\dfrac{dy}{dx} = 3x^2 - 6x - 9$ 　At stationary points $\dfrac{dy}{dx} = 0$, so $3x^2 - 6x - 9 = 0$

$$\Rightarrow \quad 3(x^2 - 2x - 3) = 0$$
$$\Rightarrow \quad (x + 1)(x - 3) = 0$$
$$\Rightarrow \quad x = -1 \text{ or } x = 3$$

Find the value of y at each of these values of x.

When $x = -1$, $y = (-1)^3 - 3 \times (-1)^2 - 9 \times -1 + 5 = 10$

When $x = 3$, $y = 3^3 - 3 \times 3^2 - 9 \times 3 + 5 = -22$

So the stationary points are $(-1, 10)$ and $(3, -22)$.

Differentiate $\dfrac{dy}{dx}$ to get the second derivative. Then find its value at each stationary point.

$\dfrac{d^2y}{dx^2} = 6x - 6$

When $x = -1$, $\dfrac{d^2y}{dx^2} = 6 \times -1 - 6 = -12$. This is negative, so $x = -1$ gives a maximum.

When $x = 3$, $\dfrac{d^2y}{dx^2} = 6 \times 3 - 6 = 12$. This is positive, so $x = 3$ gives a minimum.

So $(-1, 10)$ is a maximum and $(3, -22)$ is a minimum.

Exercise C (answers p 184)

1 Given that $f(x) = 5x^3 - 3x^2 + 7x - 2$, find 　　　**(a)** $f'(x)$ 　　　**(b)** $f''(x)$

2 Given that $y = 3x^4 + 2x^3$, find 　**(a)** $\dfrac{dy}{dx}$ 　　**(b)** $\dfrac{d^2y}{dx^2}$

3 Find the stationary points on the graph of $y = x^3 - 6x^2 + 9x + 4$ and use the second derivative to determine their types.

4 Repeat question 3 for each of these graphs.

(a) $y = x^3 + 3x^2 - 45x + 8$ 　**(b)** $y = 4x^3 - 15x^2 + 12x + 1$ 　**(c)** $y = x^3 + 12x^2 + 36x - 5$

(d) $y = 9x + 6x^2 - 4x^3$ 　　**(e)** $y = 4x^3 - 9x^2 - 30x + 1$ 　　**(f)** $y = (x - 6)(x + 6)^2$

5 The function $g(x)$ is defined by $g(x) = 3x(x^2 - 15)$.

(a) Show that 　**(i)** $g'(\sqrt{5}) = 0$ 　**(ii)** $g''(\sqrt{5}) > 0$

(b) What does the information in (a) tell you about the function $g(x)$?

D Optimisation

Optimisation means getting the best result. This might mean **minimising** the amount of material used in a design or the amount of pollution caused by an industrial process, or **maximising** the number of customers served in an hour or the number of vaccinations during an epidemic.

A problem of this kind arises in marketing when deciding on the price to charge for a product. If the price is very low, a large number of the product may be sold but the total income from sales may not amount to much. If the price is very high, very few may be sold and again the income will be small. Somewhere in between there might be a price that will give the largest income.

Example 5

The owner of a castle wants to know how much to charge for admission.

The relationship between the number N of tickets sold per day and the price £P is believed to be as shown in the graph, whose equation is

$$N = 800 - 80P$$

What price should the owner charge in order to get the maximum possible income?

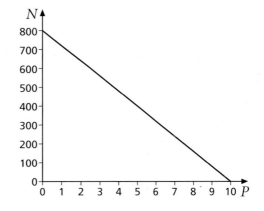

Solution

The income I gained from selling N tickets is N times P, so

$I = P(800 - 80P)$
   $= 800P - 80P^2$

For the income I to be a maximum, $\dfrac{\mathrm{d}I}{\mathrm{d}P} = 0$.

So $\dfrac{\mathrm{d}I}{\mathrm{d}P} = 800 - 160P = 0$

From which $P = \frac{800}{160} = 5$.

Check that $P = 5$ gives a maximum by using $\dfrac{\mathrm{d}^2I}{\mathrm{d}P^2}$.

$\dfrac{\mathrm{d}^2I}{\mathrm{d}P^2} = -160$, which is negative at every value of P, including $P = 5$.

So $P = 5$ gives a maximum. The owner should charge £5.

Exercise D (answers p 184)

1 For a speed of v m.p.h., the fuel economy, F miles per gallon, of a new car is found to be roughly modelled, for $30 \le v \le 80$, by the formula

$$F = 25 + v - 0.01v^2$$

What speed is most economical for this car?

2 A new housing estate started with a population of approximately 500 people.

   (a) It was planned that it should grow by roughly 100 inhabitants each year.

      (i) Find an expression for the intended population P of the estate t years after its opening.

      (ii) Find $\dfrac{dP}{dt}$ and explain what it represents.

   (b) For various reasons, the new estate did not grow as planned and the population was better modelled by the quadratic expression

$$P = 100(5 + t - 0.25t^2)$$

      (i) What was the rate of change of the population at the end of the first, second and third years?

      (ii) What was the maximum population of the estate?

      (iii) According to the model, what would happen to the population?

3 A farmer has 60 m of fencing. She wants to use it for three sides of a rectangular sheep pen with an existing hedge used for the fourth side.

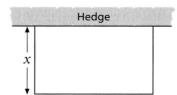

   (a) Let x metres be the length of the side shown. Write an expression for the area, $A\,\text{m}^2$, in terms of x.

   (b) Calculate the value of x for which A is a maximum.

   (c) Calculate the maximum area.

4

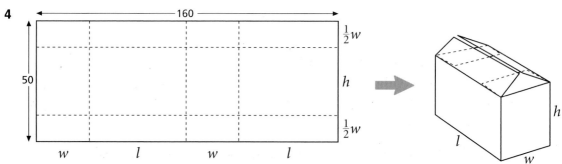

A box is to be made from a rectangular piece of card, 160 cm by 50 cm, by cutting and folding as necessary along the dotted lines shown in the left-hand diagram. The problem is to find the values of l, w and h which maximise the volume, $V\,\text{cm}^3$.

   (a) Explain why $2l + 2w = 160$. Hence express l in terms of w.

   (b) Similarly, find h in terms of w.

   (c) The volume of the box is given by $V = whl$.
Use your answers to (a) and (b) to show that $V = w(50 - w)(80 - w)$.

   (d) Find the value of w corresponding to the maximum possible volume. What dimensions will the box then have?

5 An open-topped tray is made from a rectangular piece of metal 8 cm by 5 cm. A square is cut from each corner, as shown below, and the remainder made into the tray by bending along the dotted lines and welding.

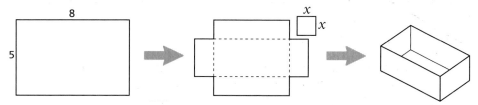

(a) If the squares cut out have side x cm, show that the volume of the tray is V cm³, where $V = x(8 - 2x)(5 - 2x)$.

(b) What should the dimensions be if the volume is to be as large as possible?

6 A box with a lid has a square base of side x cm and a height of h cm.

(a) Find an expression for the total surface area of the box in terms of x and h.

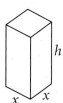

(b) The total surface area of the box is 384 cm².

  (i) Find a formula for h in terms of x.

  (ii) Hence show that, if the volume of the box is V cm³, then $V = 96x - \frac{1}{2}x^3$.

  (iii) Find the value of x for which the volume is a maximum and the corresponding value of h.

  (iv) Calculate the maximum volume of the box.

7 The end faces of a prism are in the shape of a right-angled triangle with sides $3x$ cm, $4x$ cm and $5x$ cm. The length of the prism is l cm.

The total surface area of the prism is 64 cm².

(a) Show that $l = \dfrac{16}{3x} - x$.

(b) Show that the volume V cm³ of the prism is given by $V = 32x - 6x^3$.

(c) Calculate the maximum possible volume of the prism.

*8 A bicycle manufacturer has designed a new model and wishes to fix the price so that profits are maximised. After an initial cost of £50 000 to set up the production line, it will cost £85 in labour, raw materials and components to produce each bike.

Market research suggests that the firm can hope to sell 5000 bikes if the price is fixed at £100 per bike, but they can only expect to sell 1000 if the price is £200. They assume that the relationship between price and demand is linear between these two extremes.

How many bikes would you advise the company to manufacture and at what price should they be sold?

Key points

- If the value of $\dfrac{dy}{dx}$ is positive at $x = a$, then y is increasing at $x = a$.

  If the value of $\dfrac{dy}{dx}$ is negative at $x = a$, then y is decreasing at $x = a$.

  (Alternative notation: If $f'(a) > 0$, then $f(x)$ is increasing at $x = a$;
  if $f'(a) < 0$, then $f(x)$ is decreasing at $x = a$.) (p 124)

- Points where $\dfrac{dy}{dx} = 0$ are called stationary points.

  At a local maximum, $\dfrac{dy}{dx}$ goes from positive to negative.

  At a local minimum, $\dfrac{dy}{dx}$ goes from negative to positive. (p 124)

- The second derivative, $\dfrac{d^2y}{dx^2}$ or $f''(x)$, is the derivative of $\dfrac{dy}{dx}$ or $f'(x)$. (p 127)

- If at a stationary point $\dfrac{d^2y}{dx^2}$ is positive, the point is a local minimum;
  if $\dfrac{d^2y}{dx^2}$ is negative, the point is a local maximum. (p 127)

Mixed questions (answers p 185)

1 Find the coordinates of the stationary points on the graph of $y = x^3 - 3x$ and determine their types.

2 Given that $y = (x - 5)(2x^2 + 1)$, find

   (a) $\dfrac{dy}{dx}$ (b) $\dfrac{d^2y}{dx^2}$

3 Given that $f(x) = 3 + 5x - 2x^2$,

   (a) find the coordinates of all the points at which the graph of $y = f(x)$ crosses the coordinate axes

   (b) sketch the graph of $y = f(x)$

   (c) calculate the coordinates of the stationary point of $f(x)$

4 For the curve C with equation $y = x^4 - 2x^2 + 4$,

   (a) find $\dfrac{dy}{dx}$

   (b) find the coordinates of each of the stationary points

   (c) determine the nature of each stationary point

5 The function $f(x)$ is defined by $f(x) = x^2(8x - 3)$.

(a) Find $f'(x)$.

(b) Find $f''(x)$.

(c) Determine whether the function is increasing or decreasing at the point where $x = 1$.

(d) Find the x-coordinates of the stationary points on the curve $y = x^2(8x - 3)$.

(e) Determine whether each stationary point is a maximum point or a minimum point.

6 An office worker can leave home at any time between 6:00 a.m. and 10:00 a.m. each morning. When he leaves home x **hours** after 6:00 a.m. ($0 \leq x \leq 4$), his journey time to the office is y **minutes**, where

$$y = x^4 - 8x^3 + 16x^2 + 8.$$

(a) Find $\dfrac{dy}{dx}$.

(b) Find the **three** values of x for which $\dfrac{dy}{dx} = 0$.

(c) Show that y has a maximum value when $x = 2$.

(d) Find the time at which the office worker arrives at the office on a day when his journey time is a maximum. AQA 2002

7 The function given by $f(x) = 7 + 15x - 6x^2 - x^3$ is increasing over the interval $a < x < b$. Calculate the values of a and b.

8 A simple shelter is made from a rectangular piece of sheet metal 4 m by 2 m by cutting and bending as shown below.

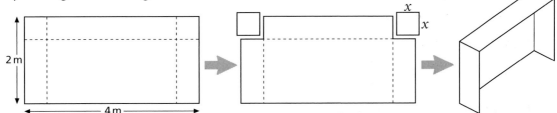

(a) If the squares removed from the sheet are each x m by x m, show that the volume, V m^3, of the shelter is given by

$$V = 2x^3 - 8x^2 + 8x$$

(b) Find the value of x for which the volume is as large as possible.

(c) Calculate the largest possible volume of the shelter.

9 An open-topped box has height h cm and a square base of side x cm. The box has capacity V cm^3. The area of its **external** surface, consisting of its horizontal base and four vertical faces, is A cm^2.

(a) Find expressions for V and A in terms of x and h.

(b) It is given that $A = 3000$.

    (i) Show that $V = 750x - \frac{1}{4}x^3$.

    (ii) Find the positive value of x for which $\dfrac{dV}{dx} = 0$, giving your answer in surd form.

    (iii) Hence find the maximum possible value of V, giving your answer in the form $p\sqrt{10}$, where p is an integer.
    (You do not need to show that your answer is a maximum.)   AQA 2001

*10 (a) The graph of the function $y = x^2(x - a)$ has a stationary point where $x = 6$. Find the value of a.

(b) The graph of the function $y = (x - 3)^2(x - b)$ has a stationary point where $x = 6$. Find the value of b.

(c) The graph of the function $y = x(x - c)^2$ has a stationary point where $x = 6$. Find the two possible values of c.

*11 A graph has the equation $y = 3x^4 + 8x^3 - 6x^2 - 24x + 1$.

(a) Find $\dfrac{dy}{dx}$.

(b) Show that the stationary points of the graph are given by the equation
$$x^3 + 2x^2 - x - 2 = 0$$

(c) Show that $x = 1$ is a solution of this equation and find the other two solutions.

(d) Find the coordinates of the stationary points of the graph and determine whether each is a local maximum or minimum.

Test yourself (answers p 187)

None of these questions requires a calculator.

1 The function f is defined for all real values of x by
$$f(x) = (x^2 + 4)(2x - 1)$$

(a) Differentiate $f(x)$ with respect to x to obtain $f'(x)$.

(b) Hence show that the gradient of the curve $y = f(x)$ is 12 at the point where $x = 1$.

(c) Prove that the curve $y = f(x)$ has no stationary point.   AQA 2001

2 The graph of the function $y = x^3 - 3x^2 - 9x$ has two stationary points.

(a) Find $\dfrac{dy}{dx}$.

(b) Is the function increasing or decreasing at the point where $x = 0$?

(c) Find the coordinates of the stationary points.

(d) Find the value of $\dfrac{d^2y}{dx^2}$ at the stationary points, and hence determine whether the stationary points are maxima or minima.

3 The size of a population, P, of birds on an island is modelled by

$$P = 59 + 117t + 57t^2 - t^3,$$

where t is the time in years after 1970.

(a) Find $\dfrac{dP}{dt}$.

(b) (i) Find the positive value of t for which P has a stationary value.

(ii) Determine whether this stationary value is a maximum or a minimum.

(c) (i) State the year when the model predicts that the population will reach its maximum value.

(ii) Determine what the model predicts will happen in the year 2029. AQA 2002

10 Integration

In this chapter you will learn
- what integration is and how it is related to differentiation
- how to integrate polynomial functions

A Thinking backwards (answers p 187)

When a ball rolls down a slope it gets faster and faster. In fact, its speed (in m/s) is proportional to the time t (in seconds) it has been travelling.

In the example shown here, the speed of the ball is equal to $2t$.

Here are a table of values and a graph showing how the speed increases over time.

t (seconds)	0	1	2	3	4
Speed (m/s)	0	2	4	6	8

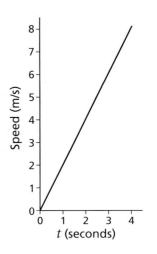

If s is the distance (in m) travelled in time t, then the speed of the ball is $\dfrac{ds}{dt}$. So the graph above shows the gradient function for the distance. The question arises: what does the distance function itself look like?

This is the reverse problem to finding a gradient function for a given function. We are given the gradient function or derivative and want to find the original function.

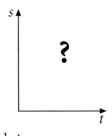

A1 Which function of t has the derivative $2t$?

Once we know the distance function we can work out, for example,

- how far the ball will travel in a given time
- how long it will take to go a given distance

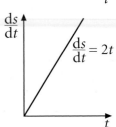

A2 On a different slope the speed of the ball is $5t$. What is the distance function in this case?

B Integration as the reverse of differentiation (answers p 187)

If you differentiate x^2 the result is the derivative, $2x$.

The reverse process is called **integration**.
Starting with $2x$ you ask: 'What function has derivative $2x$?'

D **B1** The obvious answer to the question above is x^2, but there is more to it than that.
Differentiate each of these functions: $x^2 + 1$, $x^2 + 5$, $x^2 - 9$, $x^2 + 30$
How would you answer the question: 'What function has $2x$ as its derivative?'

Because the derivative of any constant number, such as 5, is always zero,
any function such as $x^2 + 5$, $x^2 + 7$, $x^2 - 3$, and so on, also has derivative $2x$.

So the function with derivative $2x$ is $x^2 + c$, where c can be any number.
This is illustrated in the graphs on the right.

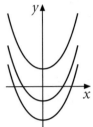

K The process of going from $2x$ to $x^2 + c$ is called **integration**.
$x^2 + c$ is called the **indefinite integral** of $2x$
('indefinite' because c can be any number).
c is called the **constant of integration**.

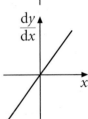

B2 **(a)** Write down the derivative of $5x^2$.

(b) Hence write down the indefinite integral of $10x$.

B3 **(a)** Write down the derivative of each of these functions of x.

(i) $3x^2$ **(ii)** $4x^2$ **(iii)** $8x$ **(iv)** x^3 **(v)** $6x$

(b) Use your answers to (a) to write down the indefinite integral of

(i) $8x$ **(ii)** $3x^2$ **(iii)** 6 **(iv)** $6x$ **(v)** 8

D **B4** The derivative of x^4 is $4x^3$. Use this fact to find the indefinite integral of x^3.

Example 1

Find the indefinite integral of $12x^2$.

Solution

You are trying to find the function whose derivative is $12x^2$.
You know that the derivative of x^3 is $3x^2$.
So if you differentiate $4x^3$ you will get $12x^2$.   The indefinite integral of $12x^2$ is $4x^3 + c$.

Exercise B (answers p 187)

1 Find the indefinite integrals of the following functions.

   (a) $4x$ (b) $12x$ (c) $20x$ (d) x

2 Find the indefinite integral of

   (a) $6x^2$ (b) $15x^2$ (c) x^2 (d) $2x^2$

3 Find the indefinite integrals of the following functions.
Check each answer by differentiating.

   (a) $4x^3$ (b) $10x^4$ (c) $5x^2$ (d) $3x$

4 (a) Copy and complete this table of indefinite integrals.

Function	x	x^2	x^3	x^4
Indefinite integral				

   (b) Use your results to help you write down a formula for the indefinite integral of the general function x^n, where n is a positive integer.

C Integrating polynomials (answers p 187)

The notation for 'the indefinite integral of $2x$' is $\int 2x \, dx$ (read as 'integral $2x$ dx').
So we write $\int 2x \, dx = x^2 + c$.

The reason for this notation will be explained in the next chapter. For now, think of $\int \ \ dx$ as a single symbol with a blank space for the function to be integrated.

C1 Use the integral notation to write each of these statements.

   (a) The indefinite integral of $3x^2$ is $x^3 + c$.

   (b) The indefinite integral of $4x$ is $2x^2 + c$.

C2 Find the indefinite integral of $5x$ and write the statement 'the indefinite integral of $5x$ is ...' using the integral notation.

C3 Repeat C2 for the function $6x^2$.

A rule for integrating a power of x emerged from the questions in exercise B.

$$\int x^n \, dx = \frac{x^{n+1}}{n+1} + c$$

In words, this rule says 'raise the index by 1 and divide by the new index'.
For example, $\int x^5 \, dx = \frac{x^6}{6} + c$.

Integrating a sum of functions

To differentiate the function $x^3 + x^2$ you differentiate each term separately and add, getting the derivative $3x^2 + 2x$.

It follows that $\int (3x^2 + 2x)dx = x^3 + x^2 + c$.

So, as with differentiation, you integrate each term separately and add.

Integrating a multiple of a function

The derivative of $5x^2$ is 5 times the derivative of x^2.
The same applies to integration. For example,

$$\int 5x^2\, dx = 5\int x^2\, dx = 5\left(\frac{x^3}{3}\right) + c = \tfrac{5}{3}x^3 + c$$

Check that this is correct by differentiating $\tfrac{5}{3}x^3 + c$.

Integrating a polynomial

Using the rules given above, a polynomial can be integrated term by term.
If you are in any doubt about a result, differentiate it and check that you get the original function.

Example 2

If $\dfrac{dy}{dx} = 2x^3 + 9x^2 - x + 3$, find y in terms of x.

Solution

y is the indefinite integral of $2x^3 + 9x^2 - x + 3$.

$$y = \int \left(2x^3 + 9x^2 - x + 3\right) dx = 2\left(\frac{x^4}{4}\right) + 9\left(\frac{x^3}{3}\right) - \left(\frac{x^2}{2}\right) + 3x + c$$

$$= \tfrac{1}{2}x^4 + 3x^3 - \tfrac{1}{2}x^2 + 3x + c$$

Example 3

Find $\int (x + 3)(x^2 - 5)\, dx$.

Solution

Multiply out the brackets to get a polynomial.

$$\int (x + 3)\left(x^2 - 5\right) dx = \int \left(x^3 + 3x^2 - 5x - 15\right) dx = \left(\frac{x^4}{4}\right) + 3\left(\frac{x^3}{3}\right) - 5\left(\frac{x^2}{2}\right) - 15x + c$$

$$= \tfrac{1}{4}x^4 + x^3 - \tfrac{5}{2}x^2 - 15x + c$$

Exercise C (answers p 188)

1 Find the following integrals.

(a) $\int x^3\, dx$ (b) $\int 4x^2\, dx$ (c) $\int 6x\, dx$ (d) $\int 5x^4\, dx$

2 Find y as a function of x for each of these.

   (a) $\dfrac{dy}{dx} = x - 4$ (b) $\dfrac{dy}{dx} = 3x^2 + x$ (c) $\dfrac{dy}{dx} = x^2 + x + 1$ (d) $\dfrac{dy}{dx} = 5x^4 + 3$

3 Given that $f'(x) = 5x + 3x^3$, find an expression for $f(x)$.

4 Find the following integrals.

   (a) $\displaystyle\int (2 - 3x + x^2)\, dx$ (b) $\displaystyle\int (5x^3 + 2x^5)\, dx$

5 Find y as a function of x for each of these.

   (a) $\dfrac{dy}{dx} = 2x^3 - 7x + 3$ (b) $\dfrac{dy}{dx} = (x + 1)(x - 2)$

6 Find the indefinite integral of each of the following functions.

   (a) $2(3x - 2)$ (b) $3x(x + 4)$ (c) $(2x - 1)^2$

7 Given that $f'(x) = (x + 2)(x - 1)(x + 4)$, find an expression for $f(x)$.

8 Find the following integrals.

   (a) $\displaystyle\int (x + 2)(x - 5)\, dx$ (b) $\displaystyle\int x^2(2x + 1)\, dx$

D Finding the constant of integration

If you are told that $\dfrac{dy}{dx} = 3x^2 - 2$, then by integration it follows that $y = x^3 - 2x + c$.

The equation $y = x^3 - 2x + c$ represents a family of graphs all having the same derivative, or gradient function.

If you are given the additional information that the graph goes through $(2, 7)$, then you can find the value of c:

$$7 = 2^3 - 2 \times 2 + c$$

$$\Rightarrow c = 3$$

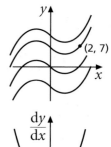

Example 4

Given that $f'(x) = 8x^3 - 6x$ and that $f(2) = 9$, find $f(x)$ in terms of x.

Solution

First find the indefinite integral of $8x^3 - 6x$. $f(x) = \displaystyle\int (8x^3 - 6x)\, dx = 2x^4 - 3x^2 + c$

Now use the fact that $f(2) = 9$ to find c. $9 = 32 - 12 + c$

$$\Rightarrow \quad c = -11$$

So $f(x) = 2x^4 - 3x^2 - 11$

Exercise D (answers p 188)

1 Given that $f'(x) = 6x^2 + 4$ and that $f(1) = 7$, find an expression for $f(x)$.

2 Express y as a function of x for each of these.

   (a) $\dfrac{dy}{dx} = 3x^2 + 4x$ and the (x, y) graph passes through $(1, 5)$.

   (b) $\dfrac{dy}{dx} = x^2 + x + 1$ and the (x, y) graph passes through $(0, 3)$.

3 The curve C passes through the point $P\,(2, 1)$.

   If $\dfrac{dy}{dx} = 2x - x^3$, find the equation of C.

4 Find an expression for $f(x)$ for each of these.

   (a) $f'(x) = 5 - 2x$ and $f(2) = 4$ **(b)** $f'(x) = 3x(3x - 2)$ and $f(0) = 2$

5 **(a)** Given that $\dfrac{dy}{dx} = (x + 1)(2x - 3)$, find y as a function of x.

   (b) If $y = 1$ when $x = 0$, find the value of y when $x = 3$.

6 The curve $y = f(x)$ passes through the points $(0, 5)$ and $(-2, k)$.

   Given that $\dfrac{dy}{dx} = 4x + 3$, find the value of k.

7 The rate of growth of a population of micro-organisms is modelled by the equation

   $$\dfrac{dP}{dt} = 3t^2 \pm 6t$$

   where P is the population size at time t hours.
   Given that $P = 100$ when $t = 1$, find P in terms of t.

8 The equation of a curve is $y = f(x)$. The curve goes through the points
   $(1, 3)$ and $(3, 7)$. Given that $f'(x) = 4x + p$, where p is a number, find

   (a) the value of p

   (b) the equation of the curve

*9 The curve with equation $y = f(x)$ goes through the points $(0, 5)$, $(1, 11)$ and $(2, 37)$.
   Given that $f'(x) = ax^2 + bx$, find

   (a) the values of a, b and c (the constant of integration)

   (b) the equation of the curve

Key points

- Integration is the reverse of differentiation. (p 137)

- The indefinite integral of a function includes a constant term. (p 137)

- The indefinite integral of a function f(x) is denoted by $\int f(x)\,dx$. (p 138)

- $\int x^n\,dx = \dfrac{x^{n+1}}{n+1} + c$ for positive integers n. (p 138)

- The indefinite integral of a sum of functions is the sum of
  the separate indefinite integrals.
  The indefinite integral of k times a function is k times
  the indefinite integral of the function. (p 139)

- Given $\dfrac{dy}{dx}$ (or f$'(x)$) and the value of y (or f(x)) for a given value of x,
  the value of the constant of integration can be found. (p 140)

Mixed questions (answers p 188)

1 Find

   (a) $\int (2x^2 + 3x - 1)\,dx$ **(b)** $\int x(5x^4 + 2)\,dx$ **(c)** $\int (2x^2 + 3)(x - 4)\,dx$

2 Given that $f'(x) = x^3 + 12x^2 - 2$ and $f(2) = 0$, find $f(x)$ in terms of x.

3 The curve C goes through the point $(3, 5)$.

   The gradient $\dfrac{dy}{dx}$ at the point (x, y) on C is given by the equation $\dfrac{dy}{dx} = \frac{1}{2}x^2 - 3x$.

   Find the equation of C.

4 Given that $\dfrac{ds}{dt} = (t + 3)(t - 1)$ and that $s = 10$ when $t = 3$, find s in terms of t.

5 Given that $f'(x) = 3x^2 + ax$, $f(-2) = 8$ and $f(1) = 2$, find

   (a) the value of a

   (b) an expression for $f(x)$ in terms of x

6 The rate of growth of a bird population is modelled by the equation

$$\frac{dP}{dt} = a + bt$$

   where P is the population at time t, and a and b are constants.

   Given that $P = 100$ when $t = 0$, $P = 172$ when $t = 4$, and $P = 202$ when $t = 6$,

   (a) find the formula for P in terms of t

   (b) find the values of t for which $P = 250$

*7 The rate of spread of an illness affecting animals in a colony is modelled by the equation

$$\frac{dN}{dt} = 5 - \tfrac{4}{9}t - \tfrac{1}{9}t^2$$

where N is the number of animals affected and t is the time in weeks since recording began.

When recording began, 36 animals were affected.

(a) Find a formula for N in terms of t.

(b) How many affected animals are there after 3 weeks?

(c) After how many weeks does the number of affected animals reach a maximum?

(d) Show that, according to the model, the number of affected animals decreases after reaching a maximum and is zero when $t = 12$.

Test yourself (answers p 188)

None of these questions requires a calculator.

1 Find

(a) $\int (x^3 + 2x^2 - x)\,dx$ (b) $\int (x^4 + 7x - 1)\,dx$ (c) $\int (x^8 + 5x^6)\,dx$

2 Find

(a) $\int 3x^2(x - 2)\,dx$ (b) $\int (4x + 1)(3x^2 - 1)\,dx$ (c) $\int (3x - 2)^2\,dx$

3 The gradient function of a curve is given by $\dfrac{dy}{dx} = 6x^2 - 1$.

The curve goes through the point $(-1, 4)$. Find the equation of the curve.

4 Given that $\dfrac{dy}{dx} = (6x + 5)(x - 1)$ and that $y = 0$ when $x = 1$, find y in terms of x.

5 Given that $f'(x) = 10x^4 - 12x^3 - 4$ and $f(2) = 10$, find

(a) $f(x)$ in terms of x (b) $f(-2)$

6 Given that $f'(x) = (x + 1)(3x - 5)$ and $f(3) = 6$, find $f(x)$ in terms of x.

7 The curve C goes through the point $(-2, 2)$.

The gradient function of C is given by $\dfrac{dy}{dx} = (3x - 1)^2$.

Find the equation of C.

11 Area under a graph

In this chapter you will learn how to calculate the area under
the graph of a polynomial function.

A Linear graphs: area function (answers p 189)

The first diagram below shows the area under the graph of $y = x$ between $x = 0$ and $x = 1$.
This area is denoted by A(1). The other diagrams show A(2), A(3) and A(4).

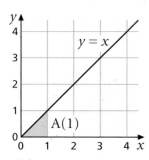 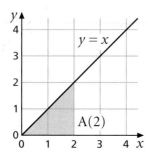 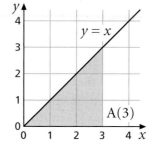 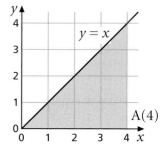

A1 (a) (i) Find the values of A(1), A(2), A(3) and A(4).

(ii) What is the value of A(0)?

(iii) Copy and complete this table of values for the function A(x).

x	0	1	2	3	4
A(x)					

(b) Plot the values of x and A(x) on a graph.

(c) What is the formula for A(x) in terms of x?

A2 Repeat for the graph of $y = 2x$.

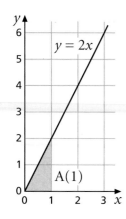 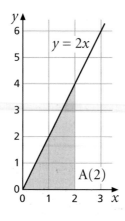 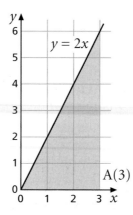 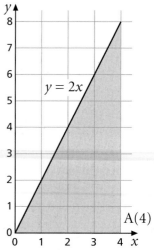

A3 Repeat for the graph of $y = x + 1$.
The last of the diagrams below should help you work out the formula for A(x).

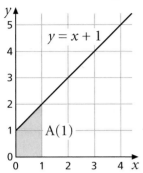 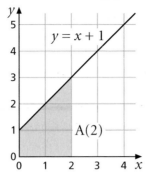 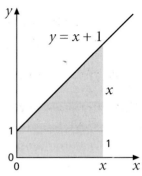

A4 The area function for the graph of $y = 3$ is simpler than any of those you have worked out so far.

What is it?

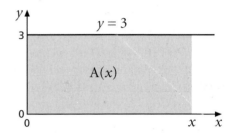

A5 Use this diagram to help you find the area function for the graph of $y = 2x + 3$.

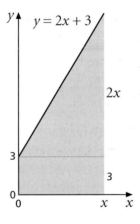

D

A6 (a) Make a table of the area functions you have found so far.

(b) What do you notice?

(c) What would you guess to be the area function for the graph of $y = x^2$?

Graph	Area function A(x)
$y = 3$	
$y = x$	
$y = 2x$	
$y = x + 1$	
$y = 2x + 3$	

It appears from the results in A6 that the area function is the indefinite integral of the given function (but without the constant of integration). In the next section we test whether this is true for the graph of $y = x^2$.

B Area function for $y = x^2$ (answers p 189)

The area under a linear graph is made up of rectangles and triangles, whose areas can easily be calculated.

The situation is different with a curved graph, but approximation is possible.

Here is the graph of $y = x^2$.
It is split up into strips, each of which is roughly a triangle or a trapezium.

A(1) is the area of the first strip,
A(2) the total area of the first two strips,
A(3) the total area of the first three strips,
and so on.

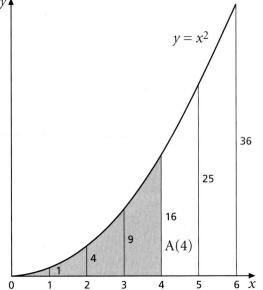

B1 (a) Calculate, approximately, the area of each strip by treating it as a trapezium. (Treat the first strip as a triangle.)

(b) Does the use of the trapezium overestimate or underestimate the true area?

(c) Work out the approximate values of A(1), A(2), A(3), and so on, and enter them in a table.

x	0	1	2	3	4	5	6
A(x)							

(d) From question A6, a guess for the actual area function is $\frac{1}{3}x^3$.
Work out the values of $\frac{1}{3}x^3$ and compare them with the approximate values of A(x). Does there appear to be any agreement?

A better approximation for the area can be found by using narrower strips (and correspondingly more of them).

Here is the start of a table in which strips of width 0.1 are used.
This calculation can be set up in a spreadsheet.

Strip from ... to ...		Value of y		Area of strip	x	Approximation to A(x)	$\frac{1}{3}x^3$
		left	right				
0	0.1	0	0.01	0.0005	0.1	0.0005	0.000333
0.1	0.2	0.01	0.04	0.0025	0.2	0.003	0.002667
0.2	0.3	0.04	0.09	0.0065	0.3	0.0095	0.009
0.3	0.4	0.09	0.16	0.0125	0.4	0.022	0.021333

There is close agreement between the approximate value of A(x) and $\frac{1}{3}x^3$.

C Definite integrals

The results of sections A and B suggest that the area under a graph is related to integration. We will assume that this is true. An explanation is given at the end of the chapter.

The area function $A(x)$ for the graph of $y = x^2$ is the integral of x^2, which is $\frac{1}{3}x^3$. (In this case there is no need to include the constant of integration; the reason will appear soon.)

The diagram shows the area under the graph of $y = x^2$ between $x = 3$ and $x = 6$.

This area is denoted by

$$\int_3^6 x^2 \, dx$$

(read as 'integral 3 to 6 of $x^2 \, dx$').

The area is the difference between $A(6)$ and $A(3)$:

$$\text{Area} = \tfrac{1}{3} \times 6^3 - \tfrac{1}{3} \times 3^3 = 72 - 9 = 63$$

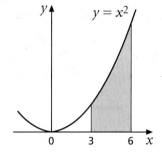

A special notation is used for calculations like this:

$\left[\tfrac{1}{3}x^3\right]_3^6$ means 'work out $\frac{1}{3}x^3$ when $x = 6$ and when $x = 3$; then subtract'.

The following example shows how the calculation above is set out in practice.

Example 1

Calculate the area under the graph of $y = x^2$ between $x = 3$ and $x = 6$.

Solution

$$\text{Area} = \int_3^6 x^2 \, dx = \left[\tfrac{1}{3}x^3\right]_3^6 = \left(\tfrac{1}{3} \times 6^3\right) - \left(\tfrac{1}{3} \times 3^3\right) = 72 - 9 = 63$$

The expression $\int_3^6 x^2 \, dx$ is called a **definite integral**. It works out to a numerical value.

The constant of integration is not included because it cancels out when the subtraction is done:

$$\text{Area} = \int_3^6 x^2 \, dx = \left[\tfrac{1}{3}x^3 + c\right]_3^6 = \left(\tfrac{1}{3} \times 6^3 + c\right) - \left(\tfrac{1}{3} \times 3^3 + c\right) = 72 + c - 9 - c = 63$$

Historical note

The notation $\int \ldots$ was introduced by Leibniz. '$\int$' is a long 's' for 'sum'. Leibniz thought of integration as summing a large number of strips of very small width ('dx').

Example 2

Evaluate the integral $\int_2^3 (x+2)(2x+3)(2x-1)\, dx$.

Solution

$$\int_2^3 (x+2)(2x+3)(2x-1)\, dx = \int_2^3 \left(4x^3 + 12x^2 + 5x - 6\right) dx$$

$$= \left[x^4 + 4x^3 + \tfrac{5}{2}x^2 - 6x\right]_2^3$$

$$= \left(3^4 + 4 \times 3^3 + \tfrac{5}{2} \times 3^2 - 6 \times 3\right) - \left(2^4 + 4 \times 2^3 + \tfrac{5}{2} \times 2^2 - 6 \times 2\right)$$

$$= 193\tfrac{1}{2} - 46 = 147\tfrac{1}{2}$$

Exercise C (answers p 189)

1 (a) Write down the integral which represents the shaded area.

    (b) Calculate this area.

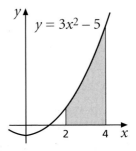

2 Evaluate $\int_1^3 \left(t^3 + t^2 + t + 1\right) dt$.

3 Evaluate these integrals.

    (a) $\int_0^1 \left(x - x^2\right) dx$ **(b)** $\int_2^4 (x+1)\, dx$ **(c)** $\int_{-2}^{-1} x^2\, dx$

    (d) $\int_0^1 \left(x^2 - 2x + 1\right) dx$ **(e)** $\int_0^1 (x+1)(x+2)\, dx$ **(f)** $\int_0^3 (x-2)^2\, dx$

4 Find the value of $a \ (> 1)$ for which $\int_1^a (2x+3)\, dx = 24$.

5 (a) Evaluate the following integrals.

        (i) $\int_2^4 x^2\, dx$ **(ii)** $\int_{-4}^{-2} x^2\, dx$

    (b) Sketch the graph of $y = x^2$ and use it to explain your results in (a).

6 Calculate the area under the graph of $y = x^3 + 2x - 3$ between $x = 1$ and $x = 4$.

7 (a) Sketch the graph of $y = 9 - x^2$, showing clearly where the curve cuts the x-axis.

    (b) Calculate the area enclosed between the graph and the x-axis.

8 (a) Sketch the graph of $y = (x-3)(6-x)$, showing clearly where the curve cuts the x-axis.

    (b) Calculate the area enclosed between the graph and the x-axis.

9 (a) Sketch the graph of $y = -x^2 + 4x - 3$, showing clearly where it cuts the x-axis.

   (b) Calculate the area enclosed by the curve and the x-axis.

10 The diagram shows part of the graph of $y = x^2(x - 1)^2$.
Calculate the shaded area.

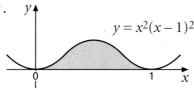

*11 The area under the graph of $y = x^2 + k$ between $x = 0$ and $x = 9$
is divided into two equal parts by the line $x = 6$.
Calculate the value of k.

D Areas below the x-axis (answers p 190)

D1 The diagram shows the graph of $y = 3x^2 - 12x$.

   (a) Calculate the area between the graph and
the x-axis between $x = 1$ and $x = 3$.

   (b) Why is the result negative?

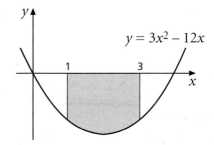

Exercise D (answers p 190)

1 (a) Evaluate $\int_0^3 (x^2 - 9)\, dx$.

   (b) Draw a sketch to explain why the result is negative.

2 (a) Find the values of x at the points where the graph of $y = (x + 1)(x - 5)$
cuts the x-axis.

   (b) Find the area enclosed between the graph and the x-axis between
these points.

3 Repeat question 2 for the graph of $y = 3x^2 - 9x$.

4 (a) Sketch the graph of $y = 4x(x + 5)(x - 2)$ showing where it cuts the x-axis.

   (b) Find the area enclosed between the graph and the x-axis between

     (i) $x = -5$ and $x = 0$ (ii) $x = 0$ and $x = 2$

*5 Evaluate $\int_{-2}^2 x(x^2 - 4)\, dx$ and draw a sketch to explain the result.

E The fundamental theorem of calculus

The fact that the area under the graph of $y = f(x)$ is found by integrating $f(x)$ is known as the 'fundamental theorem of calculus'.

Put another way, the theorem says that if A is the area under the graph of $y = f(x)$ (measured from some starting value of x), then $\dfrac{dA}{dx} = f(x)$.

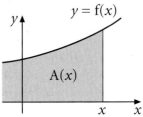

To get an idea of why the theorem is true, think what happens when the value of x is increased by a small amount δx.

Let δy be the corresponding increase in y, and δA the increase in the area (shaded lighter).

The extra area is very close to being a trapezium whose parallel sides are y and $(y + \delta y)$.

So $\delta A = \frac{1}{2}(y + y + \delta y)\delta x = (y + \frac{1}{2}\delta y)\delta x$

So $\dfrac{\delta A}{\delta x} = y + \frac{1}{2}\delta y$

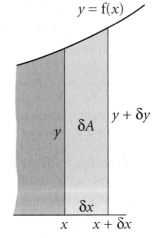

Now think what happens as δx gets smaller and smaller: δy also gets smaller and smaller, $y + \frac{1}{2}\delta y$ gets closer to y, and the ratio $\dfrac{\delta A}{\delta x}$ gets closer to $\dfrac{dA}{dx}$.

So $\dfrac{dA}{dx} = y = f(x)$.

Key points

- The area under the graph of $y = f(x)$ between $x = a$ and $x = b$ is found by evaluating the definite integral $\displaystyle\int_a^b f(x)\,dx$. (p 147)

- An area below the x-axis has a negative value. (p 149)

Mixed questions (answers p 190)

1 Evaluate these integrals.

   (a) $\displaystyle\int_0^2 \left(4x - x^3\right) dx$

   (b) $\displaystyle\int_{-1}^1 \left(x^2 - 1\right)(x - 2)\,dx$

2 The diagram shows the graph of

$$y = x^3 - x, \quad x \geq 0.$$

The points on the graph for which $x = 1$ and $x = 2$ are labelled A and B respectively.

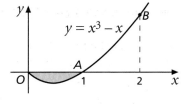

(a) Find the y-coordinate of B and hence find the equation of the straight line AB, giving your answer in the form

$$ax + by + c = 0.$$

(b) Find, by integration, the area of the shaded region.

AQA 2002

3 The diagram shows part of the graph of $y = -x^2 + 3x + 10$, which cuts the y-axis at the point $(0, 10)$.

The graph crosses the line $y = 10$ again at the point $(a, 10)$.

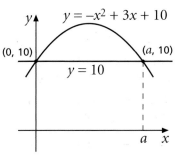

(a) Calculate the value of a.

(b) Calculate the area between the curve and the x-axis from $x = 0$ to $x = a$.

(c) Calculate the area enclosed between the curve and the line $y = 10$.

4 The function f is defined for all values of x by $f(x) = x^3 - 7x^2 + 14x - 8$. It is given that $f(1) = 0$ and $f(2) = 0$.

(a) Find the values of $f(3)$ and $f(4)$.

(b) Write $f(x)$ as a product of **three** linear factors.

(c) The diagram shows the graph of
$y = x^3 - 7x^2 + 14x - 8$.

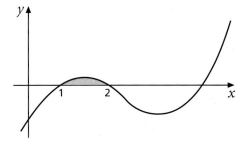

  (i) Find $\dfrac{dy}{dx}$.

  (ii) State, giving a reason, whether the function f is increasing or decreasing at the point where $x = 3$.

  (iii) Find $\int \left(x^3 - 7x^2 + 14x - 8\right) dx$.

  (iv) Hence find the area of the shaded region enclosed by the graph of $y = f(x)$, for $1 \leq x \leq 2$, and the x-axis.

AQA 2003

5 The diagram shows the curve $y = x^2 + 1$ and the straight line $y = 10$.

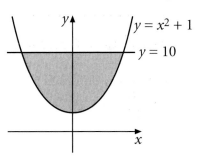

(a) Find the x-coordinates of the points where the line and the curve intersect.

(b) Calculate the area of the shaded region enclosed by the line $y = 10$ and the curve $y = x^2 + 1$.

6 (a) The graphs of $y = 4x^2$ and $y = (x-6)^2$ intersect where $x = a$ $(a > 0)$. Find the value of a.

(b) Find the shaded area.

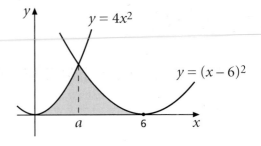

Test yourself (answers page p 190)

None of these questions requires a calculator.

1 Find the following integrals.

(a) $\displaystyle\int_0^2 \left(x^4 - 3x\right) dx$

(b) $\displaystyle\int_1^4 (x-1)\left(x^2 + 2\right) dx$

2 The diagram shows the curve $y = x^2 - 4x + 6$, the points $P(-1, 11)$ and $Q(4, 6)$, and the line PQ.

(a) Show that the length of PQ is $5\sqrt{2}$.

(b) Find the equation of the tangent to the curve at Q in the form $y = mx + c$.

(c) Find the area of the shaded region in the diagram.

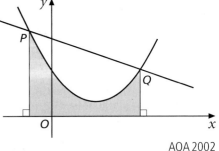

AQA 2002

3 (a) Find $\displaystyle\int (x+1)(x-2)(x-4)\, dx$.

(b) Hence find the area of the region enclosed between the graph of $y = (x + 1)(x - 2)(x - 4)$ and the x-axis for $2 \leq x \leq 4$.

4 The diagram shows the graph of $y = 12 - 3x^2$ and the tangent to the curve at the point $P(2, 0)$.

The region enclosed by the tangent, the curve and the y-axis is shaded.

(a) Find $\displaystyle\int_0^2 \left(12 - 3x^2\right) dx$.

(b) (i) Find the gradient of the curve $y = 12 - 3x^2$ at the point P.

(ii) Find the coordinates of the point Q where the tangent at P crosses the y-axis.

(c) Find the area of the shaded region.

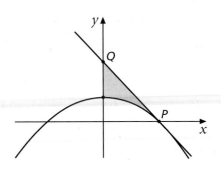

AQA 2002

Answers

1 Linear graphs and equations

A Linear graphs (p 6)

A1 A $\frac{5}{2}$ B -1 C $-\frac{1}{3}$ D $\frac{5}{2}$

A and D are parallel.

A2 (a) 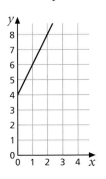   (b)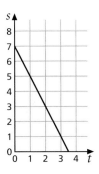

(c) 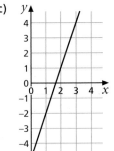   (d)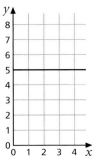

A3 (a) $4y - 24 = 0 \Rightarrow y = 6$
so the graph goes through $(0, 6)$.

(b) $3x - 24 = 0 \Rightarrow x = 8$
so the graph goes through $(8, 0)$.

A4 Sketches of straight lines going through these labelled points

(a) $(0, 4)$ and $(10, 0)$ (b) $(0, 7)$ and $(4, 0)$

(c) $(0, 2)$ and $(-4, 0)$ (d) $(0, -4)$ and $(3, 0)$

(e) $(0, -6)$ and $(-5, 0)$ (f) $(0, -1)$ and $(-5, 0)$

A5 Sketches of straight lines going through these labelled points

(a) $(0, 3)$ and $(7, 0)$ (b) $(0, -5)$ and $(-1, 0)$

(c) $(0, 4.5)$ and $(-4.5, 0)$

A6 $4x + 3y = 24$ (or an equivalent equation)

A7 (a) $y = -3x + 2$ (b) $y = \frac{1}{2}x + 3$

(c) $y = -\frac{3}{5}x + \frac{2}{5}$

A8 With gradient 3
$3x - y - 4 = 0$ $y = 3x + \frac{1}{2}$ $y = -\frac{1}{2} + 3x$

With gradient $-\frac{1}{2}$
$y = -\frac{1}{2}x + 2$ $y = 7 - \frac{1}{2}x$

With gradient -3
$y = -3x + 4$ $3x + y - 7 = 0$ $y = -2 - 3x$

A9 (a) A (gradient 1) and B (gradient -1)
C $(-\frac{3}{4})$ and D $(\frac{4}{3})$
E (3) and F $(-\frac{1}{3})$
G (-2) and H $(\frac{1}{2})$
An explanation such as:
Multiplying the two gradients together gives -1.
or:
One gradient is the negative reciprocal of the other gradient.

(b) $-\frac{3}{2}$ (c) $\frac{1}{4}$ (d) -1

A10 B and C are perpendicular.

A11 A and C, B and D, F and G

A12 Where one line is vertical and the other is horizontal.

Exercise A (p 9)

1 $\dfrac{x}{6} + \dfrac{y}{5} = 1$ and $y = -\frac{5}{6}x + 4$

2 (a) 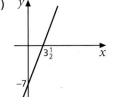   (b)

(c)

3 A, C and G with gradient $-\frac{1}{7}$
B and E with gradient $-\frac{2}{7}$
D, F and H with gradient $\frac{7}{2}$

4 (a) (i) $y = -3x - 7$ **(ii)** -3 **(iii)** -7

   (b) (i) $y = -\frac{1}{2}x + 4$ **(ii)** $-\frac{1}{2}$ **(iii)** 4

   (c) (i) $y = -\frac{4}{5}x - \frac{1}{5}$ **(ii)** $-\frac{4}{5}$ **(iii)** $-\frac{1}{5}$

   (d) (i) $y = \frac{3}{2}x - 3$ **(ii)** $\frac{3}{2}$ **(iii)** -3

   (e) (i) $y = \frac{7}{2}x - \frac{3}{2}$ **(ii)** $\frac{7}{2}$ **(iii)** $-\frac{3}{2}$

   (f) (i) $y = -\frac{2}{3}x + \frac{3}{2}$ **(ii)** $-\frac{2}{3}$ **(iii)** $\frac{3}{2}$

5 $-\dfrac{a}{b}$

6 $y = 4x + 8$ and $-8x + 2y - 7 = 0$

7 $4x + 6y + 3 = 0$ and $y = -\frac{2}{3}x$

8 $y = -\frac{1}{3}x + 2$ and $x + 3y = 1$

9 $-3x - 5y + 1 = 0$ and $y = 6 - \frac{3}{5}x$

10 AB -5, BC $\frac{1}{5}$, CA $-\frac{3}{11}$
   It has a right angle at B.

11 AB and DC $-\frac{2}{3}$, AD $\frac{3}{2}$, BC $\frac{1}{5}$
   It is a trapezium with right angles at A and D.

B Finding the equation of a linear graph (p 10)

B1   Any three points with coordinates conforming to
   $y = 3x - 1$

B2 $y = 3x - 1$

B3 (a) $y = 4x - 10$ **(b)** $y = -x + 6$ **(c)** $y = 3x + 1$
   (d) $y = \frac{1}{4}x + \frac{5}{2}$ **(e)** $y = -\frac{1}{2}x + \frac{1}{2}$

Exercise B (p 12)

1 (a) $y = 3x - 19$ **(b)** $y = \frac{1}{2}x - \frac{3}{2}$ **(c)** $y = 2x + 1$
   (d) $y = -\frac{3}{2}x + 1$

2 (a) $y = \frac{1}{3}x + 2$ **(b)** $y = -x + 3$

3 (a) $(4, 4)$ **(b)** $(1, 2)$ **(c)** $(\frac{1}{2}, -3)$

4 (a) $y = \frac{1}{2}x$ **(b)** $y = \frac{4}{3}x - 6$ **(c)** $y = -\frac{2}{5}x - \frac{12}{5}$

5 (a) (i) $(5, 7)$ **(ii)** $y = 3x - 8$
    (iii) $\sqrt{40}$ or $2\sqrt{10}$

   (b) (i) $(6, 1)$ **(ii)** $y = \frac{3}{2}x - 8$
    (iii) $\sqrt{52}$ or $2\sqrt{13}$

   (c) (i) $(-2.5, 3.5)$ **(ii)** $y = -x + 1$
    (iii) $\sqrt{18}$ or $3\sqrt{2}$

6 (a) $y = \frac{2}{3}x - \frac{1}{3}$ **(b)** $a = 8$

7 $(-4, 4.5)$

8 $y = -\frac{5}{2}x + \frac{47}{4}$ or $y = -2.5x + 11.75$

C Problem solving with linear graphs (p 12)

C1 (a) $C = 0.09E$

   (b) (and C2 (a))

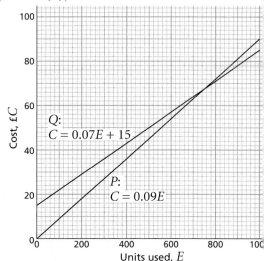

Q: $C = 0.07E + 15$

P: $C = 0.09E$

C2 (b) $C = 0.07E + 15$

   (c) £15 standing charge (or service charge) plus
    £0.07 (or 7p) for every unit of electricity used

C3 (a) P, charging £27

   (b) There is nothing to choose between them;
    they would both charge £67.50.

   (c) Q, charging £78

Exercise C (p 13)

1 (a)

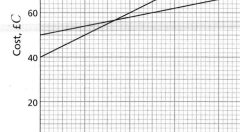

   (b) R, 750 leaflets

2 **(a)** 6 litres per second

(b) $V = 220 - 6t$

$0 = 220 - 6t \Rightarrow t = 36.7$ (to 1 d.p.)

(c) Linear graph from $(0, 220)$ to $(36.7, 0)$

(d) $V = 250 - 8t$

When the tank is empty,

$0 = 250 - 8t \Rightarrow t = 31.3$ (to 1 d.p)

Linear graph from $(0, 250)$ to $(31.3, 0)$

(e) 15 seconds from the start they will both hold 130 litres.

3 **(a)** $H = 0.3t$

(b) $H = 320 - 0.2t$

(c)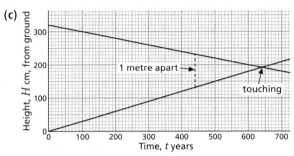

(d) About 440 years from the start

(e) They will touch after about 640 years at a point about 192 cm above the ground.

4 **(a)** Company X:

From the points $(20, 110)$, $(100, 190)$

gradient $= \frac{80}{80} = 1$

Using $y - y_1 = m(x - x_1)$ and $(20, 110)$

$C - 110 = n - 20$

$\Rightarrow C = n + 90$

Company Y:

gradient $= 2$ (because £2 per additional copy)

Using $y - y_1 = m(x - x_1)$ and $(10, 50)$

$C - 50 = 2(n - 10)$

$\Rightarrow C - 50 = 2n - 20$

$\Rightarrow C = 2n + 30$

(b) **(i)** Y (£130 instead of £140)

(ii) X (£170 instead of £190)

D Solving simultaneous linear equations

Exercise D (p 16)

1 **(a)** $p = 6, q = 1$ **(b)** $a = 2.5, b = -1.5$

(c) $h = -4, j = 3$

2 **(a)** $x = 3, y = 6$ **(b)** $x = -2, y = -3$

(c) $p = 1, q = -4$

3 **(a)** $x = \frac{1}{2}, y = \frac{5}{2}$ **(b)** $x = -4, y = 3$

(c) $x = 3, y = -5$

4 **(a)** $x = \frac{3}{2}, y = \frac{3}{2}$ **(b)** $x = \frac{3}{2}, y = 1$

(c) $t = \frac{8}{3}, s = \frac{7}{3}$

5 **(a)** $x = 5, y = -4$ **(b)** $x = -\frac{1}{2}, y = \frac{5}{2}$

(c) $x = -3, y = -2$

6 **(a)** $(6, 5)$ **(b)** $\left(\frac{5}{2}, \frac{7}{2}\right)$ **(c)** $(2, 5)$

7 **(a)** You get a nonsense statement like $2 = 6$; the two linear graphs that correspond to the equations are parallel, so do not intersect.

(b) You get a trivially true statement like $-\frac{5}{3}x - 5 = -\frac{5}{3}x - 5$; the equations are equivalent (either equation can be rearranged into the other) so both correspond to the same linear graph. This intersects itself at every point on itself.

(c) You get a nonsense statement like $-4 = 5$; the corresponding linear graphs are parallel, so do not intersect.

8 $\left(10\frac{1}{2}, 25\right)$, $(4, -1)$, $\left(-\frac{7}{8}, 2\frac{1}{4}\right)$

9 **(a)** Plumber A: $C = 40t + 40$

Plumber B: $C = 44t + 29$

(b) $2\frac{3}{4}$ hours

(c) Plumber A

10 15 seconds from the start they will both hold 130 litres.

11 They will touch 640 years from the start, at a point 192 cm from the ground.

Mixed questions (p 19)

1 A rectangle

2 **(a)** A trapezium

(b) $(5, 0)$, $(10, 0)$, $(0, 6)$, $(0, 3)$

3 **(a)** Gradient of $AB = \dfrac{5-7}{5-1} = -\dfrac{1}{2}$

Gradient of $BC = \dfrac{9-5}{7-5} = 2$

Here $m_1 m_2 = -1$ so AB and BC are perpendicular.

(b) $y = 2x - 5$

(c) (i) $y = \dfrac{1}{3}x + 5$ **(ii)** $(6, 7)$

4 (a)

(b) $(3, 2)$

(c) $4x + 3y = 28$

5 (a), (c)

(b) $y = \dfrac{4}{3}x - 7$

(d) $\left(2\dfrac{2}{5}, -3\dfrac{4}{5}\right)$

6 (a) AC: $y = \dfrac{3}{2}x - 2$
BD: $y = -\dfrac{1}{4}x + 5$
They intersect at $(4, 4)$.

(b) $(3, 6)$, $(1, 3)$, $\left(7, 1\dfrac{1}{2}\right)$, $\left(9, 4\dfrac{1}{2}\right)$

(c) Two opposite sides have gradient $\dfrac{3}{2}$.
The other two opposite sides have gradient $-\dfrac{1}{4}$.

(d) Opposite sides are parallel, so this is a parallelogram.

7 The equation of the perpendicular through the origin is $y = \dfrac{3}{4}x$. The point of intersection is $(4, 3)$. By Pythagoras, the perpendicular distance of $8x + 6y - 50 = 0$ from the origin is 5 units.

8 The points are not on the same straight line. This can be shown by finding the equation of the straight line between two of the points and showing that the third point does not satisfy it; or by calculating the gradient of the line between a pair of points and showing that it differs from the gradient of the line between a different pair.

9 (a) (i) 4 **(ii)** $\dfrac{5}{2}$

(b) $y = -\dfrac{2}{5}x - \dfrac{3}{5}$ or $2x + 5y + 3 = 0$

(c) By Pythagoras,
$AC^2 = (1 - (-6))^2 + (-1 - (-2))^2$
$= 7^2 + 1^2 = 50$
$\Rightarrow AC = \sqrt{50} = \sqrt{25} \times \sqrt{2} = 5\sqrt{2}$, which is in the form $p\sqrt{2}$, with $p = 5$.

10 (a) Through A and $(5, 7)$: $y = -x + 12$
Through B and $(6, 3)$: $y = 2x - 9$
Through C and $(10, 5)$: $y = 5$

(b) Any two of the above solved simultaneously to give the point of intersection $(7, 5)$; a check that these values of x and y satisfy the equation of the third line

11 (a) $(5, 5)$

(b) $y = \dfrac{3}{4}x + \dfrac{5}{4}$

(c) $p = 2$, $q = 13$

(d) Gradient of $AD = \dfrac{7}{1} = 7$

Gradient of $DC = \dfrac{-1}{7} = -\dfrac{1}{7}$

$7 \times -\dfrac{1}{7} = -1$, so AD and DC are perpendicular, so $\angle ADC$ is a right angle.

(e) 75 square units

Test yourself (p 21)

1 (a) $y = -5x + 4$ **(b)** $y = \dfrac{1}{2}x + 3$

(c) $y = -\dfrac{1}{2}x + \dfrac{3}{2}$ **(d)** $y = 2x + 14$

2 (a) Neither **(b)** Perpendicular

(c) Parallel **(d)** Perpendicular

3 (a) $-\dfrac{1}{4}$ **(b)** $y = -\dfrac{1}{4}x + \dfrac{7}{2}$

4 $y = \dfrac{5}{2}x$ or $5x - 2y = 0$

5 $\sqrt{13}$

6 (a) $y = 6x - 6$ **(b)** $y = -\dfrac{1}{6}x - \dfrac{1}{2}$

7 (a) $x = -1, y = 2$ **(b)** $x = -\frac{3}{10}, y = \frac{7}{10}$

(c) $x = \frac{3}{2}, y = \frac{3}{2}$ **(d)** $x = -1, y = 3$

(e) $x = \frac{15}{2}, y = \frac{3}{2}$ **(f)** $x = -6, y = -5$

8 (a) Gradient of $OA = \frac{3}{2}$

Equation of OA is $y = \frac{3}{2}x$

(b) (i) $4x + 6y = 13$

$\Rightarrow 6y = -4x + 13$

$\Rightarrow y = -\frac{2}{3}x + \frac{13}{6}$

So its gradient is $-\frac{2}{3}$.

Since $-\frac{2}{3} \times \frac{3}{2} = -1$, this line and OA are perpendicular.

(ii) The mid-point of OA is $(1, 1\frac{1}{2})$.

Solving the equations of the two lines simultaneously gives the point of intersection $(1, 1\frac{1}{2})$, which is the mid-point of OA.

9 (a) $\frac{5}{3}$

(b) (i) Gradient $= \dfrac{-2 - 4}{4 - (-6)} = \dfrac{-6}{10} = -\dfrac{3}{5}$

Since $\frac{5}{3} \times -\frac{3}{5} = -1$, AC and AB are perpendicular.

(ii) $3x + 5y = 2$

(c) $(7, 3)$

2 Surds

A Understanding surds

Exercise A (p 22)

1 (a) 7   **(b)** −9   **(c)** $\frac{1}{3}$ **(d)** 18

(e) 40   **(f)** 20   **(g)** $\frac{5}{2}$ **(h)** $\frac{5}{4}$

(i) 10   **(j)** 4   **(k)** 0.4   **(l)** 7

(m) 9   **(n)** 12   **(o)** 0.6   **(p)** 0.001

2 $\sqrt{109}$ cm

3 (a) $2\sqrt{3}$ **(b)** $4\sqrt{3}$ **(c)** $3\sqrt{3}$

(d) $9\sqrt{3}$ **(e)** $288\sqrt{3}$

4 A proof such as:

By Pythagoras, the length of a sloping edge is $\sqrt{2^2 + 5^2} = \sqrt{29}$. The perimeter is the length of the base + 2 × the length of the sloping edge, i.e. $4 + 2\sqrt{29}$.

5 Use any two adjacent points to show that the length of one edge is $\sqrt{5}$. For example, the length of the line joining $(2, 1)$ to $(4, 2)$ is

$$\sqrt{(4-2)^2 + (2-1)^2} = \sqrt{5}.$$

6 $\dfrac{4}{\sqrt{17}}$

7 $8\sqrt{3}$

B Simplifying surds (p 23)

B1 The true statements are A, B, D and F.

B2 (a) A proof such as:

$\sqrt{p^2} = p$ and $\sqrt{q^2} = q$

so $\sqrt{p^2} \times \sqrt{q^2} = pq$. Now $p^2 \times q^2 = (pq)^2$

so $\sqrt{p^2 \times q^2} = pq$.

Hence $\sqrt{p^2} \times \sqrt{q^2} = \sqrt{p^2 \times q^2}$ as required.

(b) A proof such as:

$\sqrt{p^2} = p$ and $\sqrt{q^2} = q$

so $\dfrac{\sqrt{p^2}}{\sqrt{q^2}} = \dfrac{p}{q}$. Now $\dfrac{p^2}{q^2} = \left(\dfrac{p}{q}\right)^2$ so $\sqrt{\dfrac{p^2}{q^2}} = \dfrac{p}{q}$.

Hence $\dfrac{\sqrt{p^2}}{\sqrt{q^2}} = \sqrt{\dfrac{p^2}{q^2}}$ as required.

B3 (a) One way is to use the result of the proof in B2(a) with $p = \sqrt{a}$ and $q = \sqrt{b}$

to give $\sqrt{\left(\sqrt{a}\right)^2} \times \sqrt{\left(\sqrt{b}\right)^2} = \sqrt{\left(\sqrt{a}\right)^2 \times \left(\sqrt{b}\right)^2}$,

i.e $\sqrt{a} \times \sqrt{b} = \sqrt{ab}$

(b) One way is to use the result of the proof in B2(b) with $p = \sqrt{a}$ and $q = \sqrt{b}$

to give $\dfrac{\sqrt{\left(\sqrt{a}\right)^2}}{\sqrt{\left(\sqrt{b}\right)^2}} = \sqrt{\dfrac{\left(\sqrt{a}\right)^2}{\left(\sqrt{b}\right)^2}}$,

i.e $\dfrac{\sqrt{a}}{\sqrt{b}} = \sqrt{\dfrac{a}{b}}$

B4 The easiest way is to give a counter-example such as $a = 9$ and $b = 4$, then $\sqrt{a} = 3$, $\sqrt{b} = 2$ and $\sqrt{a} + \sqrt{b} = 5$ which is not equivalent to $\sqrt{a+b} = \sqrt{13}$.

Exercise B (p 25)

1 (a) $\sqrt{10}$ **(b)** 4 **(c)** $2\sqrt{21}$ **(d)** $10\sqrt{6}$

2 (a) $2\sqrt{2}$ **(b)** $3\sqrt{6}$ **(c)** $4\sqrt{2}$ **(d)** $5\sqrt{2}$
   (e) $10\sqrt{6}$ **(f)** $15\sqrt{11}$ **(g)** $30\sqrt{2}$ **(h)** $16\sqrt{2}$

3 (a) $\sqrt{2}$ **(b)** 3 **(c)** $3\sqrt{7}$ **(d)** 6

4 (a) $\dfrac{2}{\sqrt{7}}$ **(b)** $\dfrac{\sqrt{3}}{5}$ **(c)** $\dfrac{12}{\sqrt{5}}$ **(d)** $2\sqrt{7}$ **(e)** $\dfrac{\sqrt{11}}{3}$

5 (a) (i) $2\sqrt{3}$ **(ii)** $5\sqrt{3}$
  (b) $3\sqrt{3}$

6 (a) $6\sqrt{3}$ **(b)** $\sqrt{5}$ **(c)** $13\sqrt{2}$ **(d)** $2\sqrt{2}$
  (e) 2 **(f)** $16\sqrt{3}$ **(g)** 4

7 A proof such as:
The diagonals intersect at right angles so each edge is the hypotenuse of a right-angled triangle whose shorter sides measure 7 cm and 1 cm. Hence the length of one edge is $\sqrt{7^2 + 1^2} = \sqrt{50} = 5\sqrt{2}$ cm.

8 (a) $3 + 3\sqrt{15}$ **(b)** $10\sqrt{3} - 2\sqrt{5}$

9 (a) $26\sqrt{2} - 3$ **(b)** $\sqrt{10} - 2 + \sqrt{15} - \sqrt{6}$
  (c) $9 - 14\sqrt{5}$ **(d)** $52 + 14\sqrt{3}$

10 (a) 14 **(b)** 13 **(c)** -2 **(d)** 19

11 (a) $a - b^2$ **(b)** $x^2 - y$ **(c)** $p - q$

12 Expanding the brackets gives $a^2b - c^2d$ which is a rational number for rational a, b, c and d.

C Rationalising the denominator

Exercise C (p 27)

1 (a) $\dfrac{7\sqrt{6}}{6}$ **(b)** $4\sqrt{3}$

  (c) $\dfrac{\sqrt{5}}{5}$ **(d)** $\dfrac{\sqrt{2} - \sqrt{10}}{2}$

  (e) $\dfrac{4\sqrt{6} - \sqrt{2}}{3}$

2 (a) (i) $2\sqrt{7}$ **(ii)** $3\sqrt{7}$
  (b) $5\sqrt{7}$

3 (a) $\dfrac{\sqrt{3} - 1}{2}$ **(b)** $\sqrt{6} + 1$

  (c) $\dfrac{5\sqrt{2} + 1}{7}$ **(d)** $\sqrt{10} - \sqrt{5} + 4\sqrt{2} - 4$

  (e) $2(\sqrt{5} - \sqrt{2})$ **(f)** $\dfrac{\sqrt{5} - \sqrt{3}}{2}$

  (g) $\dfrac{\sqrt{39} - 3\sqrt{3}}{4}$ **(h)** $21\sqrt{2} - 28$

  (i) $2\sqrt{2} + \sqrt{5}$ **(j)** $21 - 2\sqrt{110}$

4 $\dfrac{\sqrt{3} + 5}{3 - \sqrt{3}} = \dfrac{(\sqrt{3} + 5)(3 + \sqrt{3})}{(3 - \sqrt{3})(3 + \sqrt{3})}$

     $= \dfrac{8\sqrt{3} + 18}{6}$

     $= \dfrac{8\sqrt{3}}{6} + \dfrac{18}{6}$

     $= \tfrac{4}{3}\sqrt{3} + 3$

5 $p = \tfrac{5}{3}$, $q = \tfrac{4}{3}$

6 $a = -4$, $b = 3$

7 $\dfrac{1}{3\sqrt{2} - 4} = \tfrac{3}{2}\sqrt{2} + 2 > 2$

8 (a) (i) $4\sqrt{3} - \sqrt{33}$ **(ii)** $2\sqrt{33} - 2\sqrt{11}$
  (b) $4\sqrt{3} - 2\sqrt{11} + \sqrt{33}$

9 (a) $\sqrt{14} + 4\sqrt{7} + 9\sqrt{2}$ **(b)** $\sqrt{15} + 2\sqrt{5} + \sqrt{3}$
  (c) $2\sqrt{2} - \sqrt{3}$

10 $5\sqrt{7} - 10$

11 $\sqrt{2} + \tfrac{1}{3}\sqrt{3}$ or $\sqrt{2} + \dfrac{1}{\sqrt{3}}$

12 $\dfrac{2\sqrt{3} + 3\sqrt{2} - \sqrt{30}}{12}$ or $\tfrac{1}{6}\sqrt{3} + \tfrac{1}{4}\sqrt{2} - \tfrac{1}{12}\sqrt{30}$

D Further problems

Exercise D (p 29)

1 $4\sqrt{5}$

2 26

3 63π

4 A proof such as:

   $XY^2 + XZ^2 = (2\sqrt{3})^2 + (\sqrt{13})^2 = 12 + 13 = 25$
   Also $YZ^2 = 5^2 = 25$
   Hence $XY^2 + XZ^2 = YZ^2$ and so triangle XYZ is right-angled.

5 $2\sqrt{7}\,\pi$

6 $(\sqrt{2} - 1, 11 - \sqrt{2})$

7 A proof such as:

   Let r be the radius of the whole circle.

   The area of the quarter-circle is $\dfrac{\pi r^2}{4} = 6\pi$

   so $\dfrac{r^2}{4} = 6$. Hence $r^2 = 24$, giving $r = \sqrt{24} = 2\sqrt{6}$.

   Then the perimeter of the whole circle is

   $r + r + \dfrac{2\pi r}{4} = 2r + \dfrac{\pi r}{2}$

   $= 2 \times 2\sqrt{6} + \dfrac{\pi \times 2\sqrt{6}}{2} = 4\sqrt{6} + \pi\sqrt{6}$

   $= \sqrt{6}\,(4 + \pi)$, as required.

8 A proof such as:

   Let r be the radius of the whole circle.

   The area of the circle is $\pi r^2 = 50$ so
   $r^2 = \dfrac{50}{\pi}$. Hence $r = \sqrt{\dfrac{50}{\pi}} = \dfrac{5\sqrt{2}}{\sqrt{\pi}} = 5\sqrt{\dfrac{2}{\pi}}$,
   as required.

   The circumference of the circle is

   $2\pi r = 2\pi \times 5\sqrt{\dfrac{2}{\pi}} = 10\pi \times \dfrac{\sqrt{2}}{\sqrt{\pi}} = 10\sqrt{\pi}\sqrt{2} = 10\sqrt{2\pi}$,
   as required.

9 (a) $\sqrt{5}(2 + \pi)\,\text{cm}$ (b) $(\frac{5}{2}\pi - 4)\,\text{cm}^2$

10 A proof such as:

   Let r be the radius of the whole circle.

   By Pythagoras, $r^2 + r^2 = 100$ so $r^2 = 50$ and
   $r = \sqrt{50} = 5\sqrt{2}$.

   Then the perimeter of the quarter-circle is

   $r + r + \frac{1}{4}(2\pi r) = 2r + \frac{1}{2}\pi r$

   $= 2 \times 5\sqrt{2} + \frac{1}{2}(\pi \times 5\sqrt{2}) = 5\sqrt{2}(2 + \frac{1}{2}\pi)$ as required.

Test yourself (p 31)

1 By Pythagoras,
   $AB^2 = (4 - -2)^2 + (1 - -1)^2 = 6^2 + 2^2 = 40$.
   So $AB = \sqrt{40} = 2\sqrt{10}$, which is in the form $p\sqrt{10}$
   with $p = 2$.

2 (a) (i) $3\sqrt{5}$ (ii) $4\sqrt{5}$
   (b) $7\sqrt{5}$

3 (a) (i) $AB = \sqrt{8}, BC = \sqrt{72}, AC = \sqrt{80}$
       (ii) $AB^2 + BC^2 = 8 + 72 = 80$
          Also $AC^2 = 80$
          Hence $AB^2 + BC^2 = AC^2$ and so triangle
          ABC is right-angled.
   (b) 12

4 (a) $4 + \sqrt{3}$ (b) $8 + 2\sqrt{3}$

5 (a) $8 + 2\sqrt{7}$ (b) $-\frac{2}{3} + \frac{4}{3}\sqrt{7}$

6 A proof such as:

   Let X be the midpoint of BC.

   Triangle ABC is equilateral so $\angle AXB = 90°$ and, by
   Pythagoras, $AX^2 = 8^2 - 4^2 = 64 - 16 = 48$.

   So $AX = \sqrt{48} = 4\sqrt{3}$ cm and the area of triangle
   ABC is $4 \times 4\sqrt{3} = 16\sqrt{3}$ cm^2.

   As triangle ABC is equilateral, $\angle BAC = 60°$ and
   the area of the sector is $\frac{1}{6}\pi \times 8^2 = \frac{64}{6}\pi = \frac{32}{3}\pi$ cm^2.

   So the shaded area is
   $\frac{32}{3}\pi - 16\sqrt{3} = 16(\frac{2}{3}\pi - \sqrt{3})$ cm^2, as required.

3 Quadratic graphs and equations

A Expanding brackets: revision

Exercise A (p 32)

1 (a) $12x - 21$ **(b)** $2x^2 + 10x$
(c) $-3x^2 + x$

2 (a) $x^2 + 11x + 30$ **(b)** $x^2 + 2x - 15$
(c) $2x^2 - 7x + 5$ **(d)** $-3x^2 + 20x + 7$
(e) $x^2 - 8x + 12$ **(f)** $3x^2 + 9x - 120$
(g) $-12x^2 + 64x - 84$ **(h)** $x^2 - 4$
(i) $16x^2 - 9$ **(j)** $x^2 + 6x + 9$
(k) $2x^2 + 44x + 242$ **(l)** $x^2 - 12x + 36$

3 (a) $x^2 + ax + bx + ab$ **(b)** $x^2 + 2ax + a^2$
(c) $kx^2 + 2akx + ka^2$ **(d)** $x^2 - a^2$
(e) $a^2x^2 + 2abx + b^2$ **(f)** $a^2x^2 - b^2$

B Factorising quadratic expressions: revision

Exercise B (p 34)

1 (a) $x(5 + x)$ **(b)** $x(x - 10)$
(c) $3x(x - 2)$ **(d)** $2x(2x + 5)$
(e) $6x(2 + 3x)$ **(f)** $x(9 - x)$
(g) $3x(5 - 3x)$ **(h)** $x(-x + 7)$

2 (a) $(x + 1)(x + 5)$ **(b)** $(x - 1)(x - 5)$
(c) $(x + 3)^2$ **(d)** $(x + 1)(x + 9)$
(e) $(x - 3)(x - 6)$ **(f)** $(x - 3)(x + 7)$
(g) $(x + 3)(x - 4)$ **(h)** $(x + 1)(x - 15)$
(i) $(x - 5)^2$

3 (a) $(2x + 3)(x + 1)$ **(b)** $(3x + 1)(x + 5)$
(c) $(5x - 3)(x - 1)$ **(d)** $(3x + 1)(x - 7)$
(e) $3(2x - 1)(x + 5)$ **(f)** $(3x + 2)(x + 3)$
(g) $(3x + 1)(x + 6)$ **(h)** $2(2x - 3)(x - 4)$
(i) $(3x + 2)(x - 8)$ **(j)** $(2x - 1)^2$
(k) $(6x + 1)(x - 5)$ **(l)** $(5x - 12)(2x - 1)$

4 (a) $(x + 3)(x - 3)$ **(b)** $(x + 10)(x - 10)$
(c) $(x + 1)(x - 1)$ **(d)** $(2x + 5)(2x - 5)$
(e) $(3x + 1)(3x - 1)$ **(f)** $2(4 + 5x)(4 - 5x)$

5 (a) $(2x + 3)(x - 3)$
(b) Not possible
(c) $2(x + 5)(x - 6)$
(d) Not possible
(e) $3(2x + 5)(x - 1)$
(f) $(4x + 1)(4x - 3)$
(g) $(-x - 5)(x - 3)$ or $-(x + 5)(x - 3)$ or $(x + 5)(3 - x)$
(h) $(6x + 5)(6x - 5)$
(i) $(-2x - 9)(x - 5)$ or $-(2x + 9)(x - 5)$ or $(2x + 9)(5 - x)$

6 (a) Yes, the value is $144 = 12^2$.
(b) $x^2 + 10x + 25 = (x + 5)^2$, which is always a square number

7 (a) (i) 56   **(ii)** $56 = 7 \times 8$
(b) $x^2 + 3x + 2 = (x + 1)(x + 2)$.
As $(x + 1) + 1 = (x + 2)$, this is the product of two consecutive numbers.

8 (a) Yes, the value is $121 = 11^2$ and 121 is an odd number.
(b) $16x^2 - 8x + 1 = (4x - 1)^2$ is a square number. $4x$ is always even so $(4x - 1)$ is odd. Any odd number squared will be an odd number itself. So the expression will give an odd square number.

9 (a) (i) 99   **(ii)** $99 = 9 \times 11$
(b) $4x^2 - 1 = (2x - 1)(2x + 1)$.
$2x$ is always even so $(2x - 1)$ and $(2x + 1)$ are odd. Also $(2x - 1) + 2 = 2x + 1$ so the numbers are consecutive odd numbers.

C Parabolas (p 35)

C1 Comments such as:
Every graph is basically the same shape though, when x is negative, the graphs are 'upside down'. The shape is an open curve which has a vertical line of symmetry. The coefficient of x^2 affects how shallow or steep the curve shape is. The coefficient of x affects where the curve is positioned on the coordinate grid. The constant gives the y-intercept.

C2 (a) Each parabola shares the point $(0, 0)$.
The graph of $y = 2x^2$ can be obtained from $y = x^2$ by a stretch of scale factor 2 in the direction of the y-axis.
The graph of $y = \frac{1}{3}x^2$ can be obtained from $y = x^2$ by a stretch of scale factor $\frac{1}{3}$ in the direction of the y-axis.

(b) Each parabola shares the point $(0, 0)$.
The graph of $y = kx^2$ can be obtained from $y = x^2$ by a stretch of scale factor k in the direction of the y-axis.
When k is negative this has the effect of reflecting the graph in the x-axis as well as stretching it.

C3 The graph of $y = x^2 + q$ can be obtained from $y = x^2$ by a vertical translation of q units (up if q is positive and down when q is negative).

C4 The graph of $y = (x + p)^2$ can be obtained from $y = x^2$ by a horizontal translation of $-p$ units (left if p is positive and right when p is negative).

C5 (a) $(-5, 2)$

(b) $x = -5$

(c) (i) $(x + 5)^2 + 2 = x^2 + 10x + 25 + 2$
$\qquad = x^2 + 10x + 27$ as required

(ii) $(0, 27)$

C6 The graph of $y = (x + p)^2 + q$ can be obtained from $y = x^2$ by a horizontal translation of $-p$ units followed by a vertical translation of q units, i.e. by $\begin{bmatrix} -p \\ q \end{bmatrix}$.

C7 $(6, 9)$

C8 $x = -4$

C9 The graph of $y = 2(x + p)^2 + q$ can be obtained from $y = 2x^2$ by a horizontal translation of $-p$ units followed by a vertical translation of q units, i.e. by $\begin{bmatrix} -p \\ q \end{bmatrix}$.

C10 The graph of $y = k(x + p)^2 + q$ can be obtained from $y = kx^2$ by a horizontal translation of $-p$ units followed by a vertical translation of q units, i.e. by $\begin{bmatrix} -p \\ q \end{bmatrix}$.

C11 (a) (i) $(2, -5)$ **(ii)** $x = 2$

(b) (i) $3(x - 2)^2 - 5$
$\qquad = 3(x^2 - 4x + 4) - 5$
$\qquad = 3x^2 - 12x + 12 - 5$
$\qquad = 3x^2 - 12x + 7$

(ii) $(0, 7)$

C12 $y = (x - 6)^2 + 5$ or $y = x^2 - 12x + 41$

C13 $y = 2(x + 3)^2 + 2$ or $y = 2x^2 + 12x + 20$

C14 9 units to the right and 7 units up, i.e. $\begin{bmatrix} 9 \\ 7 \end{bmatrix}$

C15 1 unit to the left and 6 units down, i.e. $\begin{bmatrix} -1 \\ -6 \end{bmatrix}$

Exercise C (p 38)

All translations are given as column vectors.

1 $\begin{bmatrix} 4 \\ -5 \end{bmatrix}$

2 $\begin{bmatrix} -8 \\ 1 \end{bmatrix}$

3 $(5, 7)$

4 $x = -2$

5 (a) (i) $y = x^2 + 14x + 44$

(ii) 44

(b) Sketch of a parabola with a vertex of $(-7, -5)$ and a y-intercept of 44

6 (a) Sketch of a parabola with a vertex of $(2, 5)$ and a y-intercept of 9

(b) Sketch of a parabola with a vertex of $(4, 0)$ and a y-intercept of 16

(c) Sketch of a parabola with a vertex of $(-6, -20)$ and a y-intercept of 16

7 The graph is a parabola that is open at the top with a vertex of $(-3, 1)$, which is above the x-axis. Hence the whole graph is above the x-axis and does not cross it.

8 (a) $y = (x - 3)^2 + 1$ or $y = x^2 - 6x + 10$

(b) $y = (x + 4)^2 + 2$ or $y = x^2 + 8x + 18$

(c) $y = (x - 3)^2 - 2$ or $y = x^2 - 6x + 7$

9 (a) (i) $\begin{bmatrix} -1 \\ -3 \end{bmatrix}$ **(ii)** $(-1, -3)$

(b) $y = 2x^2 + 4x - 1$

(c) Sketch of a parabola with a vertex of $(-1, -3)$, a y-intercept of -1 and the axis of symmetry $x = -1$

10 (a) Sketch of a parabola with a vertex of $(-4, 1)$ and a y-intercept of 33

(b) Sketch of a parabola with a vertex of $(2, -7)$ and a y-intercept of 5

(c) Sketch of a parabola with a vertex of $(-1, -3)$ and a y-intercept of 1

11 (a) (i) $\begin{bmatrix} -2 \\ 5 \end{bmatrix}$ **(ii)** $(-2, 5)$

(b)

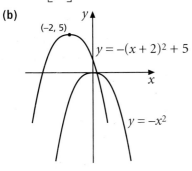

(c) 1

12 (a) $-2(x - 3)^2 + 11$
$$= -2(x^2 - 6x + 9) + 11$$
$$= -2x^2 + 12x - 18 + 11$$
$$= -2x^2 + 12x - 7$$

(b) Sketch of a parabola with a vertex of $(3, 11)$ and a y-intercept of -7

13 $y = 3(x - 8)^2 + 1$ or $y = 3x^2 - 48x + 193$

14 $y = -4(x + 5)^2 - 3$ or $y = -4x^2 - 40x - 103$

15 (a) $y = 2(x - 1)^2 + 5$ or $y = 2x^2 - 4x + 3$

(b) $y = \frac{1}{2}(x + 4)^2 - 1$ or $y = \frac{1}{2}x^2 + 4x + 7$

(c) $y = -3(x - 1)^2 - 5$ or $y = -3x^2 + 6x - 8$

D Completing the square (p 40)

D1 (a) $x^2 + 8x + 16$ **(b)** $x^2 - 18x + 81$

(c) $x^2 + 40x + 400$ **(d)** $x^2 - 2x + 1$

(e) $x^2 + \frac{1}{2}x + \frac{1}{16}$ **(f)** $x^2 - \frac{2}{3}x + \frac{1}{9}$

D2 A $(x + 5)^2$,   C $(x - 8)^2$,   F $(x - 6)^2$,   G $(x + \frac{1}{2})^2$

D3 (a) 49   **(b)** 22   **(c)** 16

D4 (a) $x^2 + 10x$ **(b)** $x^2 + 6x$

(c) $x^2 - 6x$ **(d)** $x^2 - 14x$

D5 (a) $(x + 3)^2$

(b) $(x + 3)^2 - 9$

(c) $(x + 3)^2 - 4$

(d) Sketch of a parabola with a vertex of $(-3, -4)$ and a y-intercept of 5

D6 (a) $(x - 7)^2 - 49$

(b) $(x - 7)^2 + 1$

(c) Sketch of a parabola with a vertex of $(7, 1)$ and a y-intercept of 50

D7 (a) $(x + 7)^2 - 47$ **(b)** $(x - 3)^2 + 3$

(c) $(x + 4)^2 - 19$

D8 (a) $(x + 1)^2 - 5$

(b) Sketch of a parabola with a vertex of $(-1, -5)$ and a y-intercept of -4

D9 (a) $(x + 9)^2 + 1$

(b) $(x + 9)^2 \geq 0$ for all values of x so $(x + 9)^2 + 1 > 0$

D10 (a) $(x + 2)^2 + 7$

(b) (i) $(x + 2)^2 \geq 0$ for all values of x so $(x + 2)^2 + 7 \geq 7$ so 7 is the minimum value.

(ii) $x = -2$

D11 (a) $x^2 - x + \frac{1}{4}$

(b) $(x - \frac{1}{2})^2 - \frac{1}{4}$

(c) $(x - \frac{1}{2})^2 - 5\frac{1}{4}$ or $(x - \frac{1}{2})^2 - \frac{21}{4}$

D12 (a) $(x + 1\frac{1}{2})^2 - 1\frac{1}{4}$ or $(x + \frac{3}{2})^2 - \frac{5}{4}$

(b) $(x + 2\frac{1}{2})^2 + 3\frac{3}{4}$ or $(x + \frac{5}{2})^2 + \frac{15}{4}$

(c) $(x - 4\frac{1}{2})^2 - 23\frac{1}{4}$ or $(x - \frac{9}{2})^2 - \frac{93}{4}$

D13 (a) $(x - \frac{1}{2})^2 + 1\frac{1}{2}$

(b) $(x - \frac{1}{2})^2 \geq 0$ for all values of x so $(x - \frac{1}{2})^2 + 1\frac{1}{2} \geq 1\frac{1}{2}$ so $1\frac{1}{2}$ is the minimum value

D14 **(a)** $3(x-2)^2 - 16$

(b) Sketch of a parabola with a vertex of $(2, -16)$ and a y-intercept of -4

D15 **(a)** $2(x+4)^2 + 8$

(b) $3(x-3)^2 - 28$

(c) $2(x + \frac{5}{2})^2 - 20\frac{1}{2}$ or $2(x + \frac{5}{2})^2 - \frac{41}{2}$

Exercise D (p 42)

1 **(a)** $(x+3)^2 + 1$

(b) $(x-5)^2 - 22$

(c) $(x+9)^2 - 83$

(d) $(x-2)^2 + 9$

(e) $(x + 1\frac{1}{2})^2 - 3\frac{1}{4}$ or $(x + \frac{3}{2})^2 - \frac{13}{4}$

(f) $(x - 2\frac{1}{2})^2 + 2\frac{3}{4}$ or $(x - \frac{5}{2})^2 + \frac{11}{4}$

2 **(a)** One way is to multiply out the brackets to give $(x-6)^2 + 5 = x^2 - 12x + 36 + 5 = x^2 - 12x + 41$.

(b) $(6, 5)$

(c) When $x = 0$, $y = 0^2 - 12 \times 0 + 41 = 41$ so the graph crosses the y-axis at $(0, 41)$.

3 **(a)** **(i)** $(x+3)^2 + 6$

(ii) Sketch of a parabola with a vertex of $(-3, 6)$ and a y-intercept of 15

(b) **(i)** $(x+4)^2 - 18$

(ii) Sketch of a parabola with a vertex of $(-4, -18)$ and a y-intercept of -2

(c) **(i)** $(x-1)^2 + 4$

(ii) Sketch of a parabola with a vertex of $(1, 4)$ and a y-intercept of 5

(d) **(i)** $(x-2)^2 - 7$

(ii) Sketch of a parabola with a vertex of $(2, -7)$ and a y-intercept of -3

(e) **(i)** $(x + \frac{3}{2})^2 + \frac{19}{4}$

(ii) Sketch of a parabola with a vertex of $(-\frac{3}{2}, \frac{19}{4})$ and a y-intercept of 7

(f) **(i)** $(x - \frac{7}{2})^2 - \frac{57}{4}$

(ii) Sketch of a parabola with a vertex of $(\frac{7}{2}, -\frac{57}{4})$ and a y-intercept of -2

4 In completed-square form, the equation is $y = (x-3)^2 + 4$, so the vertex is $(3, 4)$ and the minimum value for y is 4. Hence the graph is completely above the x-axis and does not cross it.

5 **(a)** $(x+1)^2 + 4$

(b) **(i)** $(x+1)^2 \geq 0$ for all x, so $(x+1)^2 + 4 \geq 4$ and so the minimum value is 4.

(ii) $x = -1$

6 In completed-square form, the equation is $y = (x+2)^2 - 3$ so the vertex is $(-2, -3)$. Hence the graph is partially below the x-axis and so crosses it twice.

7 **(a)** $(x+6)^2 - 25$ which is the form $(x+a)^2 + b$ with $a = 6$ and $b = -25$

(b) -25

8 In completed-square form, the equation is $y = (x+2)^2$, so the vertex is $(-2, 0)$ which is on the x-axis. Hence the graph just touches the x-axis.

9 **(a)** $2(x+1)^2 - 3$ **(b)** $3(x-2)^2 + 1$

(c) $5(x-1)^2 - 6$ **(d)** $2(x+4)^2$

(e) $3(x + \frac{1}{2})^2 + \frac{17}{4}$ **(f)** $4(x - \frac{3}{2})^2 - 14$

10 **(a)** $3(x+2)^2 - 19$
$= 3(x^2 + 4x + 4) - 19$
$= 3x^2 + 12x + 12 - 19$
$= 3x^2 + 12x - 7$

(b) $(-2, -19)$

(c) When $x = 0$, $y = 3 \times 0^2 + 12 \times 0 - 7 = -7$ so the graph crosses the y-axis at $(0, -7)$.

(d) $x = -2$

11 **(a)** **(i)** $y = 2(x-3)^2 + 3$

(ii) Sketch of a parabola with a vertex of $(3, 3)$ and a y-intercept of 21

(b) **(i)** $y = 3(x+1)^2$

(ii) Sketch of a parabola with a vertex of $(-1, 0)$ and a y-intercept of 3

(c) **(i)** $y = 4(x + \frac{1}{2})^2 + 2$

(ii) Sketch of a parabola with a vertex of $(-\frac{1}{2}, 2)$ and a y-intercept of 3

12 $5x^2 - 20x + 24 = 5(x - 2)^2 + 4$, so the minimum value of y is 4. So the graph does not cross the x-axis.

13 (a) (i) $3(x + 3)^2 - 2$ **(ii)** -2
     (iii) $x = -3$

   (b) (i) $2(x - 1)^2 + 3$ **(ii)** 3
     (iii) $x = 1$

   (c) (i) $2(x + \frac{7}{2})^2 - \frac{47}{2}$ **(ii)** $-\frac{47}{2}$
     (iii) $x = -\frac{7}{2}$

14 (a) $2(x + 2)^2 - 1$

   (b) (i) -1 **(ii)** $x = -2$

15 (a) $d = (t - 4)^2 + 3$ **(b)** $3\,\text{km}$

   (c) 4 hours

16 (a) $2(x + \frac{3}{4})^2 - \frac{1}{8}$ **(b)** $3(x - \frac{1}{2})^2 - \frac{11}{4}$
   (c) $4(x - \frac{3}{8})^2 - \frac{25}{16}$

17 (a) $-2(x + 1)^2 + 5 = -2(x^2 + 2x + 1) + 5$
           $= -2x^2 - 4x - 2 + 5 = -2x^2 - 4x + 3$

   (b) $(-1, 5)$

   (c) 3

   (d) Sketch of a parabola with a vertex of $(-1, 5)$ and a y-intercept of 3

18 (a) (i) $y = -(x + 3)^2 + 10$
     (ii) Sketch of a parabola with a vertex of $(-3, 10)$ and a y-intercept of 1

   (b) (i) $y = -(x - 4)^2 + 19$
     (ii) Sketch of a parabola with a vertex of $(4, 19)$ and a y-intercept of 3

   (c) (i) $y = -2(x + 3)^2 - 7$
     (ii) Sketch of a parabola with a vertex of $(-3, -7)$ and a y-intercept of -25

19 (a) 1   **(b)** 5

20 (a) $h = -5(t - 3)^2 + 45$ **(b)** 45 metres
   (c) 3 seconds

E Zeros of quadratics

Exercise E (p 46)

1 (a) $x = 0, 4$ **(b)** $x = 0, -2$ **(c)** $x = -1, -6$
   (d) $x = 3$ **(e)** $x = -2, 8$ **(f)** $x = 3, 6$
   (g) $x = \frac{1}{2}, -3$ **(h)** $x = -\frac{2}{3}, 1$ **(i)** $x = \frac{3}{2}, -7$
   (j) $x = \frac{6}{5}, 2$ **(k)** $x = \frac{1}{3}, -12$ **(l)** $x = \frac{5}{2}$

2 (a) $(-4, 0), (3, 0)$ **(b)** $(1, 0), (8, 0)$
   (c) $(-6, 0), (-\frac{1}{2}, 0)$ **(d)** $(-7, 0), (\frac{2}{3}, 0)$
   (e) $(0, 0), (7, 0)$ **(f)** $(-3, 0), (3, 0)$
   (g) $(1, 0), (3, 0)$ **(h)** $(-5, 0)$
   (i) $(-2, 0), (4, 0)$

3 (a) $y = x^2 - 5x + 4$ **(b)** $y = x^2 - 4$
   (c) $y = x^2 - 3x$

4 (a) $(-5, 0), (1, 0)$
   (b) $(0, -5)$
   (c) (i) $(x + 2)^2 - 9$ **(ii)** $(-2, -9)$
   (d) Sketch of a parabola with a vertex of $(-2, -9)$ that cuts the axes at $(-5, 0)$, $(1, 0)$ and $(0, -5)$

5 (a) Sketch of a parabola with a vertex of $(5, -9)$ that cuts the axes at $(2, 0)$, $(8, 0)$ and $(0, 16)$
   (b) Sketch of a parabola with a vertex of $(-7, -9)$ that cuts the axes at $(-10, 0)$, $(-4, 0)$ and $(0, 40)$
   (c) Sketch of a parabola with a vertex of $(\frac{7}{2}, -\frac{9}{4})$ that cuts the axes at $(2, 0)$, $(5, 0)$ and $(0, 10)$
   (d) Sketch of a parabola with a vertex of $(-3, -48)$ that cuts the axes at $(-7, 0)$, $(1, 0)$ and $(0, -21)$
   (e) Sketch of a parabola with a vertex of $(-\frac{3}{2}, -\frac{25}{2})$ that cuts the axes at $(-4, 0)$, $(1, 0)$ and $(0, -8)$
   (f) Sketch of a parabola with a vertex of $(-\frac{1}{2}, \frac{81}{4})$ that cuts the axes at $(-5, 0)$, $(4, 0)$ and $(0, 20)$

6 (a) $y = 2x^2 - 8x + 6$ **(b)** $y = -x^2 + x + 6$
   (c) $y = 3x^2 - 21x + 30$

F Solving quadratic equations by completing the square

Exercise F (p 47)

1 (a) $x = 3 - \sqrt{2},\ 3 + \sqrt{2}$

(b) $x = -5 - \sqrt{11},\ -5 + \sqrt{11}$

(c) $x = 6 - \sqrt{6},\ 6 + \sqrt{6}$

2 (a) $(x + 5)^2 - 2$ (b) $x = -5 - \sqrt{2},\ -5 + \sqrt{2}$

3 (a) $x = -2 - \sqrt{3},\ -2 + \sqrt{3}$

(b) $x = -1 - 2\sqrt{2},\ -1 + 2\sqrt{2}$

(c) $x = 3 - \sqrt{11},\ 3 + \sqrt{11}$

(d) $x = \frac{5}{2} - \frac{1}{2}\sqrt{29},\ \frac{5}{2} + \frac{1}{2}\sqrt{29}$

(e) $x = -3 - \sqrt{6},\ -3 + \sqrt{6}$

(f) $x = \frac{5}{2} - \frac{1}{2}\sqrt{15},\ \frac{5}{2} + \frac{1}{2}\sqrt{15}$

4 (a) $(-1 - \sqrt{5}, 0),\ (-1 + \sqrt{5}, 0)$

(b) $(2 - \sqrt{3}, 0),\ (2 + \sqrt{3}, 0)$

(c) $(\frac{7}{2} - \frac{1}{2}\sqrt{31}, 0),\ (\frac{7}{2} + \frac{1}{2}\sqrt{31}, 0)$

5 (a) $(x + 2)^2 + 6$

(b) You end up with the square root of a negative number. So the equation has no real roots, relating to the fact that the graph doesn't cross the x-axis.

G Solving quadratic equations by using the formula

Exercise G (p 49)

1 (a) $x = \dfrac{-5 - \sqrt{13}}{6},\ \dfrac{-5 + \sqrt{13}}{6}$

(b) $x = 1 - \sqrt{3},\ 1 + \sqrt{3}$

(c) $x = \dfrac{4 - \sqrt{10}}{2},\ \dfrac{4 + \sqrt{10}}{2}$ or

$x = 2 - \frac{1}{2}\sqrt{10},\ 2 + \frac{1}{2}\sqrt{10}$

2 (a) $x = -5.541, 0.541$ (b) $x = 0.634, 2.366$

(c) $x = -0.540, 0.740$

3 $(1.55, 0),\ (6.45, 0)$

4 (a) You end up with an expression that involves $\sqrt{-16}$ so the equation has no real roots.

(b) The graph does not cross the x-axis.

5 (a) You end up with an expression that involves $\sqrt{0}$ so the equation has just one (repeated) root.

(b) The graph just touches the x-axis.

6 c must be less than 9.

7 c must be equal to 1.

8 b must be greater than −8 but less than 8.

H Using the discriminant (p 50)

H1 If the discriminant is the square of a whole number or a fraction, then the expression will factorise. The roots of the equation are rational numbers.

Exercise H (p 50)

1 The discriminant is 52 which is larger than 0 so the equation has real roots.

2 Equations B, C and F have real roots. The values of the discriminants are 13, 40 and 21 respectively.

3 Equations A and B can be solved by factorising. The values of the discriminants are 49 ($= 7^2$) and 169 ($= 13^2$) respectively.

4 (a) $x = 2, 7$

(b) $x = 4 - \sqrt{2},\ 4 + \sqrt{2}$

(c) $x = \frac{1}{3}$

(d) No real solutions

(e) $x = \frac{1}{2}, 2$

(f) $x = -5 - \sqrt{22},\ -5 + \sqrt{22}$

5 (a) Crosses the x-axis at two points

(b) Touches the x-axis at one point

(c) Crosses the x-axis at two points

(d) Crosses the x-axis at two points

(e) Does not cross the x-axis

(f) Crosses the x-axis at two points

6 (a) $k = -20, 20$ (b) $k = 36$ (c) $k = -4, 4$

7 $k = 2, 6$

8 The discriminant is $4k^2 + 12$ which is positive for all values of k. So the equation will always have two distinct roots.

9 (a) $(2(a-3))^2 = 2(a-3) \times 2(a-3)$
$= 4(a-3)^2 = 4(a^2 - 6a + 9)$
$= 4a^2 - 24a + 36$

(b) $k = 1, 10$

Test yourself (p 52)

1 (a) $(x-6)^2 + 4$ **(b)** 4

2 (a) $(x+5)^2 - 5$

(b) Sketch of a parabola with a vertex of $(-5, -5)$ and y-intercept of 20

3 (a) $3(x-1)^2 + 7$ **(b)** $x = 1$

4 (a) $(x + \frac{5}{2})^2 - \frac{21}{4}$

(b) $\begin{bmatrix} -\frac{5}{2} \\ -\frac{21}{4} \end{bmatrix}$

5 (a) $(x-4)^2 - 12$

(b) $x = 4 - 2\sqrt{3},\ 4 + 2\sqrt{3}$

6 $x = \dfrac{-7 - \sqrt{17}}{4}, \dfrac{-7 + \sqrt{17}}{4}$

7 (a) $y = x^2 + 6x + 10$ **(b)** $y = x^2 - 4x + 4$

(c) $y = x^2 - 2x + 6$

8 (a) $x = -8 - \frac{3}{2}\sqrt{2},\ -8 + \frac{3}{2}\sqrt{2}$

(b) (i) $2(x+8)^2 - 9$ **(ii)** -9

9 (a) $4(x-4)^2 - 60$

(b) $(4, -60)$

(c) Sketch of a parabola with a vertex of $(4, -60)$ that cuts the axes at $(4 - \sqrt{15}, 0)$, $(4 + \sqrt{15}, 0)$ and $(0, 4)$

10 (a) -31 **(b)** No real roots

11 8

12 $k = \frac{4}{9}, 4$

13 $y = -\frac{1}{2}x^2 - 4x - 7$

4 Further equations

A Rearranging to solve equations: revision

Exercise A (p 55)

1 (a) $x = 0, 8$

(b) $x = -5, 3$

(c) $x = -2, 6$

(d) $x = \frac{30}{7}$

(e) $x = 2, 3$

(f) $x = \frac{3}{5}, 4$

(g) $x = \dfrac{-1 - \sqrt{61}}{6}, \dfrac{-1 + \sqrt{61}}{6}$

(h) $x = -1, \frac{5}{12}$

(i) $x = \dfrac{5 - \sqrt{33}}{4}, \dfrac{5 + \sqrt{33}}{4}$

2 (a) $x = -3, 2$

(b) $x = -3 - \sqrt{14}, -3 + \sqrt{14}$

(c) $x = -9, 1$

(d) $x = -5, \frac{3}{2}$

(e) $x = 2 - \sqrt{6}, 2 + \sqrt{6}$

(f) $x = -9, -\frac{1}{4}$

(g) $x = 7$

(h) $x = 5$

(i) $x = -3 - \sqrt{2}, -3 + \sqrt{2}$

(j) $x = \frac{9}{2}, -5$

(k) $x = -8$

(l) $x = \dfrac{9 - \sqrt{57}}{4}, \dfrac{9 + \sqrt{57}}{4}$

3 (a) $x = -1.732, 1.732$ **(b)** $x = -1.207, 0.207$

(c) $x = -0.434, 0.768$ **(d)** $x = -2.220, -0.180$

(e) $x = 0.316$ **(f)** $x = -8.243, 0.243$

B Solving problems

Exercise B (p 57)

1 $38.627\,\mathrm{m}$

2 $(-1, -\frac{3}{2}), (6, 2)$

3 $(-4, 28), (\frac{1}{2}, 1)$

4 (a) A proof such as:

'Where the graphs intersect the x-values satisfy the equation $x^2 - x - 1 = x + 1$. This rearranges to give $x^2 - 2x - 2 = 0$. Completing the square leads to $(x - 1)^2 - 3 = 0$ and $x = 1 \pm \sqrt{3}$. So $x = 1 - \sqrt{3}$ is one solution and the corresponding value of y is $1 - \sqrt{3} + 1 = 2 - \sqrt{3}$. Hence one of the points is $(1 - \sqrt{3}, 2 - \sqrt{3})$.'

(b) $(1 + \sqrt{3}, 2 + \sqrt{3})$

5 $x = \dfrac{1 + \sqrt{5}}{2}$

6 (a) $p(60 - 6p)$ or $60p - 6p^2$

(b) Solving the equation $60p - 6p^2 = 80$ leads to two solutions which correspond to profits per radio of £8.42 and £1.58. She could choose either. The lower profit might give more reliable sales. Alternatively, if she had limited space on her stall, she might prefer to sell fewer at a higher margin.

(c) No, she couldn't. One way to show that this is not possible is to show that there are no real solutions to the equation $60p - 6p^2 = 200$. The equation rearranges to $3p^2 - 30p + 100 = 0$ and the discriminant is -300 which is less than zero. Hence there are no real solutions to the equation.

C Solving simultaneous equations by substitution

Exercise C (p 59)

1 (a) $x = -7, y = 49$
$x = 1, y = 1$

(b) $x = -2, y = -1$
$x = 5, y = 6$

(c) $x = \frac{3}{4}, y = 5\frac{9}{16}$
$x = -1, y = 6$

(d) $x = -3, y = -1$
$x = 1, y = 3$

(e) $x = -3, y = -6$
$x = -1, y = -4$

(f) $x = -1, y = 2$
$x = 4\frac{3}{5}, y = -\frac{4}{5}$

2 $(-5, 4), (1, 10)$

3 $x = \frac{1}{2}, y = 5; \ x = 3, y = 0$

4 (a) Accurate graphs of $y = \frac{1}{2}x^2 - 2x + 1$ and $y = 4 - x$

(b) Estimates such as: $(-1.6, 5.6), (3.6, 0.4)$

(c) $(-1.646, 5.646), (3.646, 0.354)$

5 (a) $x = 1, y = 5; \ x = 2, y = 4$

(b) $x = -4, y = -1; \ x = 1, y = 4$

(c) $x = -3, y = 4; \ x = 5, y = 0$

6 (a) $x = 2 + 2\sqrt{2}, y = 7 + 2\sqrt{2}$
$x = 2 - 2\sqrt{2}, y = 7 - 2\sqrt{2}$

(b) $x = \dfrac{1 - \sqrt{13}}{2}, y = 2 + \sqrt{13}$

$x = \dfrac{1 + \sqrt{13}}{2}, y = 2 - \sqrt{13}$

(c) $x = 2 - \sqrt{3}, y = 3 - 2\sqrt{3}$
$x = 2 + \sqrt{3}, y = 3 + 2\sqrt{3}$

7 $\sqrt{11} - 1, \sqrt{11} + 1$

8 The length is $5 + \sqrt{2}$ and the width is $5 - \sqrt{2}$.

9 $(-2.407, 1.791), (-1.099, -2.791), (1.099, -2.791), (2.407, 1.791)$

D Counting points of intersection

Exercise D (p 62)

1 One way to show that they do not intersect is to show that there are no real solutions to the equation $x^2 + 2x + 4 = 3x + 2$. The equation rearranges to $x^2 - x + 2 = 0$ and the discriminant of $x^2 - x + 2$ is -7 which is less than zero. Hence the equation has no real roots and the graphs do not intersect.

2 One way to show that the line is a tangent is to show that there is only one real solution to the equation $x^2 - 6x + 5 = 1 - 2x$ by using the discriminant. The equation rearranges to $x^2 - 4x + 4 = 0$ and the discriminant of $x^2 - 4x + 4$ is 0. Hence the equation has one real root and the line is a tangent.

3 (a) One way to show that the line is a tangent is to show that there is only one real solution to the equation $2x^2 + 13x + 23 = 5 + x$ by completing the square. The equation rearranges to $x^2 + 6x + 9 = 0$ which is equivalent to $(x + 3)^2 = 0$. Hence the equation has one real root and the line is a tangent.

(b) $(-3, 2)$

4 (a) Meet at two points **(b)** Meet at one point

(c) Do not meet

5 One argument is that substituting $x = -1$ into $y^2 = 4x$ leads to $y^2 = -4$ which has no real solutions.

6 $k = -7$

7 $k = -\frac{1}{2}$

8 One way to show this is to let the two numbers be x and y. Then $x + y = 4$ (giving $y = 4 - x$) and $xy = 5$. Substitution gives $x(4 - x) = 5$ which rearranges to $x^2 - 4x + 5 = 0$. The discriminant of $x^2 - 4x + 5$ is -4 which is less than zero. So no real solution exists and hence it is impossible to find two such numbers.

9 $k = -7, 17$

Test yourself (p 63)

1 The length is $\sqrt{5} + 2$ and the width is $2\sqrt{5} - 4$.

2 (a) $x = -1, y = 8;\ x = 3, y = 16$

(b) $(-1, 8)\ (3, 16)$

3 $x = 1, y = 1;\ x = 3, y = -1$

4 $x = -1, y = 1;\ x = \frac{3}{2}, y = -\frac{1}{4}$

5 (a) $x = 4, y = 7$

(b) The straight line is a tangent to the parabola because they meet at only one point, $(4, 7)$.

6 $x = -1, y = 1;\ x = \frac{3}{2}, y = -\frac{1}{4}$

7 One way to show that they do not intersect is to show that there are no real solutions to the equation $y^2 + 7(2 - y) = 0$. The equation rearranges to $y^2 - 7y + 14 = 0$ and the discriminant of $y^2 - 7y + 14$ is -7 which is less than zero. Hence the equation has no real roots and the graphs do not intersect.

5 Inequalities

A Linear inequalities: revision (p 64)

A1 (a) (i) T   **(ii)** F   **(iii)** T

     (iv) F   **(v)** F

(b) $t > 3$

A2 (a) 5

(b) At $x = 2$, the graph of $y = 2x + 1$ is below the graph of $y = x + 6$.

(c) $x \geq 5$

(d) $x < 5$

A3 (a) -2 **(b)** $x < -2$ **(c)** $x > -2$

A4 (a) (i) F   **(ii)** T   **(iii)** T

     (iv) T   **(v)** T

(b) $p \leq 2.5$

A5 $<$

A6 Adding or subtracting a positive or a negative leaves the solution set unchanged, as does multiplying or dividing by a positive. However, multiplying or dividing by a negative reverses the direction of the inequality sign.

Exercise A (p 66)

1 (a) $x \geq 3$ **(b)** $y < 2$ **(c)** $z < 1$

(d) $p > 3$ **(e)** $q \geq 3$ **(f)** $a < -2$

(g) $b \geq -2$ **(h)** $x > -1$ **(i)** $y > -9$

(j) $z \leq 2\frac{2}{3}$ **(k)** $w < \frac{1}{2}$ **(l)** $d \leq -\frac{2}{7}$

2 (a) $x < 1$ **(b)** $x < 3\frac{1}{2}$ **(c)** $x \leq 4$

(d) $y > -\frac{2}{5}$ **(e)** $y \leq 3$ **(f)** $y < -8$

3 (a) $x > 4$ **(b)** $x > -3\frac{1}{7}$ **(c)** $x \leq 6\frac{1}{4}$

B Linear inequalities: solving problems

Exercise B (p 67)

1 Using h for the number of hours gives $8h + 11 > 73$ and so $h > 7\frac{3}{4}$.

So National Insurance needs to be paid if the number of hours worked is greater than $7\frac{3}{4}$.

2 Using d for the number of days gives
$2d + 10 < 3.5d + 5$ and so $d > 3\frac{1}{3}$.
So Cutting Edge is less expensive if the chain saw
is hired for more than 3 days.

3 (a) (i) Each shorter edge is $(l - 6)$ cm so the total
length of the two shorter edges is
$(2l - 12)$ cm. Now, in a triangle, the total
length of the two shorter edges must be
greater than the length of the longest edge.
So $2l - 12 > l$ which leads to $l > 12$.

   (ii) The total length of wire is
$2l - 12 + l = 3l - 12$. Now $l > 12$ so we
know that $3l > 36$ and that $3l - 12 > 24$ as
required.

  (b) $3l - 12 \le 100$
$\Rightarrow$ $3l \le 112$
$\Rightarrow$ $l \le 37\frac{1}{3}$ as required

4 (a) If $w \ge 20$ then the length of the edge parallel
to the wall would be zero or negative. So w
must be less than 20.

  (b) $40 - 2w$

  (c) (i) The length of the edge parallel to the wall
is $40 - 2w$. Hence the total perimeter of the
rectangle is $2w + 2(40 - 2w) =$
$2w + 80 - 4w = 80 - 2w$. The total
perimeter cannot be more than 60 metres
so $80 - 2w \le 60$ as required.

   (ii) The solution is $w \ge 10$ so the minimum
value of w is 10.

C Quadratic inequalities (p 68)

C1 (a) (i) F   (ii) T   (iii) T
      (iv) F   (v) F

  (b) $-3 < x < 3$

C2 (a) $A\,(-5, 0)$, $B\,(5, 0)$ (b) $x \le -5$, $x \ge 5$

C3 (a) $P\,(-2, 3)$, $Q\,(1, 6)$ (b) $-2 < x < 1$

C4 $x \le -4$, $x \ge 7$

C5 $-5 \le x \le 3$

C6 One way is to show that the inequality can be
written as $x^2 - 5 < 0$ and then work graphically to
obtain $-\sqrt{5} < x < \sqrt{5}$.

C7 One way is to show that the inequality can be
written as $x^2 - 5 > 0$ and then work graphically to
obtain $x < -\sqrt{5}$, $x > \sqrt{5}$.

Exercise C (p 70)

1 (a) $-5 < x < 2$ (b) $x \le -9$, $x \ge -2$
  (c) $x < 3$, $x > 6$ (d) $-2 \le x \le 7$
  (e) $x \le 0$, $x \ge 3$ (f) $x < -2$, $x > 2$

2 (a) $-5 < q < \frac{1}{2}$ (b) $k < -\frac{1}{3}$, $k > 4$
  (c) $y \le -4$, $y \ge 0$ (d) $-3 \le p \le \frac{1}{2}$
  (e) $0 < a < \frac{1}{3}$ (f) $t \le -\frac{3}{2}$, $t \ge \frac{2}{3}$

3 (a) $-\sqrt{2} < x < \sqrt{2}$
  (b) $x \le 1 - \sqrt{2}$, $x \ge 1 + \sqrt{2}$
  (c) $-1 - \frac{1}{2}\sqrt{6} < x < -1 + \frac{1}{2}\sqrt{6}$

4 (a) $k < -5$, $k > 5$
  (b) $-1 < k < 3$
  (c) $k \le -5$, $k \ge 2$
  (d) $k < -4$, $k > \frac{1}{2}$
  (e) $0 < k < 5$
  (f) $-\sqrt{5} < k < \sqrt{5}$
  (g) $k < 1 - \sqrt{3}$, $k > 1 + \sqrt{3}$
  (h) $k < -1$, $k > \frac{1}{4}$
  (i) $-\frac{3}{2} < k < \frac{3}{2}$

5 (a) $6x - x^2 < 5$
$\Rightarrow$ $6x - x^2 - 5 < 0$
$\Rightarrow$ $x^2 - 6x + 5 > 0$ as required
  (b) $x < 1$, $x > 5$

6 (a) $(2 - x)(x - 3) > 0$
$\Rightarrow$ $2x - 6 - x^2 + 3x > 0$
$\Rightarrow$ $-x^2 + 5x - 6 > 0$
$\Rightarrow$ $5x - x^2 > 6$ as required
  (b) $2 < x < 3$

7 (a) $-3 < x < 3$ (b) $x < -1$, $x > 4$
  (c) $x < -7$, $x > 2$

8 (a) $y(y + 2) < 8$
$\Rightarrow$ $y^2 + 2y < 8$
$\Rightarrow$ $y^2 + 2y - 8 < 0$ as required
  (b) $-4 < y < 2$

9 (a) $3 < x < 4$ **(b)** $-7 < y < 1$

(c) $k < -\frac{2}{3}$, $k > 1$

10 (a) $(x + 1)^2 - 16$ **(b)** $-5 < x < 3$

11 (a) $x^2 + 4x + 5 = (x + 2)^2 + 1$ and so
$x^2 + 4x + 5 > 0$ for all values of x.

(b) $x^2 + 2x + 1 = (x + 1)^2$ which is greater than or equal to 0 for all values of x. Hence $x^2 + 2x + 1 < 0$ has no real solutions.

12 $1 < x \leq 4$

13 (a) $x < -5$, $x > -3$ **(b)** $-4 \leq x \leq -2$, $x \geq 1$

(c) $x < -5$, $1 < x < 6$

14 (a) $-1 < x < 6$ **(b)** $-13\frac{1}{2} < x < -5$

D Inequalities and the discriminant (p 72)

D1 (a) 5   **(b)** $5 \geq 0$

D2 (a) -3 **(b)** $-3 < 0$

D3 (a) $k^2 - 4$ **(b)** $k \leq -2$, $k \geq 2$

D4 (a) $k^2 - 4k$ **(b)** $0 < k < 4$

Exercise D (p 73)

1 (a) The equation has real roots so the discriminant must be greater than or equal to 0.
The discriminant here is $k^2 - 4 \times 16 = k^2 - 64$ so $k^2 - 64 \geq 0$ as required.

(b) $k \leq -8$, $k \geq 8$

2 (a) $k \leq -10$, $k \geq 10$ **(b)** $k \leq 0$, $k \geq \frac{4}{9}$

(c) $k \leq -9$, $k \geq -1$

3 $k < 0$, $k > 1\frac{1}{4}$

4 (a) $k < 0$, $k > 16$ **(b)** $-\frac{3}{2} < k < \frac{3}{2}$

(c) $\frac{6}{7} < k < 2$

5 The equation does not have real roots when the discriminant is less than 0.
The discriminant here is $k^2 - 8$ and $k^2 - 8 < 0 \Rightarrow -\sqrt{8} < k < \sqrt{8}$ i.e. $-2\sqrt{2} < k < 2\sqrt{2}$ as required.

6 (a) $-\sqrt{3} < k < \sqrt{3}$ **(b)** $-6 < k < 2$

(c) $k < -\frac{1}{7}$, $k > 1$

7 The discriminant here is
$(-(k + 4))^2 - 4 \times k \times 4$
$= (k + 4)^2 - 16k$
$= k^2 + 8k + 16 - 16k$
$= k^2 - 8k + 16$
$= (k - 4)^2$
Now $(k - 4)^2 \geq 0$ for all values of k so the equation will have real roots for all values of k.

8 $k > -\frac{1}{4}$

9 $1 < k < 9$

E Quadratic inequalities: solving problems

Exercise E (p 75)

1 (a) $n(2n - 1) > 465$ has solution set given by
$n < -15$ and $n > 15\frac{1}{2}$. Hence the relevant value of n is 16.

(b) 496

2 The width must be greater than or equal to 5 metres but less than or equal to 15 metres.

3 (a) $\frac{n(n + 1)}{2} > 100$ has solution set
given by $n < -\frac{1}{2} - \frac{1}{2}\sqrt{801}$ and $n > -\frac{1}{2} + \frac{1}{2}\sqrt{801}$.
Now $-\frac{1}{2} + \frac{1}{2}\sqrt{801} = 13.6509\ldots$ Hence the relevant value of n is 14.

(b) 105

(c) 45

4 (a) The perimeter is 50 metres so the length must be $25 - w$. Both the width and length cannot be negative or zero so both w and $25 - w$ must be greater than 0. Hence $w > 0$ and $w < 25$ so $0 < w < 25$ as required.

(b) $0 < w \leq 10$, $15 \leq w < 25$

Test yourself (p 77)

1 (a) $x > 6\frac{1}{2}$ **(b)** $x \leq 2\frac{1}{4}$

2 Using w for the number of words gives
$50w + 250 < 20w + 500$ and so $w < 8\frac{1}{3}$.
So it is cheaper to use the *Cadzow Times* for a message of 8 words or fewer.

3 (a) $y < -3$ **(b)** $x < -6$, $x > 2$

4 $-9 < x < \frac{1}{2}$

5 (a) $x = -2 - \frac{1}{2}\sqrt{2}$ or $-2 + \frac{1}{2}\sqrt{2}$

  (b) $x < -2 - \frac{1}{2}\sqrt{2},\ x > -2 + \frac{1}{2}\sqrt{2}$

6 (a) The equation has distinct real roots so the discriminant must be greater than 0. The discriminant here is
$(-5k)^2 - 4k = 25k^2 - 4k = k(25k - 4)$
so $k(25k - 4) > 0$ as required.

  (b) $k < 0,\ k > \frac{4}{25}$

7 The inequality is $12t - 5t^2 < 4$ which leads to $(5t - 2)(t - 2) > 0$ and $t < \frac{2}{5},\ t > 2$. So the height of the ball is less than 4 metres before 0.4 seconds and after 2 seconds.

8 The width must be greater than or equal to 15 metres and less than or equal to 35 metres.

9 $k < -4,\ k > 4$

10 $-10 < k < 10$, where k is the y-intercept of the line.

6 Polynomials

A Indices: revision

Exercise A (p 78)

1 (a) 81   (b) 36   (c) 18   (d) 125
  (e) 48   (f) 12   (g) 477   (h) 28
  (i) 40   (j) 35

2 (a) $\frac{3}{2}$ (b) 0   (c) $-\frac{1}{8}$

3 (a) 10   (b) -1 (c) 32

4 (a) $5x^3$ (b) $12x^3$ (c) $10x^5$ (d) $2x^4$
  (e) $\frac{5}{3}x^3$ (f) $8x^3$ (g) $9x^4$ (h) $\frac{1}{4}x^6$

B Cubic graphs (p 79)

B1 The shape of each graph is always a curve with a 'kink' in the middle. It is always one of the three basic shapes shown below and, if the value of a is negative, then it will be a reflection in the x-axis of one of these shapes.

B2 The graphs cross or touch the x-axis one, three and two times respectively.

B3 Comments such as:
$y = x^3$ increases from left to right.
The graph has rotation symmetry about the origin.
Near the origin the curve 'wiggles', being momentarily flat at $(0, 0)$.

$y = x^3 - x$ has rotation symmetry about the origin. Near the origin the curve has a pronounced 'wiggle', decreasing for a little while before beginning to increase again.

$y = x^3 + x$ increases from left to right like $y = x^3$ and has rotation symmetry about the origin. The curve 'wiggles' near the origin too but doesn't flatten out like $y = x^3$.

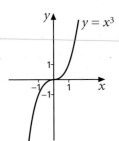

$y = x^3$

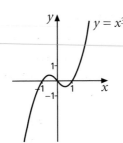

$y = x^3 - x$

B6 (a)

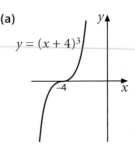

$y = (x + 4)^3$

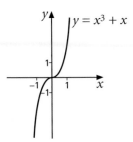

$y = x^3 + x$

(b)

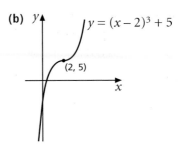

$y = (x - 2)^3 + 5$

(2, 5)

(c) $y = (x + 6)^3 - 7$

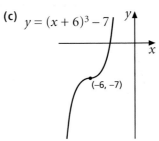

(−6, −7)

B4 (a)

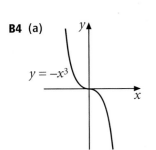

$y = -x^3$

(b)

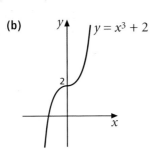

$y = x^3 + 2$

2

(c)

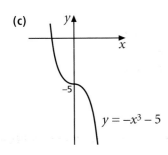

−5

$y = -x^3 - 5$

B7 (a) **B:** $y = (x - 3)^3 - 1$ (c) $(0, -28)$

B8 (a) $y = (x + 2)^3 + 4$ (b) $(0, 12)$

B9 $\begin{bmatrix} 5 \\ 3 \end{bmatrix}$

B10 (a) **D:** $y = (x - 2)^3 + (x - 2) - 9$ (c) $(0, -19)$

Exercise B (p 81)

1 (a) $\begin{bmatrix} 1 \\ 2 \end{bmatrix}$ (b) $\begin{bmatrix} 3 \\ -5 \end{bmatrix}$ (c) $\begin{bmatrix} -7 \\ 1 \end{bmatrix}$

2 (a) $\begin{bmatrix} 4 \\ 5 \end{bmatrix}$ (b) $\begin{bmatrix} -2 \\ -1 \end{bmatrix}$ (c) $\begin{bmatrix} -6 \\ 3 \end{bmatrix}$

3 (a) $y = (x - 3)^3$

(b)

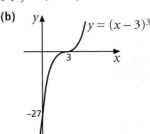

$y = (x - 3)^3$

3

−27

B5 (a), (b)

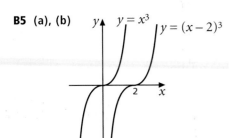

$y = x^3$ $y = (x - 2)^3$

2

4 $y = (x - 5)^3 - 3$

5 $y = (x - 2)^3 + (x - 2)$

6 (a) $y = (x - 1)^3 + x + 2$ (b) $(0, 1)$

7 $y = (x + 3)^3 - x - 5$

C Further graphs and manipulation (p 82)

The important elements of sketches here are the x- and y-intercepts and the general shape. There is no need to be any more precise.

C1 $y = x^3 + 9x^2 + 27x + 27$

C2 (a) $x^3 + 9x^2 + 23x + 15$ (b) $2x^3 - x^2 - 13x - 6$

C3 (a) $x = -3, -2, 1$

(b) It crosses the x-axis at $(-3, 0)$, $(-2, 0)$ and $(1, 0)$.

(c) -6

(d)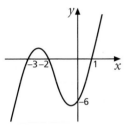

(e) $y = x^3 + 4x^2 + x - 6$

C4 (a) (i) $(-1, 0)$, $(\frac{1}{2}, 0)$ $(3, 0)$ (ii) 3

(b)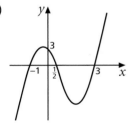

(c) $y = 2x^3 - 5x^2 - 4x + 3$

C5 (a)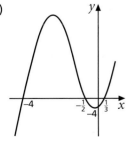

(b) $y = 6x^3 + 25x^2 + 3x - 4$

C6 (a) $x = -3, 1$

(b) It meets the x-axis at two points: $(-3, 0)$ and $(1, 0)$. Since it is a cubic shape, it must just touch the x-axis at one of these points.

(c) $(0, 3)$

(d)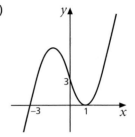

(e) $y = x^3 + x^2 - 5x + 3$

C7 (a) $(x + 3)^3 + 1$
$= (x + 3)(x^2 + 6x + 9) + 1$
$= x^3 + 9x^2 + 27x + 27 + 1$
$= x^3 + 9x^2 + 27x + 28$

(b)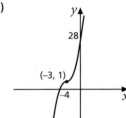

C8 (a) $(x + 4)(x - 5)(2 - x)$
$= (x + 4)(-x^2 + 7x - 10)$
$= -x^3 + 3x^2 + 18x - 40$

(b) **D**

Exercise C (p 84)

1 (a) (i) 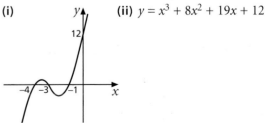   (ii) $y = x^3 + 8x^2 + 19x + 12$

(b) (i) 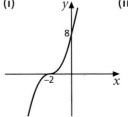   (ii) $y = x^3 + 6x^2 + 12x + 8$

(c) (i) 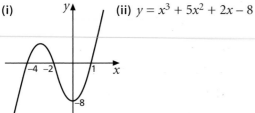 **(ii)** $y = x^3 + 5x^2 + 2x - 8$

(d) (i) 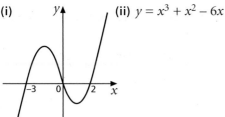 **(ii)** $y = x^3 + x^2 - 6x$

(e) (i) 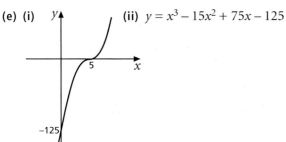 **(ii)** $y = x^3 - 15x^2 + 75x - 125$

(f) (i) 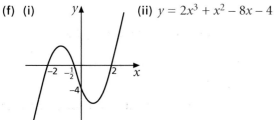 **(ii)** $y = 2x^3 + x^2 - 8x - 4$

(g) (i) 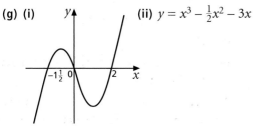 **(ii)** $y = x^3 - \frac{1}{2}x^2 - 3x$

(h) (i) 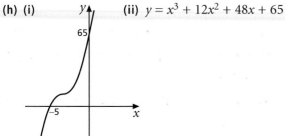 **(ii)** $y = x^3 + 12x^2 + 48x + 65$

2 (a) $x = -1, 3$

(b) 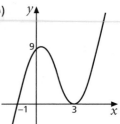 **(c)** $y = x^3 - 5x^2 + 3x + 9$

3 (a) 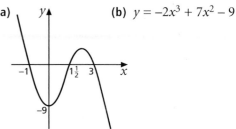 **(b)** $y = -2x^3 + 7x^2 - 9$

4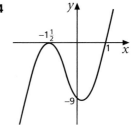

D Polynomial functions

Exercise D (p 86)

1 $x^3 - x^2 + 11x - 2$

2 (a) 30 **(b)** 43 **(c)** 0

3 (a) $x^5 + 2x^4 + 3x^2 + 7x + 2$

(b) $x^4 + 12x^2 + 36$

(c) $2x^5 + 6x^4 - x^3 + 8x^2 + 14x - 5$

(d) $-x^4 + x^3 + 7x - 1$

(e) $3x^4 - x^3 + 10x^2 - 3x$

(f) $x^6 - 3x^4 + 3x^2 - 1$

(g) $x^4 - 15x^2 + 10x + 24$

(h) $-6x^3 - 27x^2 + 41x - 12$

4 (a) 5 **(b)** 6 **(c)** 26 **(d)** 11 **(e)** 50

5 (a) $g(5) = 0$, $g(-5) = 0$ and $g(-2) = 0$

(b) $(5, 0), (-5, 0), (-2, 0)$

6 (a) x^5

(b) $-x^5 + 5x^2 + 5$

(c) $x^7 + x^5 - 2x^4 - 4x^2 - 2$

(d) $x^{10} - 4x^7 - 4x^5 + 4x^4 + 8x^2 + 4$

7 (a) (i) 0   (ii) 12   (iii) 0   (iv) 0   (v) 2

(b)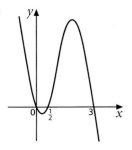

8 (a) $f(x) = 2x^3 + 13x^2 + 8x - 48$

(b)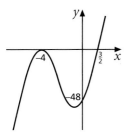

E Division (p 87)

E1 (a) $x + 4$ (b) $x + 4$

E2 (a) $3x + 1$ (b) $2x + 3$

E3 (a) $x^2 + 2x + 5$ (b) $x^2 - 5x - 2$ (c) $x^2 + 2x + 3$

E4 (a) $x + 2$ (b) $x + 3$ (c) $x - 5$

E5 (a) $(x + 5)(x + 1) + 2$ (b) 2

E6 (a) $(x - 3)(x - 7) + 10$ (b) 10

E7 (a) $(x - 3)(x - 7) - 10$ (b) −10

Exercise E (p 89)

1 (a) $x^2 + 3x + 4$ remainder 5

(b) $x^2 + 4x - 1$

(c) $x^2 - x + 6$ remainder −1

(d) $2x^2 + x + 3$ remainder 3

(e) $3x^2 + 2x - 5$

(f) $5x^2 - 2x - 1$ remainder −2

(g) $x^2 - 1$

2 $x^2 - x - 1$

3 (a) $x^2 + x - 12$

(b) $x^2 - 2x + 5$ remainder 2

(c) $2x^2 + x - 3$

(d) $3x^2 + 6x + 7$ remainder 15

(e) $4x^2 - 5x + 5$ remainder −2

4 $x^2 + x + 1$

5 (a) A demonstration that f(x) divided by $(x + 5)$ is
$x^2 + 2x - 3$

(b) $f(x) = (x + 5)(x^2 + 2x - 3)$

(c) $f(x) = (x + 5)(x + 3)(x - 1)$

6 (a) (i) 6   (ii) 12   (iii) 12   (iv) 0   (v) −30

(b) $(x + 1)$

(c) $(x + 1)(x^2 - 7x + 12)$

(d) $(x^2 - 7x + 12) = (x - 3)(x - 4)$ so
$p(x) = (x + 1)(x - 3)(x - 4)$

(e) $x = -1, 3, 4$

7 (a) $2x^2 - 6x - 9$ remainder 1

(b) $x^2 - 3$

(c) $x^2 - \frac{1}{2}x + \frac{1}{4}$ remainder $12\frac{3}{4}$

F Remainders and factors (p 90)

F1 (a) (i) $x^2 + 4x - 1$ remainder 8

(ii) 8

(iii) The value of p(2) is the remainder after division by $(x - 2)$.

(b) (i) $x^2 + x - 10$ remainder 20

(ii) 20

(iii) The value of p(−1) is the remainder after division by $(x + 1)$.

(c) The value of p(a) is always the remainder after division by $(x - a)$. See the explanation on page 91.

F2 (a) 2   (b) $x^2 + 6x + 4$ remainder 2

F3 $f(3) = 0$ so we know that $(x - 3)$ divides f(x) exactly.

F4 (a) (i) −30   (ii) −24   (iii) −12   (iv) 0   (v) 6

(b) $(x + 2)$

(c) $(x + 2)(x^2 + x - 12)$

(d) $(x + 2)(x + 4)(x - 3)$

(e) $x = -2, -4, 3$

(f)

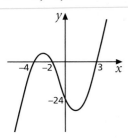

F5 $p(3) = 0$ so $(x - 3)$ is a factor.

Exercise F (p 93)

1 10

2 (a) $p(3) = 0$ so $(x - 3)$ is a factor.

(b) $(x - 3)(x + 1)(x + 7)$

3 (a) $f(-2) = 0$ so $(x + 2)$ is a factor.

(b) $(x + 2)(x - 1)(x - 5)$

4 (a) $f(1) = 0$; $f(-1) = -4$

(b) $(x - 1)(x + 2)(x + 3)$

5 (a) $q(-7) = 0$ so $(x + 7)$ is a factor.

(b) $(x + 7)(x + 2)(x - 3)$

(c) $x = -7, -2, 3$

6 (a) $(x - 1)(x - 1)(x + 6)$

(b) $x = 1, -6$

(c)

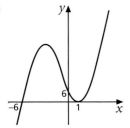

7 (a) $p(1) = 0$ so $(x - 1)$ is a factor

(b) $(x - 1)(x^2 + 2x + 5)$

(c) (i) -16

(ii) $p(x) = 0$ when
$(x - 1)(x^2 + 2x + 5) = 0$,
i.e. when $(x - 1) = 0$ or $(x^2 + 2x + 5) = 0$.
Since the discriminant of $x^2 + 2x + 5$ is
negative, $(x^2 + 2x + 5) = 0$ has no real
solutions. So $p(x) = 0$ has just one real
solution, $x = 1$.

8 (a) $p(-1) = 0$ so $(x + 1)$ is a factor.

(b) $(x + 1)(x^2 - 7)$

(c) $x = -1, \sqrt{7}, -\sqrt{7}$

9 (a) $(x - 2)(x + 1)(x + 5)$

(b) $(x - 1)(x + 2)(2x + 3)$

(c) $(x - 2)(x^2 + x - 1)$

(d) $(x + 1)(x + 2)(x + 4)$

(e) $(x + 1)(2x^2 - 5)$

(f) $(x + 2)(x + 3)^2$

G Further problems

Exercise G (p 95)

1 $k = 1$

2 $a = -10$

3 $b = 4$

4 $a = 1$

5 $p = 4, q = -37$

6 $a = 0, b = -7$

7 $p = 1, q = 6$

8 $a = 7, b = 11$

9 $h = 2, k = -1$

Mixed questions (p 96)

1 (a) C: $y = (x - 4)^3 + 1$

(b) $y = x^3 - 12x^2 + 48x - 63$

2 (a) -6

(b)

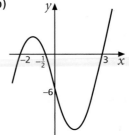

(c) $y = 2x^3 - x^2 - 13x - 6$

3 $x^2 + x - 6$

4 (a) $(x + 1)(6x^2 + 11x + 3)$
  $a = 6, b = 11, c = 3$

(b) $x = -1\frac{1}{2}, -1, -\frac{1}{3}$

5 (a) $p(-2) = 0$ so $(x + 2)$ is a factor

(b) $(x + 2)(x - 1)^2$

(c)

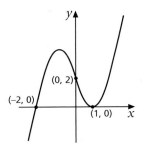

6 $p = 5, q = -9$

7 (a) $p(2) = 0$ so $(x - 2)$ is a linear factor.
  $p(x) = (x - 2)(x^2 - 3)$ and $(x^2 - 3)$ cannot be factorised. Hence the polynomial has only one linear factor.

(b) $x = 2, \sqrt{3}, -\sqrt{3}$

8 (a) $(x + 1)(x + 2)(x + 3)$

(b) The factorisation shows that f(a) can be written as the product of three consecutive integers when a is an integer. One of these must be a multiple of 3 so the product f(a) must also be a multiple of 3.

Test yourself (p 97)

1 (a) $y = x^3 - 6x^2 + 13x - 11$ **(b)** $(0, -11)$

2 (a) 0 **(b)** $(x - 2)$

(c) $(x - 2)(x + 1)(x + 4)$

3 (a) $p(-2) = 0$ so $(x + 2)$ is a factor.

(b) $(x + 2)(x - 2)(2x - 1)$

4 (a) $(x - 1)(x - 2)(x - 4)$

(b)

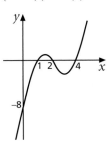

5 $p = -3$

6 $(x - 2)$ is a factor so p(2) = 0.
  Hence $42 - 2k = 0$ so $k = 21$.

7 $a = -3, b = 0$

8 $p = -2, q = -5$

9 (a) $k = -15$

(b) $(x - 3)(x^2 + 4x + 5)$

(c) One method is to note that
  $x^2 + 4x + 5 = (x + 2)^2 + 1 > 0$
  for all x. So $x^2 + 4x + 5 = 0$ has no real solution. Hence there is only one real solution, i.e. when $x - 3 = 0$.

7 Equation of a circle

A A circle as a graph (p 98)

A1 (a) 17   (b) 10   (c) 12.5   (d) 14.5

A2 (a) (i) On the circle   (ii) On the circle

     (iii) Inside   (iv) Outside

     (v) On the circle

     (b) $x^2 + y^2 = 13^2$

A3 A plot of the graph of $x^2 + y^2 = 13$

A4 Centre $(0, 0)$, radius 7

A5 5

A6 (a) (i) On the circle   (ii) On the circle

     (iii) On the circle   (iv) On the circle

     (v) Outside   (vi) On the circle

     (vii) Inside

     (b) Three other points that satisfy the condition
$(x - 2)^2 + (y - 1)^2 = 25$, for example:
$(6, 4), (5, 5), (2, 6), (-1, 5), (-3, 1), (-2, -2),$
$(-1, -3)$

A7 In the case shown in
the diagram, the base
of the right-angled
triangle is $2 - x$,
which is $-(x - 2)$.

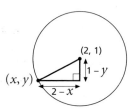

So $(2 - x)^2 = (-(x - 2))^2 = (x - 2)^2$.

The height of the triangle is $1 - y$ but, as above,
$(1 - y)^2 = (y - 1)^2$.

So $(x - 2)^2 + (y - 1)^2$ still works as the equation of
the circle in this case and similarly all round the
circle.

A8 A plot of the graph of $(x - 2)^2 + (y - 1)^2 = 5^2$

A9 $(x - 5)^2 + (y + 2)^2 = 16$

A10 Centre $(-4, 7)$, radius 6

A11 $x^2 - 10x + y^2 + 4y + 13 = 0$

Exercise A (p 100)

1 (a) $(x - 6)^2 + (y - 3)^2 = 4^2$

     (b) $(x + 2)^2 + y^2 = 5^2$

(c) $(x - 1)^2 + (y + 6)^2 = 3^2$

(d) $(x + 2)^2 + (y + 2)^2 = 7^2$

2 (a) (i) $(2, 6), 4$

     (ii) $x^2 - 4x + y^2 - 12y + 24 = 0$

     (b) (i) $(-3, 4), 5$

     (ii) $x^2 + 6x + y^2 - 8y = 0$

     (c) (i) $(4, 0), \sqrt{7}$

     (ii) $x^2 - 8x + y^2 + 9 = 0$

     (d) (i) $(-1.5, 0.5), 2$

     (ii) $x^2 + 3x + y^2 - y - 1.5 = 0$

3 Radius $= \sqrt{3^2 + 4^2} = 5$
Equation is $(x + 2)^2 + (y + 3)^2 = 5^2$
(or an equivalent equation)

4 The centre is the mid-point of the diameter,
$(3, -5)$.
By Pythagoras the radius is $\sqrt{194}$.
The equation is $(x - 3)^2 + (y + 5)^2 = 194$ or
$x^2 - 6x + y^2 + 10y - 160 = 0$.

5 $(x + 4)^2 + (y + 2)^2 = 10$ or
$x^2 + 8x + y^2 + 4y + 10 = 0$

6 The centre is $(1, 4)$ and the radius is 3 (or $\sqrt{9}$).
By Pythagoras the distance from the centre to
$(-1, 2)$ is $\sqrt{2^2 + 2^2}$, which is $\sqrt{8}$, which is less
than $\sqrt{9}$. So $(-1, 2)$ lies inside the circle.

7 (a) $2, (2, 1)$ (b) $3, (1, -3)$ (c) $\sqrt{11}, (-5, 2)$

     (d) $7, (0, 5)$ (e) $6, (-4, 3)$ (f) $2, (0.5, 3.5)$

8 B could not be a circle, because the x^2 and y^2
terms have different coefficients.

9 $(x - 6)^2 + y^2 = 16$

10 (a) Substituting $x = 0$ and $y = 0$ into the LHS
gives 0, which is the RHS. So the circle goes
through the point $(0, 0)$.

     (b) $(-6, 4)$

11 (a) From the equation of the circle, its centre is
$(2, 3)$.
The mid-point of PQ is $(2, 3)$.
So PQ is a diameter.

     (b) $a = 7$

     (c) PR: -3, RQ: $\frac{1}{3}$; PR and RQ are perpendicular.

     (d) An angle in a semicircle is 90°.

12 By completing the square, the equation becomes
$(x + 1)^2 + (y - 3)^2 = -4$
But the negative value -4 cannot be the square of
the radius, so this cannot be a circle.

B Tangent and normal to a circle

Exercise B (p 102)

1 (a) $y = \frac{2}{3}x + 3$ (b) $y = -\frac{3}{2}x + 16$

2 (a) $\sqrt{10}$, $(-1, 3)$ (b) $y = -3x + 10$

3 (a) $(1, 8)$, 4

  (b) 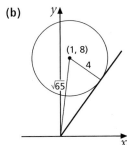   (c) 7

4 (a) $y = -x + 5$ (b) $y = x - 1$

  (c) $(3, 2)$ (d) $(x - 5)^2 + (y - 4)^2 = 8$

5 Equation of normal is $y = -3x - 5$.
Solving this and the given equation
simultaneously gives the contact point $(-3, 4)$.
By Pythagoras the radius is $\sqrt{10}$.
So the circle's equation is $(x + 2)^2 + (y - 1)^2 = 10$.

6 (a) $(4, 2)$

  (b) (i) $\dfrac{b - 2}{a - 4}$ (ii) $\dfrac{4 - a}{b - 2}$

7 (a)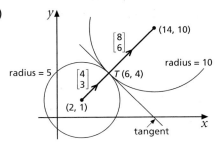

  The line segments are on the same line,
because they are both perpendicular to a
tangent where the two circles touch.

  (b) $(14, 10)$

  (c) A: $(x - 2)^2 + (y - 1)^2 = 25$
     B: $(x - 14)^2 + (y - 10)^2 = 100$

C Intersection of a straight line and a circle
(p 103)

C1 At $(1, 2)$ and $(7, 8)$

C2 (a) There is only one point, $(3, 6)$.

  (b) There are no solutions to the quadratic in x.

Exercise C (p 105)

1 (a) Intersects   (b) Is a tangent

  (c) Intersects   (d) Does not meet

2 (a) Intersects at $(1, 3)$ and $(3, 7)$

  (b) Does not meet circle

  (c) Touches at $(6, 2)$

  (d) Intersects at $(1, 3)$ and $(2, 2)$

3 (a) $(5, -1)$ (b) $(12, 0)$, $(-2, 0)$, $(0, -6)$, $(0, 4)$

  (c)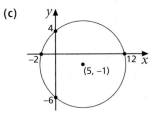

4 (a) $x = -2$, $y = -3$

  (b) The line is a tangent to the circle at the point
$(-2, -3)$ because the quadratic equation
obtained in solving simultaneously the
equations for the line and the circle has a
single (repeated) root.

5 (a) $x^2 - 2x + y^2 = 9$

  (b) $y = 2x + 3$ intersects at $(0, 3)$ and $(-2, -1)$.
$y = 2x - 7$ intersects at $(2, -3)$ and $(4, 1)$.
The two given lines are parallel (gradient 2).
The line through $(0, 3)$ and $(4, 1)$ has
gradient $-\frac{1}{2}$, as does the line through $(-2, -1)$
and $(2, -3)$; so these lines are parallel and are
perpendicular to the two given lines.
By Pythagoras the line segment from $(0, 3)$ to
$(4, 1)$ (for example) is the same length
($\sqrt{20}$ units) as the line segment from $(-2, -1)$
to $(0, 3)$. So the vertices form a square.

6 $(x - 9)^2 + (y - 7)^2 = 74$

7 (a) $a = 3$, $b = 6$

(b) The line through the centre perpendicular to PQ has the equation $y = \frac{3}{5}x + 1$.

PQ has the equation $y = -\frac{5}{3}x + 18$.

Solving these simultaneously gives the point of intersection $(7.5, 5.5)$, which by considering the coordinates of P and Q is the mid-point of PQ.

8 $a = 4$

9 Centre $(-2, 2)$, radius $\sqrt{50}$
$(x + 2)^2 + (y - 2)^2 = 50$

10 $(-4, 2)$

Test yourself (p 107)

1 (a) $x^2 + y^2 - 8x - 2y + 13 = 0$
(b) $x^2 + y^2 + 4x + 6y + 4 = 0$
(c) $x^2 + y^2 - 5x - 8y + 18\frac{1}{4} = 0$
(d) $x^2 + y^2 - 2x + 14y + 43 = 0$

2 (a) $6, (2, 1)$ **(b)** $5, (0, -3)$
(c) $\sqrt{3}, (-2, -4)$ **(d)** $3, (1.5, 2.5)$

3 (a) Equation of circle is $(x + 1)^2 + (y + 2)^2 = 13$.
Substituting 1 for x, $2^2 + (y + 2)^2 = 13$
$\Rightarrow y + 2 = 3$ or -3
$\Rightarrow y = 1$ or -5, the first value being that of the point to be verified.
(b) $y = \frac{3}{2}x - \frac{1}{2}$

4 (a) Radius 7, centre $(-2, 7)$
(b)   **(c)** 4

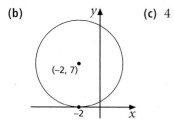

5 (a) $x = 2, y = 3$
(b) The line is a tangent to the circle at the point $(2, 3)$ because the quadratic equation obtained in solving simultaneously the equations of the line and the circle has one (repeated) root.

8 Rates of change

A Gradient as rate of change (p 108)

A1 (a) $3\,°C$
(b) $7\,°C$
(c) (i) $37\,°C$ **(ii)** $46\,°C$ **(iii)** $82\,°C$
(d) $2000\,m$

A2 (a) -0.007 degrees per metre; the negative sign shows a rate of decrease.
(b) $0.7\,°C$
(c) $-14\,°C$

A3 (a) 2
(b) (i) 2   **(ii)** 5   **(iii)** $\frac{1}{2}$ **(iv)** 4

A4 (a) -3
(b) (i) -2 **(ii)** -1 **(iii)** $-\frac{1}{2}$ **(iv)** $\frac{7}{2}$

A5 (a)

$s = 4t + 5$

(b) 4
(c) The speed of the vehicle.

A6 (a) It is of the form $y = 3x + c$.
(b) $y = 3x - 1$

A7 0 (with a sketch of $y = 5$)

Exercise A (p 110)

1 (a) 3   **(b)** -7 **(c)** 1   **(d)** 0   **(e)** $\frac{3}{2}$

2 (a) $C = 900 + 5n$
(b) $\dfrac{dC}{dn} = 5$; the cost per unit, in pence

3 $y = 5x + 7$

4 $y = -2x + 8$

5 $\dfrac{dy}{dx} = 2$; $y = 2x + 3$

6 $\dfrac{dy}{dx} = -\frac{1}{2}$; $y = -\frac{1}{2}x + 9$

7 (a) (i) $C = 30 + 20t$ **(ii)** 20

(b) $\dfrac{dC}{dt} = 25$; this plumber's charge for labour is
£25 per hour.

B Gradient of a curve (p 111)

B1 (a) 8

(b) The gradient represents the speed in m/s when $t = 3$.

B2 At (2, 2) gradient $= 1$; at (5, 2.75) gradient $= -\dfrac{1}{2}$

B3 (a) 3

(b)

x	−2	−1.5	−1	0	1	1.5	2
$\dfrac{dy}{dx}$	−4	−3	−2	0	2	3	4

(c) 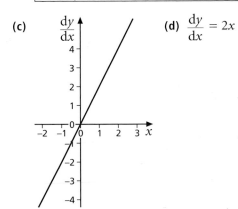   **(d)** $\dfrac{dy}{dx} = 2x$

B4 (a)

x	−1	0	1	2	3
$\dfrac{dy}{dx}$	6	4	2	0	−2

(b) 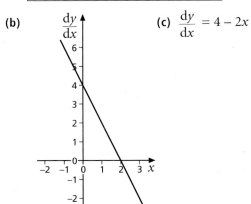   **(c)** $\dfrac{dy}{dx} = 4 - 2x$

B5 (a)

x	−3	−2	−1	0	1	2	3	4
$\dfrac{dy}{dx}$	1.7	0.2	−0.7	−1	−0.7	0.2	1.7	3.8

(b) 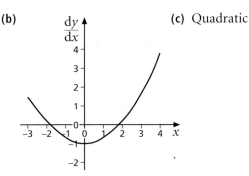   **(c)** Quadratic

Exercise B (p 114)

1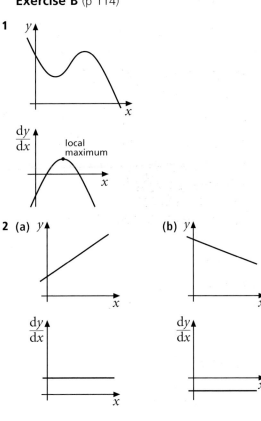

2 (a)   **(b)**

(c)

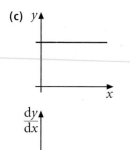

(d)

local maximum

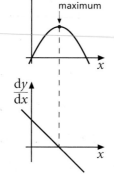

(e)

local maximum

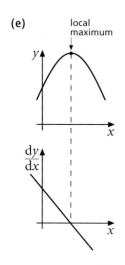

(f)

local minimum

local maximum

local minimum

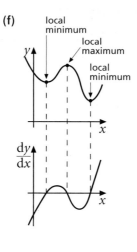

3 (a)

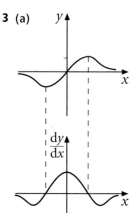

(b)

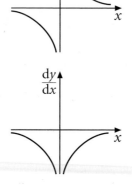

C Calculating the gradient of a curved graph

(p 115)

C1 (a) Gradient of $AB = 6.001$ **(b)** 6

C2 Gradient of tangent at $(4, 16) = 8$

C3 (a)

x	0	1	2	3	4	5	6
$\dfrac{\mathrm{d}y}{\mathrm{d}x}$	0	2	4	6	8	10	12

(b) $\dfrac{\mathrm{d}y}{\mathrm{d}x} = 2x$

C4 (a) The gradient is as shown in this table.

x	0	1	2	3	4	5
$\dfrac{\mathrm{d}y}{\mathrm{d}x}$	5	7	9	11	13	15

(b) $\dfrac{\mathrm{d}y}{\mathrm{d}x} = 2x + 5$

C5 The graph of $y = x^2$ is stretched in the y-direction by a factor of 3, making the gradient 3 times as large.

C6 (a) Gradients are 0, 3, 12, 27, 48, 75.

(b) 3, 12, 27, 48, 75

(c) A quadratic function

(d) $\dfrac{\mathrm{d}y}{\mathrm{d}x} = 3x^2$

Exercise C (p 119)

1 $6x^2 - 5$

2 (a) $8x - 1$ **(b)** $12x^3 - 15x^2$

(c) $4 - 12x + 21x^2$

3 -3

4 (a) -12 **(b)** 31

5 (a) $8x^3 - 3$ **(b)** $5x^4 + 9x^2 - 2$

(c) $4x^3 - 9x^2 + 1$

6

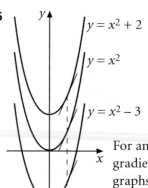

$y = x^2 + 2$

$y = x^2$

$y = x^2 - 3$

For any given value of x, the gradient is the same for all three graphs because they are translations of one another.

7 88

8 (a) $(0, 0)$, $(2, 0)$, $(3, 0)$

(b)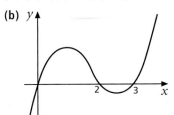

(c) Gradient at $(0, 0)$ is 6
Gradient at $(2, 0)$ is -2
Gradient at $(3, 0)$ is 3

9 $p = 8$

10 $a = 2$, $b = 7$

11 (a) $t = 0$ and $t = 8$ **(b)**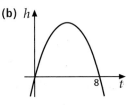

(c) 10. The stone is travelling upward at $10\,\text{m/s}$.

(d) -20. It is travelling downward at speed $20\,\text{m/s}$.

12 $a = 3$, $b = -5$

D Tangents and normals

Exercise D (p 121)

1 $y = 6x - 9$

2 Tangent: $y = 3x + 2$ Normal: $y = -\frac{1}{3}x - \frac{4}{3}$

3 Tangent: $y = 2x - 15$ Normal: $y = -\frac{1}{2}x - 10$

4 Tangent: $y = 16x - 64$ Normal: $y = -\frac{1}{16}x + \frac{1}{4}$

5 $y = 7x - 16$

6 $y = \frac{1}{8}x - \frac{1}{2}$

7 (a) $y = x - 12$ **(b)** $y = -x - 12$

8 (a) $\dfrac{dy}{dx} = 2x$. At (k, k^2), $\dfrac{dy}{dx} = 2k$.
The equation of the tangent at (k, k^2) is
$$y - k^2 = 2k(x - k)$$
$$\Rightarrow \qquad y = 2kx - k^2$$
which cuts the y-axis at $(0, -k^2)$.

(b) The gradient of the normal at (k, k^2) is $-\dfrac{1}{2k}$.
The equation of the normal is
$$y - k^2 = -\frac{1}{2k}(x - k)$$
$$\Rightarrow \qquad y = -\frac{1}{2k}x + k^2 + \frac{1}{2}$$
which cuts the y-axis at $(0, k^2 + \frac{1}{2})$.

Mixed questions (p 122)

1 (a) $4x^3 - 6x + 5$ **(b)** 25

2 (a) 4

(b) It is travelling at $4\,\text{m/s}$ after 5 seconds from the start.

3 $3x^2 - 6x + 4$

4 -9

5 (a) $y = 7x - 5$
(b) $y = -\frac{1}{7}x + \frac{15}{7}$ or $y = \dfrac{15 - x}{7}$

6 (a) $y = 2x - 6$ **(b)** $y = -\frac{1}{2}x - 1$

7 (a) $y = x + 3$ **(b)** $(1, 4)$

8 $k = 17$

9 $a = 2$, $b = -7$

10 $p = -4$, $q = -3$, $r = 14$

11 (a) $(x + \delta x)^3 = x^3 + 3x^2\,\delta x + 3x(\delta x)^2 + (\delta x)^3$

(b) $\dfrac{\delta y}{\delta x} = \dfrac{3x^2\,\delta x + 3x(\delta x)^2 + (\delta x)^3}{\delta x} = 3x^2 + 3x\,\delta x + (\delta x)^2$

(c) $\dfrac{\delta y}{\delta x}$ gets closer and closer to $3x^2$. (So $\dfrac{dy}{dx} = 3x^2$.)

Test yourself (p 123)

1 (a) $3x^2 + 6x + 3$ **(b)** 30

2 (a) $3x^2 - 4x + 3$ **(b)** $y = 2x - 6$

3 (a) $\dfrac{dy}{dx} = 3x^2 + 6x - 7$ **(b)** -3

(c) $y = 2x - 6$ **(d)** $3\sqrt{5}$

4 $y = \frac{1}{2}x - 26$

9 Using differentiation

A Increasing and decreasing functions, stationary points

Exercise A (p 125)

1 (i) $(3, -3)$ (ii) Minimum

(iii)

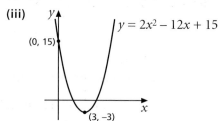

2 (a)

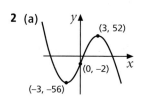

(b)

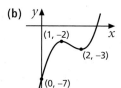

(c)

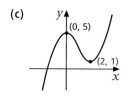

(d)

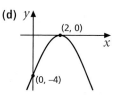

(e)

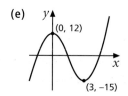

(f)

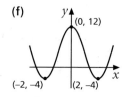

B Increasing and decreasing functions again

Exercise B (p 126)

1 $p = 0, q = 4$ (i.e. $0 < x < 4$)

2 $x < -3, x > 3$

3 $-5 < x < 5$

4 $0 \leq t < 10$

C Second derivative (p 127)

C1 (a) $f'(x)$ is decreasing at $x = 1$.

(b) $f''(x)$ is negative at $x = 1$.

(c) $f''(x)$ is positive at $x = 3$.

Exercise C (p 128)

1 (a) $15x^2 - 6x + 7$ (b) $30x - 6$

2 (a) $12x^3 + 6x^2$ (b) $36x^2 + 12x$

3 Maximum at $(1, 8)$; minimum at $(3, 4)$

4 (a) Maximum at $(-5, 183)$; minimum at $(3, -73)$

(b) Maximum at $(\frac{1}{2}, 3\frac{3}{4})$; minimum at $(2, -3)$

(c) Maximum at $(-6, -5)$; minimum at $(-2, -37)$

(d) Minimum at $(-\frac{1}{2}, -2\frac{1}{2})$; maximum at $(1\frac{1}{2}, 13\frac{1}{2})$

(e) Maximum at $(-1, 18)$; minimum at $(2\frac{1}{2}, -67\frac{3}{4})$

(f) Maximum at $(-6, 0)$; minimum at $(2, -256)$

5 (a) (i) $g(x) = 3x^3 - 45x$
$g'(x) = 9x^2 - 45$
$g'(\sqrt{5}) = 45 - 45 = 0$

(ii) $g''(x) = 18x$
$g''(\sqrt{5}) = 18\sqrt{5} > 0$

(b) $g(x)$ has a (local) minimum where $x = \sqrt{5}$.

D Optimisation

Exercise D (p 129)

1 $\dfrac{dF}{dv} = 1 - 0.02v$

For maximum fuel economy, $\dfrac{dF}{dv} = 0$,

so $v = \dfrac{1}{0.02} = 50$.

The most economical speed is 50 m.p.h.

2 (a) (i) $P = 500 + 100t$

(ii) $\dfrac{dP}{dt} = 100$

This represents the rate at which the population increases.

(b) (i) $\dfrac{dP}{dt} = 100 - 50t$

When $t = 1$, $\dfrac{dP}{dt} = 50$; when $t = 2$, $\dfrac{dP}{dt} = 0$;

when $t = 3$, $\dfrac{dP}{dt} = -50$.

(ii) P is a maximum when $\dfrac{dP}{dt} = 0$,
i.e. when $t = 2$.
When $t = 2$, $P = 600$.

(iii) The population would decrease to zero.

3 (a) Length of side parallel to hedge $= 60 - 2x$

$A = x(60 - 2x) = 60x - 2x^2$

(b) $\dfrac{\mathrm{d}A}{\mathrm{d}x} = 60 - 4x$

For maximum A, $60 - 4x = 0$ so $x = 15$

(c) Maximum area $= 15 \times (60 - 30) = 450 \,\mathrm{m}^2$

4 (a) Length of card $= w + l + w + l = 2w + 2l$

So $2w + 2l = 160$

$\Rightarrow \quad w + l = 80$

$\Rightarrow \qquad l = 80 - w$

(b) Width of card $= \frac{1}{2}w + h + \frac{1}{2}w = w + h$

So $w + h = 50$

$\Rightarrow \qquad h = 50 - w$

(c) $V = whl = w(50 - w)(80 - w)$

(d) $V = w^3 - 130w^2 + 4000w$

$\dfrac{\mathrm{d}V}{\mathrm{d}w} = 3w^2 - 260w + 4000$

For maximum V, $3w^2 - 260w + 4000 = 0$

$\Rightarrow \qquad (3w - 200)(w - 20) = 0$

$\Rightarrow \qquad w = 20 \text{ or } 66\frac{2}{3}$

$w = 66\frac{2}{3}$ is impossible, so $w = 20$ gives the maximum volume.

The dimensions of the box are 20 cm, 30 cm, 60 cm.

5 (a) Length of tray $= 8 - 2x$

Width of tray $= 5 - 2x$

So volume $V = x(8 - 2x)(5 - 2x)$

(b) V is a maximum when $x = 1$.

The dimensions are 6 cm, 3 cm, 1 cm.

6 (a) Total surface area $=$ top $+$ bottom $+$ 4 sides

$= x^2 + x^2 + 4hx$

$= 2x^2 + 4hx$

(b) (i) $2x^2 + 4hx = 384$

$\Rightarrow \quad h = \dfrac{384 - 2x^2}{4x}$

(ii) $V = x^2 h = x^2\left(\dfrac{384 - 2x^2}{4x}\right) = \dfrac{384x}{4} - \frac{1}{2}x^3$

$= 96x - \frac{1}{2}x^3$

(iii) V is a maximum when $x = 8$.

The corresponding value of h is 8.

(iv) $512 \,\mathrm{cm}^3$

7 (a) Area of each end $= 6x^2$

Area of rectangular faces $= 3xl + 4xl + 5xl$

$= 12xl$

Total surface area $= 12x^2 + 12xl$

$12x^2 + 12xl = 64$

$\Rightarrow l = \dfrac{64 - 12x^2}{12x} = \dfrac{64}{12x} - \dfrac{12x^2}{12x} = \dfrac{16}{3x} - x$

(b) Volume $=$ area of end $\times$ length

$= 6x^2 l = 6x^2\left(\dfrac{16}{3x} - x\right) = 32x - 6x^3$

(c) $\dfrac{\mathrm{d}V}{\mathrm{d}x} = 0$ when $32 - 18x^2 = 0$

$\Rightarrow \qquad x^2 = \frac{16}{9}$

$\Rightarrow \qquad x = \frac{4}{3} \ (-\frac{4}{3} \text{ impossible})$

When $x = \frac{4}{3}$, $V = 32 \times \frac{4}{3} - 6 \times (\frac{4}{3})^3$

$= \frac{128}{3} - \frac{128}{9} = \frac{384 - 128}{9} = \frac{256}{9} \,\mathrm{cm}^3 = 28\frac{4}{9} \,\mathrm{cm}^3$

8 Let the price per bike be £P. The number sold drops by 40 for each increase of £1 in the price, and so the number sold is

$5000 - 40(P - 100) = 9000 - 40P$

Total revenue $= £(9000 - 40P)P$

Total costs $= £(50\,000 + 85(9000 - 40P))$

Profit $=$ revenue $-$ costs

$= £(-815\,000 + 12\,400P - 40P^2)$

$\dfrac{\mathrm{d(Profit)}}{\mathrm{d}P} = 0$ when $12\,400 - 80P = 0$,

i.e. $P = 155$

Number sold $= 9000 - 40P = 2800$

Approximately 2800 should be manufactured and they should be sold at a price of £155 each.

Mixed questions (p 132)

1 Maximum at $(-1, 2)$; minimum at $(1, -2)$

2 (a) $6x^2 - 20x + 1$ **(b)** $12x - 20$

3 (a) $(0, 3), (3, 0), (-\frac{1}{2}, 0)$

(b) 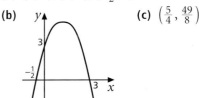   **(c)** $\left(\frac{5}{4}, \frac{49}{8}\right)$

4 (a) $4x^3 - 4x$

(b), (c) $(-1, 3)$ minimum; $(0, 4)$ maximum; $(1, 3)$ minimum

5 (a) $24x^2 - 6x$

(b) $48x - 6$

(c) $f'(1) = 24 - 6 = 18$
$f'(1) > 0$, so f is increasing

(d) $f'(x) = 0$ when $24x^2 - 6x = 0$
$$\Rightarrow \quad 6x(4x - 1) = 0$$
$$\Rightarrow \quad x = 0 \text{ or } \tfrac{1}{4}$$

(e) $f''(0) < 0$, so y is a maximum when $x = 0$
$f''(\tfrac{1}{4}) > 0$; so y is a minimum when $x = \tfrac{1}{4}$

6 (a) $4x^3 - 24x^2 + 32x$

(b) $4x^3 - 24x^2 + 32x = 0$
$$\Rightarrow \quad x^3 - 6x^2 + 8x = 0$$
$$\Rightarrow \quad x(x^2 - 6x + 8) = 0$$
$$\Rightarrow \quad x(x - 4)(x - 2) = 0$$
$$\Rightarrow \quad x = 0, 2 \text{ or } 4$$

(c) $\dfrac{d^2y}{dx^2} = 12x^2 - 48x + 32$

When $x = 2$, $\dfrac{d^2y}{dx^2} = 48 - 96 + 32 < 0$
So y has a maximum value when $x = 2$.

(d) When $x = 2$, $y = 24$. He arrives at 8:24 a.m.

7 $f'(x) = 15 - 12x - 3x^2$
$$= 3(5 - 4x - x^2)$$
$$= 3(5 + x)(1 - x)$$

	−5		1	
$5 + x$	− −	0	+ + + + + +
$1 - x$	+ + + + + +	0	− −
$(5 + x)(1 - x)$	− −	0	+ + +	0 − −

$f'(x) > 0$ in the interval $-5 < x < 1$
so $a = -5$ and $b = 1$

8 (a) Length of shelter = $4 - 2x$
Height of shelter = $2 - x$
So $V = x(4 - 2x)(2 - x)$
$$= x(8 - 8x + 2x^2)$$
$$= 2x^3 - 8x^2 + 8x$$

(b) $\dfrac{dV}{dx} = 6x^2 - 16x + 8$

$\dfrac{dV}{dx} = 0$ when $6x^2 - 16x + 8 = 0$
$$\Rightarrow \quad 2(3x^2 - 8x + 4) = 0$$
$$\Rightarrow \quad 2(3x - 2)(x - 2) = 0$$
$$\Rightarrow \quad x = \tfrac{2}{3} \text{ or } 2$$
$x = 2$ is impossible, so $x = \tfrac{2}{3}$

(c) $\tfrac{64}{27}$ m^3 or $2\tfrac{10}{27}$ m^3

9 (a) $V = x^2h$
$A = x^2 + 4xh$

(b) (i) $x^2 + 4xh = 3000$
$$\Rightarrow h = \frac{3000 - x^2}{4x}$$
$$V = x^2h = x^2\left(\frac{3000 - x^2}{4x}\right)$$
$$= 750x - \tfrac{1}{4}x^3$$

(ii) $\dfrac{dV}{dx} = 750 - \tfrac{3}{4}x^2$

$\dfrac{dV}{dx} = 0$ when $750 - \tfrac{3}{4}x^2 = 0$
$$\Rightarrow \quad x^2 = \tfrac{3000}{3} = 1000$$
$$\Rightarrow \quad x = 10\sqrt{10}$$

(iii) Maximum V
$$= 7500\sqrt{10} - \tfrac{1}{4}(1000 \times 10 \times \sqrt{10})$$
$$= 5000\sqrt{10}$$

10 (a) $y = x^2(x - a) = x^3 - ax^2$
$$\dfrac{dy}{dx} = 3x^2 - 2ax$$
$\dfrac{dy}{dx} = 0$ when $x = 6$, so $108 - 12a = 0$
$$\Rightarrow \quad a = 9$$

(b) $y = (x - 3)^2(x - b)$
$$= (x^2 - 6x + 9)(x - b)$$
$$= x^3 - (b + 6)x^2 + (6b + 9)x - 9b$$
$$\dfrac{dy}{dx} = 3x^2 - 2(b + 6)x + 6b + 9$$
$\dfrac{dy}{dx} = 0$ when $x = 6$,
so $108 - 12(b + 6) + 6b + 9 = 0$,
$$\Rightarrow \quad b = 7\tfrac{1}{2}$$

(c) $y = x(x - c)^2$
$$= x(x^2 - 2cx + c^2)$$
$$= x^3 - 2cx^2 + c^2x$$
$$\dfrac{dy}{dx} = 3x^2 + 4cx + c^2$$
$\dfrac{dy}{dx} = 0$ when $x = 6$, so $108 - 24c + c^2 = 0$
$$\Rightarrow \quad (c - 6)(c - 18) = 0$$
$$\Rightarrow \quad c = 6 \text{ or } 18$$

11 (a) $12x^3 + 24x^2 - 12x - 24$

(b) $\dfrac{dy}{dx} = 0$ when $12x^3 + 24x^2 - 12x - 24 = 0$
Divide through by 12: $x^3 + 2x^2 - x - 2 = 0$

(c) When $x = 1$, $x^3 + 2x^2 - x - 2 = 1 + 2 - 1 - 2 = 0$
$x - 1$ must be a factor of $x^3 + 2x^2 - x - 2$
(by the factor theorem). By dividing by $x - 1$,
the other factor is $x^2 + 3x + 2$, which factorises
as $(x + 1)(x + 2)$. So the other two solutions
are $x = -1$ and $x = -2$.

(d) $(-2, 9)$ minimum; $(-1, 14)$ maximum;
$(1, -18$ minimum$)$

Test yourself (p 134)

1 (a) $f'(x) = 6x^2 - 2x + 8$

(b) $f'(1) = 6 - 2 + 8 = 12$

(c) $f'(x) = 0$ when $6x^2 - 2x + 8 = 0$
$\Rightarrow \quad 3x^2 - x + 4 = 0$
Discriminant = '$b^2 - 4ac$' $= 1 - 48 < 0$
There are no real roots, so no stationary
points.

2 (a) $\dfrac{dy}{dx} = 3x^2 - 6x - 9$

(b) When $x = 0$, $\dfrac{dy}{dx} = -9$.

$\dfrac{dy}{dx} < 0$, so the function is decreasing.

(c) $(3, -27)$, $(-1, 5)$

(d) $\dfrac{d^2y}{dx^2} = 12$ when $x = 3$

$\dfrac{d^2y}{dx^2} = -12$ when $x = -1$

So $(3, -27)$ is a minimum and $(-1, 5)$ is a
maximum.

3 (a) $117 + 114t - 3t^2$

(b) (i) $t = 39$ (ii) Maximum

(c) (i) 2009

(ii) When $t = 59$, $P = 0$.
The population dies out.

10 Integration

A Thinking backwards (p 136)

A1 t^2

A2 $\frac{5}{2}t^2$

B Integration as the reverse of differentiation
(p 137)

B1 The derivative of each of them is the same, $2x$.
The function $x^2 + c$, where c is a number, has
derivative $2x$.

B2 (a) $10x$ (b) $5x^2 + c$

B3 (a) (i) $6x$ (ii) $8x$ (iii) 8

(iv) $3x^2$ (v) 6

(b) (i) $4x^2 + c$ (ii) $x^3 + c$ (iii) $6x + c$

(iv) $3x^2 + c$ (v) $8x + c$

B4 $\frac{1}{4}x^4 + c$

Exercise B (p 138)

1 (a) $2x^2 + c$ (b) $6x^2 + c$

(c) $10x^2 + c$ (d) $\frac{1}{2}x^2 + c$

2 (a) $2x^3 + c$ (b) $5x^3 + c$

(c) $\frac{1}{3}x^3 + c$ (d) $\frac{2}{3}x^3 + c$

3 (a) $x^4 + c$ (b) $2x^5 + c$

(c) $\frac{5}{3}x^3 + c$ (d) $\frac{3}{2}x^2 + c$

4 (a)

Function	x	x^2	x^3	x^4
Indefinite integral	$\frac{x^2}{2} + c$	$\frac{x^3}{3} + c$	$\frac{x^4}{4} + c$	$\frac{x^5}{5} + c$

(b) $\dfrac{x^{n+1}}{n+1} + c$

C Integrating polynomials (p 138)

C1 (a) $\int 3x^2 \, dx = x^3 + c$ (b) $\int 4x \, dx = 2x^2 + c$

C2 $\int 5x \, dx = \frac{5}{2}x^2 + c$

C3 $\int 6x^2 \, dx = 2x^3 + c$

Exercise C (p 139)

1 (a) $\frac{1}{4}x^4 + c$ (b) $\frac{4}{3}x^3 + c$ (c) $3x^2 + c$ (d) $x^5 + c$

2 (a) $y = \frac{1}{2}x^2 - 4x + c$

(b) $y = x^3 + \frac{1}{2}x^2 + c$

(c) $y = \frac{1}{3}x^3 + \frac{1}{2}x^2 + x + c$

(d) $y = x^5 + 3x + c$

3 $f(x) = \frac{5}{2}x^2 + \frac{3}{4}x^4 + c$

4 (a) $2x - \frac{3}{2}x^2 + \frac{1}{3}x^3 + c$ (b) $\frac{5}{4}x^4 + \frac{1}{3}x^6 + c$

5 (a) $y = \frac{1}{2}x^4 - \frac{7}{2}x^2 + 3x + c$

(b) $y = \frac{1}{3}x^3 - \frac{1}{2}x^2 - 2x + c$

6 (a) $3x^2 - 4x + c$ (b) $x^3 + 6x^2 + c$

(c) $\frac{4}{3}x^3 - 2x^2 + x + c$

7 $f(x) = \frac{1}{4}x^4 + \frac{5}{3}x^3 + x^2 - 8x + c$

8 (a) $\frac{1}{3}x^3 - \frac{3}{2}x^2 - 10x + c$ (b) $\frac{1}{2}x^4 + \frac{1}{3}x^3 + c$

D Finding the constant of integration

Exercise D (p 141)

1 $f(x) = 2x^3 + 4x + 1$

2 (a) $y = x^3 + 2x^2 + 2$ (b) $y = \frac{1}{3}x^3 + \frac{1}{2}x^2 + x + 3$

3 $y = x^2 - \frac{1}{4}x^4 + 1$

4 (a) $f(x) = 5x - x^2 - 2$ (b) $f(x) = 3x^3 - 3x^2 + 2$

5 (a) $y = \frac{2}{3}x^3 - \frac{1}{2}x^2 - 3x + c$

(b) $5\frac{1}{2}$

6 $k = 7$

7 $P = t^3 + 3t^2 + 96$

8 (a) $p = -6$ (b) $y = 2x^2 - 6x + 7$

9 (a) $a = 6, b = 8, c = 5$

(b) $v = 2x^3 + 4x^2 + 5$

Mixed questions (p 142)

1 (a) $\frac{2}{5}x^3 + \frac{3}{2}x^2 - x + c$ (b) $\frac{5}{6}x^6 + x^2 + c$

(c) $\frac{1}{2}x^4 - \frac{8}{3}x^3 + \frac{3}{2}x^2 - 12x + c$

2 $f(x) = \frac{1}{4}x^4 + 4x^3 - 2x - 32$

3 $y = \frac{1}{6}x^3 - \frac{3}{2}x^2 + 14$

4 $s = \frac{1}{3}t^3 + t^2 - 3t + 1$

5 (a) $a = 10$ (b) $f(x) = x^3 + 5x^2 - 4$

6 (a) $P = 20t - \frac{1}{2}t^2 + 100$ (b) 10 and 30

7 (a) $N = 5t - \frac{2}{9}t^2 - \frac{1}{27}t^3 + 36$

(b) 48

(c) After 5 weeks

(d) $\dfrac{dN}{dt} = -\frac{1}{9}(t + 9)(t - 5)$

When $t > 5$, $\dfrac{dN}{dt} < 0$, so N is decreasing.

When $t = 12$, $N = 5 \times 12 - \frac{2}{9} \times 12^2 - \frac{1}{27} \times 12^3 + 36$

$= 0$

Test yourself (p 143)

1 (a) $\frac{1}{4}x^4 + \frac{2}{3}x^3 - \frac{1}{2}x^2 + c$ (b) $\frac{1}{5}x^5 + \frac{7}{2}x^2 - x + c$

(c) $\frac{1}{9}x^9 + \frac{5}{7}x^7 + c$

2 (a) $\frac{3}{4}x^4 - 2x^3 + c$ (b) $3x^4 + x^3 - 2x^2 - x + c$

(c) $3x^3 - 6x^2 + 4x + c$

3 $y = 2x^3 - x + 5$

4 $y = 2x^3 - \frac{1}{2}x^2 - 5x + \frac{7}{2}$

5 (a) $f(x) = 2x^5 - 3x^4 - 4x + 2$

(b) -102

6 $f(x) = x^3 - x^2 - 5x + 3$

7 $y = 3x^3 - 3x^2 + x + 40$

11 Area under a graph

A Linear graphs: area function (p 144)

A1 (a) (i) $A(1) = \frac{1}{2}$, $A(2) = 2$, $A(3) = 4\frac{1}{2}$, $A(4) = 8$

(ii) $A(0) = 0$

(iii)
x	0	1	2	3	4
$A(x)$	0	$\frac{1}{2}$	2	$4\frac{1}{2}$	8

(b)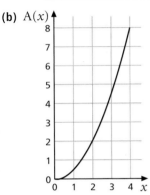

(c) $A(x) = \frac{1}{2}x^2$

A2 (a) (i) $A(1) = 1$, $A(2) = 4$, $A(3) = 9$, $A(4) = 16$

(ii) $A(0) = 0$

(iii)
x	0	1	2	3	4
$A(x)$	0	1	4	9	16

(b) The graph of $A(x) = x^2$

(c) $A(x) = x^2$

A3 $A(x) = \frac{1}{2}x^2 + x$

A4 $A(x) = 3x$

A5 $A(x) = x^2 + 3x$

A6 (a)
Graph	Area function $A(x)$
$y = 3$	$3x$
$y = x$	$\frac{1}{2}x^2$
$y = 2x$	x^2
$y = x + 1$	$\frac{1}{2}x^2 + x$
$y = 2x + 3$	$x^2 + 3x$

(b) The area function is the indefinite integral (but without the constant of integration).

(c) $\frac{1}{3}x^3$

B Area function for $y = x^2$ (p 146)

B1 (a) The areas are 0.5, 2.5, 6.5, 12.5, 20.5, 30.5

(b) Overestimate

(c)
x	0	1	2	3	4	5	6
$A(x)$	0	0.5	3	9.5	22	42.5	73

(d) The values of $\frac{1}{3}x^3$ (to 2 d.p.) are:

0, 0.33, 2.67, 9, 21.33, 41.67, 72

There is close agreement, especially for larger values of x.

C Definite integrals

Exercise C (p 148)

1 (a) $\int_2^4 \left(3x^2 - 5\right) dx$ (b) $\left[x^3 - 5x\right]_2^4 = 46$

2 $\left[\frac{1}{4}t^4 + \frac{1}{3}t^3 + \frac{1}{2}t^2 + t\right]_1^3 = 34\frac{2}{3}$

3 (a) $\frac{1}{6}$ (b) 8 (c) $2\frac{1}{3}$ (d) $\frac{1}{3}$ (e) $3\frac{5}{6}$ (f) 3

4 The information given leads to the equation $a^2 + 3a - 4 = 24$ from which $a = 4$ (or -7, which is rejected since $a > 1$).

5 (a) (i) $18\frac{2}{3}$ (ii) $18\frac{2}{3}$

(b)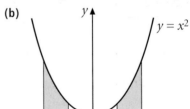

The areas are equal because of the symmetry of the graph.

6 $69\frac{3}{4}$

7 (a) 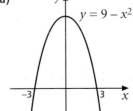 (b) 36

8 (a)

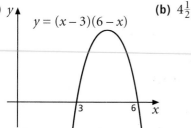

$y = (x-3)(6-x)$

(b) $4\frac{1}{2}$

9 (a)

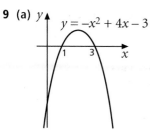

$y = -x^2 + 4x - 3$

(b) $1\frac{1}{3}$

10 $\frac{1}{30}$

11 $k = 33$

D Areas below the *x*-axis (p 149)

D1 (a) Area $= \left[x^3 - 6x^2\right]_1^3 = (27 - 54) - (1 - 6)$

$$= -27 + 5 = -22$$

(b) Because the area is below the *x*-axis, where values of *y* are negative.

Exercise D (p 149)

1 (a) -18 **(b)**

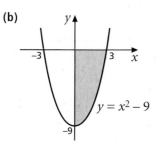

$y = x^2 - 9$

2 (a) $x = -1$ and $x = 5$ **(b)** -36

3 (a) $x = 0$ and $x = 3$ **(b)** $-13\frac{1}{2}$

4 (a)

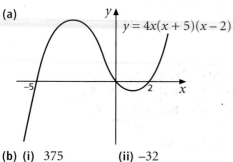

$y = 4x(x + 5)(x - 2)$

(b) (i) 375 **(ii)** -32

5 The value of the integral is 0. The negative and positive areas cancel each other out.

Mixed questions (p 150)

1 (a) 4   **(b)** $2\frac{2}{3}$

2 (a) *y*-coordinate of $B = 6$
Equation of AB is $6x - y - 6 = 0$

(b) $-\frac{1}{4}$

3 (a) $a = 3$ **(b)** $34\frac{1}{2}$ **(c)** $4\frac{1}{2}$

4 (a) $f(3) = -2$, $f(4) = 0$

(b) $f(x) = (x - 1)(x - 2)(x - 4)$

(c) (i) $\frac{dy}{dx} = 3x^2 - 14x + 14$

(ii) When $x = 3$, $\frac{dy}{dx} = 3 \times 3^2 - 14 \times 3 + 14 = -1$.
This is negative, so f is decreasing.

(iii) $\frac{1}{4}x^4 - \frac{7}{3}x^3 + 7x^2 - 8x \, (+ c)$

(iv) $\frac{5}{12}$

5 (a) $x = -3$ and $x = 3$ **(b)** 36

6 (a) $a = 2$ **(b)** 32

Test yourself (p 152)

1 (a) $\frac{2}{5}$ **(b)** $51\frac{3}{4}$

2 (a) $PQ^2 = 5^2 + 5^2 = 50$
$PQ = \sqrt{50} = \sqrt{25 \times 2} = 5\sqrt{2}$

(b) $y = 4x - 10$ **(c)** $21\frac{2}{3}$

3 (a) $\frac{1}{4}x^4 - \frac{5}{3}x^3 + x^2 + 8x \, (+ c)$

(b) $-5\frac{1}{3}$ (area below axis)

4 (a) 16

(b) (i) -12 **(ii)** $(0, 24)$

(c) 8

Index